`from the Heart

From the Heart

Conversations, Visions, and Answers
From God's Angels and Saints

JOYCE ANN STEVENS

DIVINE POWER PUBLISHING
SPRINGFIELD, MASS.

Copies of this book may be purchased for educational, business, or sales promotional use. For information, please contact Joyce Ann Stevens at:
Divine Power Publishing
121 Garfield Street
Springfield, MA 01108
JoyceAnnStevens@AOL.com

Publisher's Cataloging-in-Publication Data
Stevens, Joyce Ann.
    From the heart: conversations, visions, and answers from God's
angels and saints / Joyce Ann Stevens — Springfield, Mass.: Divine Power
Publishing, 2003.
         p. ill. cm.
Includes index.

    ISBN 0-9708645-2-3

    Library of Congress Control Number: 2002111443

    1. Stevens, Joyce Ann—Diaries. 2. Religious life. 3. Spirituality.
4. Visions. 5. Angels. 6. Prophecies. 7. Spiritual journals. I. Title.

BL628.5 .S74   2003
248.46—dc21   CIP

07 06 05 04 03 † 5 4 3 2 1

Printed in the United States of America

Project coordinated by To The Point Solutions ♦ zazattc@traverse.net

A special thank you to Moria Neville, for her support and assistance.

Cover illustration is explained on pages 82-83.

A gift from God,
which I give to *all*
of His very Loved children.

Please realize when I mention any holy spirit, saint or angel
it is to the Glory of our Heavenly Father.

Contents

Preface

$\mathcal{I}$ HAVE SEEN AND EXPERIENCED SOME EXTREMELY WONDER-
ful things, things that only God could have allowed. Only
through the Grace of God was I able to write what I did in
these pages, and only through the Grace of God am I here at all . . .
God knew I would share these experiences with you.

There are some vast differences in the things God allowed me
to see and become aware of. I've seen the enormously Good, good
way beyond what I could have imagined, good to the point of being
pure; to seeing the enormously bad, completely evil. The amazingly
good things, love and light, are in our reach; and the bad things,
hate and darkness, are also there about us.

Please be patient as this book begins a bit slowly, but this will
only be for the first ten or so pages. I had to explain a bit about my
past, in order for you to fully understand why God presented His
gifts to me the way He did; but the book will work its way up.

Also, I saw some devil's spirits, and I explained these visions
vividly, as they were vivid. Have Faith and continue reading. Well
over ninety percent of the book tells about pure and loving visions,
and this all intertwines. In order for you to understand the spirit

world, and the world about you better, you must be aware of the bad as well as the good.

I hope that this book will help you to make correct choices in your life. Please choose to love and not to hate. We make our own choices. As you read, I hope you will understand and feel, how your heart can help you make choices for your soul . . . for eternity.

I will try and tell you everything exactly as He let me experience it. Dears, God wants so much to have all of us with Him in Heaven. We are all His children.

May God always Bless and Keep You.
Joyce Ann Stevens

From
the
Heart

I give you a new commandment: love one another.
As I have loved you, so you also should love one another.
This is how all will know tht you are my disciples,
if you have love for one another.

John 13:34-35

Chapter 1

My Spiritual Introduction

M Y FATHER'S DAD DIED BEFORE MY FATHER WAS born, and the siblings from his deceased step-mother were much older than him. Therefore, my father, who was the youngest of his immediate siblings, was very close to his mother. He always talked about her with the greatest respect; she was certainly very loved by him.

Although my father's mother passed away shortly after he married and before any of us children were born, the love that was between my father and his mother did overflow into our lives. Throughout his life our father showed love and emphasized the importance of a mother.

My father was a good, hardworking man. He went to church almost every Sunday, and even as a child, I noticed he had Faith.

Now there will be some fussing, but I must tell you, at times my mother seemed angry or uncaring. I know as children, when my siblings did face this, none of us knew why our mother was not always caring.

Growing up as I did, the way I handled the hurt I saw around me was by keeping quiet, as I felt helpless and I did not want to hurt anyone. Strangely enough, because I did not want to hurt anyone and was quiet, I became independent and strong. Later, as life went on and troubles came my way, my kindness helped my independence and strength grow even more.

Now, thank God, He has let me see where anger really comes from. I'm writing not for myself, as this may very well cause me problems. But all of us should know where hate and anger in the people around us comes from; and especially in those whom we love.

My religious education consisted of attending a Catholic school until the third grade, attending three or four C.C.D. (Confraternity of Christian Doctrine. Religious education for children in public schools.) classes as a teenager, sitting in on three Bible study classes as a young adult, and, of course, attending church. (I am telling you this to give you an idea of just how little education I had.) However, even though my religious education was limited, I remember having a strong belief and Faith in God.

I think watching my father go to Mass on Sunday, and unhesitatingly showing his Faith and love, helped guide me. He never pressured us into accepting the Catholic faith, but he did set a good example of belief and humility. I can still remember him kneeling and being very respectful in, and about the church.

I believed in Jesus, the Holy Spirit, the Blessed Mother Mary, and in Heaven and God. I believed in the Catholic religion. As a child my first and strongest love was for the Holy Mother of Jesus, the Blessed Mary. I can still remember the beautiful picture of her that my father had hung on my bedroom wall.

Even in junior high school, every night before going to bed, I kneeled and said my evening prayers before the picture of the Blessed Mother. Especially then, and even now, cruel thoughts rarely entered my mind. I was very good then, and I think I am also good now.

At a very young twenty years old, I thought I had found love. My relationship with this boyfriend lasted for over a year and a half. During this time I thanklessly told God that I loved this man more than Him and I put my religion second. I was wrong.

Shortly after this relationship ended I decided to go shopping downtown. Shopping makes me feel better. As I was walking down Main Street, I suddenly started to cry. Trying to hide my tears, I quickly entered a nearby office building. Right inside the double set of glass doors I saw some hallway steps and I sat down on them; feeling hidden and safe, I put my head down and cried.

I didn't hear anyone come through the glass doors, but for some reason I looked up, and there, in front of the inside set of doors, stood a man looking at me. Even though I couldn't remember ever seeing him before . . . he felt so very familiar to me. I also knew I could ask him my question. I asked, 'Why can't I have him?'

He answered, "You will never be alone."

Somehow, from the way he said this, I knew he was also saying to me, "You will never marry."

I looked down for just a second, then I looked up again . . . he was gone. I knew if he had left through the glass doors, the doors would still be slowly closing, but they weren't. Suddenly I stopped crying. I got up from the steps and looked around, but there was no sign of him anywhere. I calmly left the building and returned to my shopping.

When I told my girlfriend about this she kept asking me more and more questions. I realize she knew then what I now know, that this man was one of God's helpers. I am now over fifty years old and I have never been married, nor have I ever really been alone.

I was the homebody. I would have been happy spending my time at home or going no further than my own neighborhood. This was to change.

At thirty-two years old I became pregnant, even though ten years earlier two doctors had told me that I probably would never have any children. I had prayed for a child and I was excited to be pregnant. However, the pregnancy was to be both a blessing and a hardship. Thank God I had a healthy child, but the father was not ready for the responsibility of raising a child. I would be a single mother.

When my son was a year and a half I decided to move. I had always believed that other people were trying to control my life, and especially at that time I felt this. I wanted to have a normal family life for my child and myself and I thought I could not have this unless I was totally running my life. At the time I thought my family was trying to control my life, so, determined me, I packed up and left my hometown. When I moved to our state capital, many miles away, I thought I could leave my troubles behind.

A year later I moved to another state and broke off all communications with my family. Even though I was angry (I thought I had good reason to be), I did not realize that I shouldn't have been angry with my family.

Today I am very sorry that I hurt my parents and my family. I can only hope that they will forgive me. You see, it wasn't my family that was trying to control my life or hurt me.

I moved several more times over the next nine years. In 1991 my son and I were living in an apartment in southern New Jersey, which we had been living in for eight months or so. I still did not understand why I never felt as though I was in control of my life, but I didn't want to give up. My poor child, I knew he felt it every time we moved.

In August of that year, even though my phone number was

unpublished, my older sister phoned me. She told me that our mother had passed away. She gave me the funeral dates, etc. I was still a bit angry with my family and I decided not to go home for the services. However, I have to say, a lot of my decision not to go home was because I did not want any more trouble in my life.

Thank God, now I can say I was wrong in not going home at that time. He has helped me to say this.

Three nights after my mother's wake I saw my first spirit. It was about 9:30 p.m., my son was asleep in his room and I was sitting on my bed watching TV. My windows were open; usually in the summer I keep my windows open all the time. I love the fresh air and our apartment was on the second floor.

I turned from the TV and looked at the window. My mother's spirit flew through the screen of the open window, and she stopped just inside the screen to look at me for a second or two. Although she did not talk, the peaceful look on her spirit's face spoke for her . . . she had come to see me. Then her spirit left, departing by the same screen she had come in.

I cannot even begin to describe the overwhelming look of peace that shone through, and so immensely, on her face. Try to imagine the most peaceful person you have ever seen on Earth, then multiply that peace by seven or eight times. This is the best I can do to explain her enormous inner peace, an inner peace that was so strong . . . it even spoke for her.

Her spirit was only visible from the waist up. She wore ordinary clothes, which I can only suppose were the clothes she was buried in. She looked the same as I remembered her when she was much younger, many years ago.

When my mother's spirit left, I just turned my head and calmly continued to watch TV. This is how calm I felt after seeing her familiar and peaceful spirit. After I had seen that my mother was now so peaceful, I was no longer afraid of her.

I had seen my first spirit. God allowed me into His spirit world. But I never told anyone—not for years.

In October of 1991, I called my father and asked him if we could visit for a few days and stay with him. He said OK—and we went home. I was still a little weary and cautious of this controlling family, but I was happy to see them. As it was, the visit went fine.

During our stay my father took us to visit my brother, Peter, and his relatively new wife and family. Peter was a fighter—boy was he stubborn. However, his back had been bothering him and giving him pain for at least ten years, and because of this pain his face looked tense. I could also tell that he didn't feel well.

I went back to New Jersey, and about a month later, in November, my sister called me again. This time she told me, Our brother had passed away. I just couldn't believe it. He was only forty-five years old, and all that kept going through my mind was that he was too young to be gone. She said he had smoked too much and this probably greatly contributed to his first, and fatal, heart attack.

Peter, the only boy in our family, had a hard life, but I always thought he was a good brother and a good person. He was very good to our mother. Since my brother had not gotten married until he was in his forties, he left two small children with his widow; they were two and three years old when their father died. I can only hope that someday they will realize how much their father loved them.

I did not go back to my hometown at that time. I did not go to the funeral, but I was told many of my brother's friends were there. He had numerous friends, most of whom he had known since his childhood. I was foolishly angry because I had lost my brother and I had lost him at a young age. I was selfish and I was blaming other people. I was very wrong, again. I should have paid my respect to my brother, to his family, and to my family.

About two weeks after my brother's funeral I saw my
second spirit. I was in my kitchen cooking supper, and it was
a beautiful day so my child was outside playing. My windows were
open. My brother's spirit flew through the screen of the open
kitchen window. There his spirit stopped, just inside the screen, and
he looked at me for two or three seconds before he left. I knew,
because I could feel it from him, that he had just come to see me.

Amazingly . . . my brother's spirit's face shone with the same
great peace that my mother's spirit's face had shone with shortly
after she had passed away. Many times, long ago, my brother would
become peaceful and his face would show peace. However, his
peace back then did not come close in comparison to the awesome
peace I now saw in him and in my mother's spirit's face. Their spirits' peace was so overwhelming; this was the very first clear message
I got from them when I looked into their faces: Peace. I could only
see my brother's spirit from the waist up and he had on ordinary
clothes. I thought, The look of physical pain is gone from his face,
after all those years. I was so glad. Again, this was a familiar and
peaceful spirit, and I felt calm after his spirit left. For many years, I
never mentioned this to anyone.

Within a month I saw my brother's spirit again. It was about the
same time of the day that I had seen him before, and again, I was in
my kitchen. I was sitting alone at the kitchen table when his spirit
came in through the same window he had come in before. Dears,
(that's you) he had lost that overwhelming look of total peace that
was *so* strong on his spirit's face shortly after his death. He looked a
little confused and worried, and as his spirit came into my kitchen,
he said something, and then his spirit vanished. Still, his spirit wore
ordinary clothes.

At the time I did not understand why my brother said what he
did, or why he looked so confused. Now I think I do. A part of his
confusion was, of course, since he himself was now a spirit, he could
see the spirit world. This world was new to him and must have been

very confusing. I'm sure it probably even seemed a bit scary to him. This was the last time I saw my brother's spirit. However, I did hear his voice after this, and the next time I heard his voice, out of respect for my father, I told my father what his son had said.

When Christmas of 1991 came, we went home to visit, spending Christmas Eve and a few more days at my father's house. I remember that during this visit I felt uncomfortable, because after all these years, when I was with my family I finally felt as if I were an adult, not just a child. However, I wasn't sure how I should interact with them as an adult. I also remember I felt a little anger toward my older sister.

I was sad for my father because I knew he felt alone that Christmas. He took the recent deaths of his wife and son very hard. I wanted to give my father our company for those few days and I tried to be good to him. I knew my father had tried to be good to me when I was a child and needed him.

Well, that Christmas Eve I put my son to bed, said, Good night, to my Dad, and then I went to bed. As I lay in bed, I peacefully looked around at my old bedroom. Within no more than a few minutes, I saw my mother's spirit for the second time. She still wore ordinary clothes and her spirit was only visible from the waist up. But her spirit had lost its peace, the peace that had shone so overwhelmingly on her face the first time I had seen her spirit.

As her spirit looked into my eyes, I looked back into her eyes. I knew, this time, she realized that I could see her spirit. Her mouth did not open, but I could hear from her a frantic, 'She can see me.' When she said this, I saw guilt show throughout her face and she quickly flew into the closet, where I could no longer see her. I just lay there, amazed she actually felt guilt. I could not ever remember her feeling guilty. I wasn't scared, nor did I get up to look into the closet. I just turned around and went to sleep. Of course, I never told my father or anyone.

About six months later, I moved from New Jersey. As I was still a bit apprehensive and worried about moving back to my hometown, I moved to Connecticut, a state next to my home state. I rented an apartment that was about 40 miles away from my father's home. I was testing my ground. Although this homebody was homesick, I was also worried. I was worried for myself and for my child.

Even though I had seen spirits and realized that there is a spirit world here with us, I still didn't realize what was going on. I was extremely calm about everything. I did not think much about it, and I still did not talk about it at all. God must have given me this strength.

I now fully realize God had let me see spirits, however, this was just the beginning. God and His helpers went slowly with me, and as you will see, they do have tremendous, Heavenly patience. Also, amazingly, and as I will write later in a much better way, everything will all fit together as a puzzle does. Please, continue to read . . . this is just the beginning of a wonderful awareness.

I was hired for a temporary government job, and for the first time I was to get training and experience on computers. I was very excited about the job, and after working for several weeks I even had the opportunity to attend a one-day paid class for Word Perfect. I thought this was great.

Since the class was for government employees from a large New England area, the training center was seventy or so miles north of my job. I drove my car on the long trip to the training center. In class, although the students were from a variety of jobs and locations, everyone seemed excited about learning.

After the class, as I was driving home on the highway, my car started to make noises, and more noises. Then the engine just stopped. I had to coast my car over to the breakdown lane, and there I sat, still some 60 plus miles away from home and stuck on the highway. I was so glad when a state policeman came by and called a tow truck for me.

My car was towed to a garage in Holyoke, Massachusetts, a town close to my hometown. However, when I got to the garage it was 4:15 p.m. and their closing time was 5:00 p.m. I called my father for help, a ride to his house, or something. He said OK, and then suddenly he started to yell at me. Now, I knew he was old, however, I could feel myself starting to cry. I just said, Good-bye, and I hung up the phone.

I was still crying when I realized that I had to call my son. I managed to stop crying for a few minutes and I called him, telling him my car was stuck and he would be alone that night. From his voice I could tell that he was scared and my heart just broke. I told him I would be home the next night for sure, and don't forget to go to school the next morning. I was so glad that he would be in school the next day and not home alone. After I had hung up the phone I sat down and continued to cry. Desperate and only having seven dollars in my purse, I called the police and asked them to drive me to a shelter in the city for the night. I could see that the garage attendant felt so sad for me.

The next morning I got a ride back to the garage. Come to find out, my car's engine was blown, so basically I had no car. After much debating, the new garage attendant agreed to give me a break on the cost of towing my car home for me. I was so glad that I got home that morning, hours before my son was home from school.

That night, at home, as my son and I sat on the couch watching TV, he couldn't seem to be able to get close enough to me. I felt we were safe, and for the first time in two days I finally relaxed.

Again I saw my mother's spirit. She was to our left, watching us. I was to learn a lot from this last vision of her. Although her mouth never opened, I could hear her yell out, 'God. I was wrong. I have to tell them.' Then her spirit quickly turned around and flew away.

Now, she desperately wanted to tell them, but I am not sure either what, or whom she wanted to tell. She still wore ordinary clothes. The look on my mother's spirit's face was of total awareness. I could see she was now aware of right and wrong. This was the first time I had ever seen that look on her face, and I knew she was now, finally, aware of what she had <u>done</u> in her lifetime. Thank God, He gave her this awareness. (As I typed the word <u>done</u>, God's helper let me know this was an important word.)

Also, God helped me when He let me see that my mother's spirit now had an awareness of knowing right from wrong. When He let me see this, I think one of the things He was trying to do was to help me to forgive. It is much easier to forgive someone when you know they now know right from wrong.

Importantly, I'll never forget the way she yelled the name, God. When her spirit said His name, she said it as if she was talking to the dearest, oldest friend she had ever had. **There certainly is a God.** You will know.

✝As I looked at the previous paragraph to retype it again, years later, an angel's tiny light lit up (Keep reading.), and I knew she was crying—so after I retyped this paragraph I looked at it again. Dears, God is a friend, of course, but—He is Our Father, whom we should always adore, listen to, and obey. This angel knew that my mother felt as if Our Loving God was a dear friend, more—than as her Heavenly Father. This made God's angel cry.✝

✝Much later, I thought, Both my brother's and mother's spirits had lost their peace. Why? To begin, I can only assume that after they died, they met God, Our Father; and that just from being in His great presence and radiant Light alone, their spirits received a heavenly peace. After this meeting, at least for my mother, it seemed as if her spirit's heart ultimately had the final outcome, if you will, on her soul. This seemed to be why she had lost her peace. Her heart felt guilt, and this feeling eventually overtook any love or peace she had received. This was not a swift judgment on her, but an inevitable outcome. I can see that guilt, hate, and unforgiving hearts can set our eternity. Please let your heart fill with love, here and now. This will allow your heart to burst with love for Eternity. ✝

Back to my temporary job. It ended. I couldn't get another job and I couldn't pay the rent. I wasn't doing well. I finally got brave and decided to go home. I called my father and told him I wanted to move back, knowing he really wanted me home and he would try to help me. My father wanted our family together. We soon made arrangements and moved into one of my older sister's apartments.

Even though my father was in his eighties, his health was good. He was relatively strong both physically and mentally, but he was to have his first major setback. Before we moved, my father had his first stroke and had to be hospitalized. This stroke left his right side paralyzed. Thank God, with physical therapy he did recover, and within weeks he was able to walk and get about fairly well by himself.

We lived in the apartment quietly, for a while.

Now it is time to explain more.

Many of the things that the spirits said are in quotes, either single quotes ' ' or double quotes " ". The words or sentences in double quotes are what God's helpers, or lights, had said. All of the single quotes were said by other spirits or people. Any words in quotes are exactly as they were said at the time.

When spirits talk, what they say may be just a part of what their souls can convey to you. Remember, spirits can speak and also communicate with their thoughts, their eyes, and their facial expressions. From within their souls.

When God's lights talk, they can convey two thoughts at one time. Also their spirits radiate feelings. Therefore, when God's heavenly beings talked to me, one or two thoughts and also feelings, could, and did, come across and radiate to me. Thus many meanings to some of my visions.

I will try to explain everything communicated to me, both the good and the bad. I will try to tell you all of the things that were said, conveyed, and radiated.

And, as I have done before, and will continue to do, I will underline words that God's lights helped me with. They would say these words to me as I wrote or thought about writing. They did help.

There are parenthesis ( ) around my personal thoughts. When I reached a growing point, I put crosses ✝ around these important thoughts or lessons.

I hope this is clear.

Most of the time I was oblivious to everything that was going on around me. I was preoccupied with working, trying to be a mother, and running my household. So although God had begun my journey back to Him by letting me see spirits, oblivious me, almost needed things to be written down in big, bold letters and put in front of my face. I still missed the point. But God knew my heart, and He was patient.

What was a bit of a mystery to me, begins here. The man who was to bring me back to God and my Faith (through much persistence and hard work, I have to admit), came to me. You could say he came knocking on my front door. For a while after meeting this man I had a lot of unanswered questions. Some things I saw still do not make complete sense to me, however, I will tell you about the things I have been allowed to see and experience.

When I first noticed this man, right away, I could see he had a quiet peace about him, and when I met him, I knew he had Heaven's compassion and love within him. But still, even after seeing Heaven's compassion, foolishly, I did not move closer to my religion. It took more time.

(I didn't realize it then, but I know now, God and His lights are always helping us and guiding us. Eventually they did get through to me, and after they did, every day I learned more and more. I would really just like to say, 'Thank God for His wonderful and patient helpers; they work so hard for Him and for us. Thank God they are persistent in their efforts to save our souls.)

One day, while we were still living in my sister's apartment, my son and I decided to go to the mall. If I had some free time I would take my son to the mall, as we liked being out and he enjoyed 'shopping' in the toy stores. At the mall, in three completely different instances, three completely different people said to me, "Go out tonight." They said this directly to me and this was all they said. Still, being me, I didn't think too much about it.

That night, although we usually never have pizza, I decided to have a pizza delivered. After I paid the delivery boy for the pizza, he said to me, "Thank you. Go out tonight." Well, I thought, If even the pizza delivery boy wanted me to go out, I was going to go out. I was extremely curious at this point, and I thought someone must want to meet me. I figured I would go out to a lounge, one that I had gone to several times before.

In the lounge I saw an old friend and I told him why I was out that night. He didn't say too much about it. Then I decided to wait alone, so I anxiously sat at the bar to wait. In the large crowded room I noticed a man across the bar from me, although I have to say he was just average looking. I noticed him because he looked as if he had such an inner peace, and in his peace he looked like a very good man, which is important to me. He sat alone in his quiet. Later, a couple, a man and a woman, came up to this man and started talking to him. The woman touched him from time to time, but he showed no interest and talked very little. He never moved from his chair. (Days later, when I talked to my same old friend again, he told me that he had also noticed this man in the lounge. He noticed he didn't move a muscle, not even to go to the bathroom. To my friend, and now even I realized, this man looked scared.)

As I sat in the lounge a man came up to me and introduced himself. He said he knew my family as his mother used to watch me when I was a child. I remembered his mother and I politely talked to him, but I knew he was not the person I was waiting for. When it was closing time at the lounge, most of the lights went on and many of the people left. I still sat there, waiting, but I began to feel sad.

I glanced over at the man I had first noticed when I had sat down. When I looked into his eyes, I noticed he was looking at the bartender. Strangely, I could hear his thoughts, as he talked to the bartender with his thoughts. He never opened his mouth. I could also see these inner thoughts showing throughout his face and eyes, as his emotions were so intense. (Now, remember that I had seen this form of communication previously, but I had only seen this in spirits. At that time I didn't think about this.) I especially liked this form of communication in this man. It seemed to so quietly come from within him.

As he looked at the bartender, he said, "You said I could have her." I knew the bartender and I were the only ones that heard his thoughts. The bartender said, 'OK.' Then, and only then, did this man get up from his seat. He came over to me. When he stood in front of me I started talking to him.

He told me his name was Bob. My other friend stayed and the three of us talked. (Much later, you will see that I call him Robert. I will call him Robert with the deepest respect. I must tell you, right now, as I sit in this seemingly empty church writing this, I hear an animal growl at the mere mention of his name, Bob. For months, I have heard this growl every time I think of Bob or say his name. I know this may be confusing, but it will all make sense later on, when I explain more about the spirit world.)

I thought, I want to know Bob better, but I had just met him and it was time to go. So, I suggested that we go out for breakfast. At this, the bartender came over to us and said to the first man I had met, 'Don't leave them alone, not even for a minute. Don't let them touch' and 'Watch them' and 'Don't leave them alone.' As usual for oblivious me, although the bartender was having a fit, I didn't give it too much thought.

When we had gotten outside, both of them came up with excuses why they could not drive to the restaurant. So I said I would drive, grumbling, 'I'm with two men and I have to drive.' Bob smiled and seemed to like my bluntness. I don't know why. Then Bob looked at the other man, and with his eyes and thoughts only, I heard him say, "She can't see it. She'll know." (That night, I *thought* I knew why he said he didn't want me to, ". . . see it." And why he wanted me to drive my car. As later that night when I did see Bob drive away, I noticed he had a beautiful, expensive looking red sports car. So I thought, Well, he didn't want me to see his car because he didn't want me to know he had money. I think that many people with money don't want you to know they have it when they first meet you. I think they want you to like them for themselves. However, now I think this thought was what Bob wanted the other man to think.)

✝As I learn more about God's spirit world, and as I think back to this time, there were probably other reasons why Bob wanted me to drive my car. I was to learn that many of the Heavenly beings are very humble; therefore they will wait for you to invite them before they come into your car, your home, or your life. So, when I *invited* Bob, who had a very heavenly presence, into my car, in fact, I was opening the door of my life for Bob to enter. He had received his invitation.✝

For whatever reasons, and although I did grumble that night, I really didn't care that I had to drive. I invited Bob into my car. Bob sat in the front seat of my car, while the other man sat in the backseat. The other man, more than once, said very cruelly to Bob, 'I really like the backseat.'

Bob was so full of peace: I could see it in everything he did and said. Almost every time he talked to me he first said my name. In addition to getting my attention, this somehow left me with a little peace in my soul.

While in the car, Bob said, "Joyce, more than anything else you want another child." I was set back a little. This was a dear thought, a thought that I had hardly mentioned to anyone, and I wondered, How did he know? I had just met him. Although this was true, I didn't answer. When Bob talked I noticed his jaw had wires in it. I had only seen this once before, when a friend's jaw had been broken in a fight. But he hadn't had as many wires in his jaw as Bob did.

Although the restaurant was open twenty-four hours, there were hardly any customers inside when we got there, so we were able to sit in the large booth we chose by the back of the restaurant. Bob sat next to the window, I sat beside him, and our friend sat across from us.

Both the other man and I let Bob order his food first. I liked Bob, and also out of respect, when I was asked by the waitress what I wanted, I said, 'Same as him.' Bob enjoyed this. From just this little bit of friendship by me, in response, he showed such warmth in his face.

Then Bob turned and looked out of the window and I could see his reflection in the glass. With his compassion showing throughout his face, and seemingly talking for him, because he never opened his mouth, I could hear from him, "It was worth it." I looked out the window but there was no one there. I wondered what Bob saw, and for some reason I thought of the past, and I thought about spirits. I wondered if there was an angel out there. I must say he loved to eat.

When we were almost done eating, several couples came into the restaurant and sat in the booths around us. I joked and said, 'We're surrounded.'

Then one of the men from the table across from us said to Bob, 'I know who you are.' At this Bob got upset and started to talk nervously.

I wanted to help . . . so I put my hand on his arm and said, 'Don't worry about anyone else but the people you are with.' I was glad to see this calmed him down.

After I took my hand off of Bob's arm the other man got angry and said, 'You let her touch you.' That night people did seem to want to touch Bob, but he really showed no interest. Anyway, Bob knew I only wanted to comfort and console him when I touched his arm, and he was fine with that. I must say, later in the restaurant, I did want to put my arm around him, but I didn't.

As we were driving back from the restaurant I looked over at Bob. For a few amazing seconds, as he looked at some people driving toward us on the other side of the two-lane road, his eyes shown of a great Heavenly compassion and sadness. I'll never forget his eyes. Only a saint from Heaven could have had such an enormous inner compassion. It was awesome.

After this great saintly look left him, he still had a terrible sadness on his face. I wanted to lessen his pain, and I thought I could do this if I could remind him of some past happy memories. I said to him, 'Where are you from?'

He replied, "Everywhere."

I continued, 'Where is your home?'

He said, "I don't have a home."

Trying again and trying to act cheerful (thinking that we all have some happy childhood memories), I said, 'Oh, come on. Everyone has a place where they grew up.'

He didn't say anything, but he didn't look so sad. This made me feel good also.

Back where we started, after I had parked my car, I asked Bob if I would see him again. He said, "I don't know." We just sat there for a while as he seemed a little reluctant to leave, but then he left. I watched him as he walked behind a building. Soon he drove away very fast, and noisily shifting his car gears. Therefore, I could not help but hear him or see his red sports car. I remember thinking, If there's a policeman around, he will notice him and give him a ticket for speeding. (I now know Bob wanted me to see him, knowing someday I would understand more about our meeting and his invitation.)

✝Today as I was typing the above and making corrections, I heard a devil's spirit say evilly, 'You're close.' So I know that although I am now closer to the meaning of my meeting with Bob, I do not yet fully realize all of the events that took place that night. As I become more aware, I will write things down. I am writing a second book.✝

As soon as Bob, left the other man asked, and then got into the front seat of my car. He said, 'I'll take you out.' Out of respect for his mother I said, 'OK.' He came to my house a few times after that.

I saw so little of what was really going on that night. Now I understand a lot more. However, I did realize that I had been allowed to have seen a saint's eyes, or heart, if you will. This is what I remember most about Bob from that night . . . his eyes that shown with the Heavenly compassion of his loving spirit. Remembering this saintly compassion, has continually reinforced my belief in Our Loving God and His saints. Ultimately, God's Love and His helpers' would rekindle my Faith once again, guide me, and keep my Faith growing and strong. Thank God.

For the following month I can't tell you how many times I saw Bob in his red sports car. Although he always seemed to be around my street, he never drove down it. One day I saw Bob in his red car talking to an elderly man that lived on the street next to mine. Later I went to this man's house and asked him what Bob had said to him. He said, 'The man in the red car, he wants to give you something.' His eyes lit up as he said, 'He really likes you.' I still thought it was strange that Bob never came too close to me. Sometimes it almost seemed as if he was just watching me. At times I would go out looking for him, but I never seemed to be able to bump into him. Then, after a month, Bob started to drive around in an old, beige car. Still, he always seemed close to me. He was always alone.

Well, people I did not even know, or that I might just be passing on the street, began to tell me, 'He promised' or 'He would only give it to you.' †When people said things like this, they would be communicating to me only using their inner thoughts and facial expressions. This is important to remember. Spirits communicate like this. Because I hadn't figured this fact out completely yet, I never thought too much about the way they were communicating with me.† Of course my friends said Bob must have been trying to give me money. Although I still didn't understand what was going on, I thought money would be nice.

Nevertheless, Bob certainly got my attention.

†I was to learn that after we see one of God's Heavenly beings, the devils get very upset with you. They are very bitter and jealous. So therefore, after I had seen the Heavenly presence that Bob had, I had a hard time of it, and at times things did confuse me. **For me, my weakness lasted until I opened the Bible and read and read. When I opened my heart to Jesus, I regained my inner strength.** (Just now, as I was proofreading the above, God's saint said, "Yes, Joyce.")†

Later, there were times that my life was threatened by people I did not even know. Importantly, again, when these people threatened me they did not talk to me using their mouths, as you and I do. These people communicated their thoughts to me from within themselves, and used their eyes and facial expressions. I never even thought enough about the way they were getting their point across, to realize that this is the way spirits communicate. Sometimes they would even say, 'We want it' or 'We want what he gives you.' I thought, Well, I don't have anything; they must want what Bob had, what some people thought he wanted to give me. These threats went on daily for about one month, then not as frequently, but for many more months.

One night, when I was sure it was my last, I called my father and asked him to take my son overnight. I didn't tell him or anyone else that I did not want my son with me that night because I was scared for him. At my father's house I told my son I loved him, and I went home to wait. I stayed in bed awake and very scared until about 3:00 a.m., then exhausted, I fell asleep. When I woke up the next morning, I got myself together and got my son. Then, even though I was still threatened, I decided to ignore it.

I know Bob had some powers, and I know they were good, or at least I knew he would use them for good. At the time I thought that many people wanted what Bob had. I was to find out, as time went on, that it wasn't people or even humans that wanted what Bob had.

One day when I was out driving my car, hoping to see Bob, I

saw something else. It was a clear day, about 3:00 p.m., and the sky was a beautiful blue. I looked into the sky and I saw a large lightning bolt, which seemed to come from high above. Of course, this was the only lightning in the sky on this beautiful, clear day. With this I heard a man's voice, that also seemed to come from high in the sky. He said to me, "This is yours." I was really amazed. Then I became completely puzzled. At that time I couldn't even begin to figure out what this meant.

Fall semester of 1993 was beginning at the local community college. I signed up for two evening classes. As I was leaving class one night I saw Bob standing by the far door, the door I had gone out of on my previous night of class. Dear God, he looked so scared. I looked into his eyes, he never opened his mouth, but from his thoughts, from inside of him, I could hear him say, "It's been a long time." As much as I had wanted to see him, I did not even walk toward him or by him. I left the building by another door. At the time I did not know why I left without talking to him, because I did want Bob. I wanted him because of his goodness and compassion.

Not until well over a year later was I to know what held me back that night. Not until then would I know what made Bob so scared. (I know this may all seem a bit confusing, but it won't be. Please continue to read, there is so much in this book.)

One evening I took my break from night class and went outside with some students. I was hoping Bob would drive by. I was so sorry I had missed him. A student that I didn't even know, said to me, 'All he wants is half.' I thought, I know he's talking to me, but he wants half of what? Then I thought, Maybe he means half of what Bob is to give me. Again, I thought of money, and stubbornly I said, 'No.' Still not even sure of what I had just said no to. I had no idea what was going on.

Then the student let me know, through his thoughts, that if Bob talked to me again, or even came close to me, they had told him they would kill me. Things were a little clearer to me now. I thought, This is why I see him about, but he never comes close.

Still, I would see persistent Bob, in his old, beige car.

One night I decided to go to the local lounge again, and while I was there I met a man and his friend. Then we decided to go out for breakfast so I followed them to the twenty-four hour restaurant, the one I had gone to with Bob. This time the restaurant was crowded. Later, every seat seemed to be taken and people were even waiting for seats.

Before we had gotten our food, I noticed a man out of the crowd. It was like an awareness, a very calm and gentle awareness, that directed me to notice him. He was sitting with some other people two booths behind our booth. (At the time I didn't realize why I had been allowed to notice him.) A short time afterward the same calm and gentle awareness directed me to notice another man, a man who was sitting in another booth that was by the door. Somehow I knew this man by the door was connected to something good, and to Bob. This is the best I can do to explain this awareness.

We had just gotten our food and started to eat. Suddenly, I had an enormous, Heavenly feeling of compassion overtake me. (My Guardian Angel just told me, as I'm typing, "It was him." By the way, him, is a saint. You will understand this all much better as you read on.) I have never felt such a strong, loving compassionate feeling as this. I would have never thought this much love and compassion was possible. At this, I turned and looked at the man sitting beside me. I felt so much overwhelming compassion inside of me, and for him, that I could actually feel this man's inner hunger. I could not help but take my fork and feed this poor man some of the food from my plate. Then the feeling left me.

Right after the feeling left, I even still had my fork in my hand, I heard the thoughts of the man I had noticed sitting in the booth by

the door. He never opened his mouth, but from within him, and from it also showing on his face, he calmly said to the man who was two booths behind me, "He just wanted you to know how it felt."

I knew only the man sitting two booths behind me, and I, heard this man's thoughts. I also knew that somehow the man behind me could feel this tremendous saintly compassion I had just been allowed to feel. (I do not know anything else that was said between the two men.) When I left the restaurant, I noticed that the man who had been two booths behind me was standing outside with three or four male friends. Only he got into the backseat of a black limousine. I was to see him again, and be told who he was.

Shortly after December of 1994 we moved into a duplex, which was in a town close to my hometown. How my poor hometown had changed. It was now crowded and had many of the problems of a city.

Even at this time, I would sometimes still look for Bob; I could not forget his Heavenly compassionate eyes. A few times, when I was driving, I heard his voice. He would say, "Joyce, it's yours." Although I had no idea what he meant, what was mine, his calm voice always put me at peace. Somehow I sensed, I knew, that he had come for me, and somehow I knew that he had stayed to keep me safe. However, again, a few of my friends said that he must have surely wanted to give me money, and greed at that time was a strong emotion in me. So greed would, at times, overtake my senses.

Two times as I drove close to home, Bob tried, patiently I must say, to make me aware and to show me the gifts he had to give. He wanted me to know. Please, let me explain both times:

The first time, I was driving at night down a quiet, two-lane road that runs alongside a river. Coming toward me on the other side of the deserted road, I saw a car that looked like Bob's old, beige car. Although I could not see the face of the driver clearly, I could see that this heavyset man was alone.

As he looked toward me, he almost stopped his car beside mine. I heard Bob's voice. He was very excited as he said, "Joyce, look."

I turned my head and looked toward the river. I saw thousands of tiny, bright white spiritual stars, in an oval cluster. The cluster was about seven feet tall and seemed to hover over the water. The white stars shown brightly over the river at nighttime. It was beautiful, but at the time, I didn't realize it. I looked back at the driver and angrily thought, 'Fine, where's my money?' At this I could feel an enormous sadness coming from the driver of the car, and he very slowly drove away.

Bob had given me this beautiful gift . . . this vision, and I still didn't realize what gifts he had to give.

The second time, I was driving on the same two-lane road at night. The same old, beige car drove toward me and almost stopped beside me. I heard the driver say,

"Joyce, look." I looked in the sky, a little to my right. In the distant sky, I saw a white spiritual light that seemed to be going from Heaven to Earth. I remember thinking vaguely, This is a stairway to Heaven.

This spiritual light seemed to lead the way for smaller, brighter, spiritual lights or stars, which were moving slowly in the light. The brighter lights followed each other, forming two rows that moved in two directions, up and down. The row of small, bright lights closest to me were moving down toward Earth, while on the other side, the small, bright lights were moving up toward Heaven.

The small, bright white spiritual lights seemed very well organized and were spaced equally in distance from one another, a good distance. They were not crowded at all. I remember thinking, This is a comfortable distance. It seemed as if these, small, bright lights, were being moved by a spiritual cloud within the light. This cloud was on both sides of them, and also went up to Heaven and down to Earth. There was a beautiful, white, seemingly soft cushion, that looked like a bit thicker cloud between the two rows. This seemed like a divider or railing, for the small, bright, white lights going in the two directions.

Again, I did not realize the wonder of what I was being allowed to see. I looked back at the driver of the beige car, and still thinking of money, I said to myself, 'So.' As the beige car slowly drove away I could feel the driver's sadness. After this, I went home. I felt so lost and alone. I was still not totally aware of what I had just seen.

Well, I have to say (a bit ashamed), God definitely has some very, very patient helpers.

It was the spring of 1995. I was still thinking I would like to see Bob, but for about five days I kept thinking, Bob is dead. One night, after we had just finished eating supper, my son got up from the table and sat on the couch to watch TV. I started taking the dishes from the table to the nearby sink, as I usually did.

As I was doing this, just inside the kitchen door, appeared Bob's spirit. He had on ordinary clothes. (I know I haven't explained the clothes to you yet, but I will later on. This is important.) From within his spirit, very sadly, he said to me, "Joyce, I am dead." His spirit disappeared. His face shown a look of complete sadness; he looked sadder than I had ever seen him or anyone else. I knew that I had seen his spirit because he knew I wanted to see him, and also—he knew God would let me see him. I realized God allowed this.

After Bob died I saw more of God's spirit world. One night as I lay in bed I saw a bright, small, white star slowly blink. It couldn't have been larger than one-half inch, and looked like a small Christmas light. This beautiful spiritual light was suspended in midair on the side of my room. At the time I just looked, because I had seen these tiny stars a few other times in my life, but all the other times the lights were smaller and had blinked much quicker, so I had just thought, No, it couldn't be.

Well, not even a minute later, the small star blinked again and in the same place in my room, but this time the star blinked its bright light a little longer and a little brighter. This star seemed determined, and I could even, ever so slightly, feel his determination. He wanted to get my attention and to let me know that he was definitely there. As this star blinked the second time I could hear his spirit say, "Show her." All of a sudden, I saw hundreds of tiny white stars blink everywhere in my bedroom. These white stars were smaller than the first one, but there must have been three hundred white stars showing bright for that second. I was totally amazed.

Another night I was upstairs. I heard a car come down my quiet street and stop in front of my house. Then I saw a tiny star light up as it flew into my open dresser drawer. As the star lit up, I heard a voice say very quietly, "Hide." I knew the man outside was not good and these lights were trying to tell me to be careful. But I looked out of the window anyway. No one got into or out of the car; the driver just stayed parked for a few minutes and then he drove away.

Another night at home, I saw the biggest and brightest star I had seen to that time. It was about one and a half inches, and its very bright, white, spiritual light also seemed to sparkle. I was sitting down and the white star was suspended in the air about a foot or so in front of my face. There it shown so brightly.

I calmly looked at the star in front of me. I was so impressed by its beauty that I reached out, very slowly and gently, with my right pointing finger, to touch it. As my finger touched it, it disappeared. But I could feel it, *ever so slightly*, as it gently and quickly sped through the right side of my body to my calf. I waited a bit for it to reappear, but it didn't. I went to bed.

For the longest time I thought this would certainly be the most amazing and exciting thing that could ever happen to me . . . being allowed to see and touch this large, bright, white star!

I also saw two beautiful, light blue, spiritual lights; they were about three to four inches and round. These beautiful spiritual lights were always close to each other and they seemed to be continually playing happily. Like children, they circled and followed each other.

Twice these lights were at my back door by the doorknob. I thought, Well, they may want me to open the door for them so they can go out. When I opened the door, they quickly sped outside together, making circles around each other. More than once I saw two squirrels outside playing together as the lights did. When I saw this, I couldn't help but wonder if these beautiful, spiritual, blue lights were in the squirrels.

One time when I was lying on my couch, I started to get angry about something that had happened that day. Then I saw tiny stars around me and I heard Bob's voice. He said, "You must stay calm." I did not know what was happening, but I think, When we are calm, it is much more possible for God's bright spirits to stay in and close to us.

†Now, Bob was talking to me at this time, but I think it is very important that we all try to stay calm, for the reason above . . . to keep God close to us. And, it seems that when we become angry, the evil spirits become very excited and may even become attracted to us.†

During the next six to seven months I heard Bob's voice again; it was strong and clear. This happened while I was at home.

One time after I just walked up the stairs to my second floor, Bob said, "Joyce, they're not human." I had no idea what he meant. His voice was very calm and peaceful, so I took this calmly and continued doing what I had been doing. Remember, all the spirits I had seen had been peaceful or familiar.

Two months later, when I was upstairs, again, Bob said, "They're not human."

Two to three months later, again, "They're not human."

Only once in that time did Bob's voice seem sad. He said, "They never let us touch." I knew what he meant. Although I had touched his arm, we had never really touched. I also became sad.

Then, for the last time in that house, I heard Bob's voice. I was upstairs alone and getting ready for my shower. I always wear a crucifix on a chain around my neck, and the only time it comes off is before I take my showers. I would take my crucifix and chain off, kiss Jesus, and then put it down on a table. After my shower I would kiss Jesus again and put my crucifix back around my neck.

I was about to take off my crucifix for a shower when I heard Bob's voice. Very clearly and distinctly, he said, "Joyce, don't ever take your cross off." I kissed my crucifix and kept it on.

This was my first awakening. At that time, and for the first time, I thought, What was Bob trying to warn me about? What had he been trying to warn me about? I then realized that whatever he was trying to make me aware of, and probably protect me from, it wasn't human. I began to become aware, that Jesus, through my crucifix, would help me.

✝As I have made my journey back to God, I have taken several steps along the way where I have remembered this warning from Bob—when I have remembered dear Jesus.✝

One night, when both my son and I were home in our beds, I heard the voice of a very old man say, "There are thirty-nine of them." (I wasn't going to write this, because I couldn't remember if the number the man said was thirty-nine or twenty-nine. I think the number was thirty-nine, but I will tell you what happened.) The very second the man finished talking I heard a gunshot. I knew that this older man had been shot on the left side of his head, just above his ear. Within one minute, I saw a white, oval spirit in my room and I could feel this spirit. I could feel he was scared. His spirit was huddled in the corner of my room by the ceiling. I could not see a face, but I knew this white spirit figure was the man who had just died. I felt extremely sad for him. Now, I have to say, Because I knew how this man had died, the whole experience scared me a bit.

Although I knew the man could hear me, and I wanted to make him feel better, I was not sure what to say. Then I remembered my mother's spirit's voice, when she had said the name of God. I remembered how her voice expressed such a comfortable and close friendship with Him. I was also aware that this man had to see God now that his life here was over. I said to the spirit, 'Have you seen God yet?' As I was saying this, I could sense that he had led a good life and God would be good to him. Within three to four seconds I briefly and vaguely saw a white spirit come from my right; and I felt that this angel took this man's hand to lead him on his way to God. They were gone.

About a month later I heard this same man's voice. Peacefully he said to me, "I met God." I knew God had let him come back to answer me. I also knew, by the calm way he talked, that he was happy with his meeting with God. I knew God was good to this man who had led a good life here.

When summer came I began to exercise a lot in my home. One time, when I was alone at home and exercising, I heard my brother's voice, but this time I did not see his spirit. His voice was full of concern as he said, 'My children.' I had also been worried about his children, but I had so little to offer them or his widow.

Well, for the first time I told someone about my experience with spirits. I told my father, as I thought he would like to know about

his son. When I told my father he said, 'Yes, this was Peter.' He said, 'Peter had a great concern and love for his children, and he would worry about them.' My brother was a good man and a good father.

I will tell you about the next time that I heard from my mother's spirit. This time, I did not see her spirit. I just heard her voice. I had decided to have a mole on my face removed, so I asked my father if he could drive me to the hospital and home afterwards, as the doctor had said I should not drive. On the way to the hospital, all of a sudden, my father started to yell at me and I started to cry. While I was crying I heard my mother's voice. Her voice was very faint as she said, 'I'm sorry.' (Now, as I was at home and typing this, I said to myself, She finally said she was sorry. I was angrily thinking about the other times I had seen her spirit and she had never even thought about saying it.)

✝So, I am going to put this here, although I know I haven't explained my Guardian Angel or saint yet. In response to my some-what sarcastic thought of, She finally said she was sorry, God's angel said to me, with her angelic enthusiasm, "Yes." And God's saint said to me, "You must forgive." I thought, Forgiveness is important for our souls.

Just now, I saw a white spirit flash in front of me as I typed this previous sentence. **Forgiveness is important for our souls.** Dears, how can we become white or pure spirits if we carry bitterness or hatefulness . . . darkness in our souls? How can we enter Heaven, with this in our souls . . . if we don't Forgive? Please, Forgive.✝

Please continue to read.

Remember, I could see and hear both my mother's and brother's spirits for some time after they passed away. They were still on Earth. I really wonder, Did God let them stay here to become aware of their mistakes and to learn more? This may be one reason.

With Bob's spirit, some things were different. First of all, his spirit came to me because I had wanted to see him. He came to me, for me; and he had an enormous sadness after he passed away. He had on ordinary clothes after he passed away, but this was to change. Also, Bob's spirit was, and still is, here to protect, guide, and help me. He has a great love for all of God's creations. You will see this, and more, as you read on.

My father had another stroke. Again, he had to stay in the hospital and he needed therapy to walk by himself. Although he had almost totally recovered from his first stroke, his eighty-seven years were beginning to gain on him and this stroke left him exhausted. The first week my father was in the hospital, my son and I would visit him in the evenings, after supper. This time was convenient for us and we knew Dad would be awake and quiet.

Well, the weekend came and my son went with his father. Early that Sunday morning, although it was unusual for me to go anyplace, even to church, on my lazy Sunday mornings, I wanted to visit my Dad. So there I was, 9:30 Sunday morning, at the hospital. For as long as I can remember my father had always gone to the 10:30 morning Mass at his church, however, the previous Sunday he had missed this Mass because he was unable to leave the hospital. That was the only Sunday I can ever remember him missing a Mass.

This Sunday, since he was stronger, the doctor had said he could go to Mass if he had someone to take him, someone who could lift him. That someone was my brother-in-law. My sister and him had the doctor's permission to sign Dad out of the hospital for Mass. I wanted him to get out and to go to Mass and I knew I could not take him. I also wanted to go to church; however, I was still foolishly angry with my sister. So I told my father that I would meet them in church and I left the hospital before my sister and her husband got there. (Donna, that's God's angel, just said to me, "You were wrong." I will explain more about her soon.) Now I know I was wrong in leaving the hospital when I did.

In church, the Mass had been going on for a few minutes before my father, sister, and brother-in-law arrived. They all sat in the pew in front of me. The Mass was on forgiveness and I tried to listen, but forgiving was very hard for me. During the Mass the priest said, "Shake hands in the sign of Peace, and Forgiveness." Of course, the priest always says, "Shake hands in the sign of Peace." This Sunday, and for the only time that I have ever heard, the priest added, "And Forgiveness."

When my sister turned around to shake my hand, I didn't extend my hand out to her. I just said, 'Never.' I was angry. I was wrong. At that time I could not forgive. As my sister slowly turned back around she quietly, but very angrily said, 'O . . . .K.' I knew, and I knew my father knew that she was going to get me for this one. Right after she said that my father turned around to me and angrily said, 'You always cause trouble. Don't come around again.' I knew why my father said this and I knew when he said it my sister did calm down. My father had said it to protect me. I knew, but I still felt very hurt.

Suddenly, to the right of my father . . . an angel appeared. She seemed to come from behind me, as she flew in front of my sister and her husband. Now, the angel was all white, a pure white, except for her brown hair, which she wore in a pageboy. All around her was an aura, also of pure white. She was a light of God's, and she was beautiful. What made this spirit so very beautiful was the purity and goodness from inside of her that shone throughout her, especially on her face. I could only see her spirit from the waist up.

Mass continued as usual, no one even turned their heads slightly to look at the angel. I knew my father and I were the only ones that could see her. With a compassion for my hurt and a concern for my father because of what he had just said, the angel said to him, "Why did you say that?" As with the other spirits her mouth never opened. I heard her thoughts, and the goodness that was so visible on her beautiful face of light spoke very clearly for her.

My father looked to his right, to the angel. He said, 'Because they would kill her.' Her spirit vanished. My father was referring to my sister and her husband. I knew that they really wouldn't kill me; however, I thought, Something isn't right here. I just watched and said nothing; even though this white angel was the very first spirit I had seen that was not familiar to me. Her goodness and compassion left me calm. As soon as Mass ended, I left the church without talking to anyone. I wanted to avoid any arguments.

When I got home . . . I really got excited. I had seen an angel! I was amazed! God's angels are so white, so beautiful, and so very good. The goodness on her face was overwhelming. I'm sorry I can't explain her purity and goodness any better to you than by saying, It was Heaven's light.

I told no one about the angel. I first wanted to talk to my father about her. I wanted to ask him so many questions. Within a day my father went home from the hospital. However, I waited a couple of more days to call him. I wanted to make sure he wasn't still mad at me because I did not want to get yelled at.

When I finally did call my father, he did not seem angry with me. Although I knew he had seen the angel, I said to him, 'Did you see her?' He answered, 'I did. She *was* good.' This was all we said about her, even though I sensed that he wanted me to ask him more questions, right then and there on the phone. I really wish I had.

I didn't ask him any more questions because I felt I really needed to sit down and talk to him in person about the angel. I felt if we sat down, more of my questions would be answered. I wanted to know so much. Still not wanting to get into an argument, I thought, I'll wait a few more days before I visit my Dad at home.

While we were on the phone my father told me he didn't feel good. This was only the third time in his life that I had ever heard him complain, and all three of those times had been in the last one to two months. I am very sorry that when he said this, it went right by me. I guess I was still just so used to seeing him strong. I was to later find out that when he was in the hospital the doctors had found cancer in his stomach.

Before I was able to see my father again, he had a fatal heart attack. It was May of 1995. But I will never forget . . . the last time I saw my father he was talking to an angel.

At home, my son started to act terrible. He seemed to be very angry and he would not listen to me, regardless of what I said. His grades in school dropped and for the first time he got a few E's on his report card. None of this was like him at all. When we went out in the car he would wave to people that neither of us knew. When I asked him, 'What are you doing? Please stop it.' He would say he didn't do anything and look at me as if to say, What are you talking about? He truly didn't remember waving and I knew he thought, What is wrong with you, Mom?

Twice, when we were sitting at the supper table he jumped as if someone had hurt him, then he would start to yell at me. When he yelled, I do not think either of us were sure why he was yelling. He wasn't himself and I did not know what to do. I became very worried for him.

I also began acting differently. I was so tense. I spent less time at home, gave my son less time, and at times I even left my son alone. I had never left him alone before.

I was worried because I thought, There's something that's starting to bother us, but I couldn't figure it out. I thought, What is it? Was this what Bob had been trying, all the time he had been around us, to protect us from? Was this what Bob was trying to warn me about after he died? Could it hurt us since Bob and my father had died? It seemed that frightening problems were coming into my home and becoming overwhelming. At that time, the thought did not even occur to me that these problems might be caused by bad spirits. I just got scared for my poor son. I wanted him safe.

I planned on moving again. When I told my son, he became outraged. His father had just started taking our son out, over the last three to four months, every other weekend. My son, who was almost thirteen years old, asked if he could live with his father. I knew my son's father had been really selfish, and naively I was hoping he had changed. I asked his father to take his son for just the summer, thinking that after a summer with his father, the child might be more settled. However, his father said he would only take him if he could have him. In the back of my mind I thought, If I let my son go, at the end of the summer I could get started again and get my son back anyway.

My basic concern was that I desperately wanted my son to be safe. I figured whatever it was that was making trouble in my home wanted me. Since I thought it would be safer for my son, on June 12, 1995, he moved to live with his father and his father's new family, whom I really barely knew. The day after my son left, I left my home. At that time, I was relieved. I thought, I would not have to worry about my child. He would now be safe.

. . . . .

As things went, at the end of the summer I wasn't able to get my child back. Now I realize my son was not himself and I should not have let him go. I really wish I had turned to my religion and to God for help, and I feel if I had, much of this would not have happened. This move was to break my heart.

THE FIRST TRIP

THIS WAS THE FIRST OF TWO TRIPS I WOULD TAKE IN THE summer of 1995. I needed answers. I had usually run or hid from my problems, and you could say I was doing this here, but I wasn't. This time, although I was still hoping I could lose this problem, I really wanted to make whatever it was that was upsetting my life come out and face me. I thought, Enough is enough. I was ready to fight. So I got into my car and just kept driving south, keeping my atlas beside me and deciding which road to take as I went along.

Now God would let me see more; it was time and I was ready. I would see the side of the spirit world that has no light, the side of darkness. Some things were frightening at first, but through Faith (God's angel just told me that word is important, Faith) I am now stronger. Remember, even though I had seen spirits for years, I did not connect any of my problems with them, because all of the spirits I had seen had been calm and had left me calm. If I had known more about my religion and the Bible, I would have known what was causing me problems.

I drove continually my first day out, and most of the night. At about 2:00 or 3:00 a.m. I found myself in Virginia. I was extremely tired and just about all that I could think of was that I wanted to find a quiet place to sleep. I did not want to drive much further.

As I was driving down this small, winding interstate, I had noticed several small signs for churches, which directed cars off the main routes and down small, dirt roads. I thought the churches in this area must have been very small. Since I was so tired and I felt safer near a church, I thought, Well, I'll turn down the next road that has a church sign and sleep in my car by the church. I didn't have to drive too much further. The next small church sign pointed to a narrow dirt road. This narrow road was just wide enough for one, maybe two, cars, and had lots of trees and bushes on both sides of it.

As I drove down the dirt road, from the left side of the woods came a large black dog. He stopped in the middle of the road, and then he turned his head to look at me. Because of the trees and bushes I couldn't drive around him, so I stopped my car to wait for him to go by. The dog's head turned again, sideways to me, and then seemingly involuntarily, he opened his mouth. I saw a fog, of sorts, come from the right side of the woods and float into the dog's open mouth. When the fog totally entered the dog's mouth, he closed his mouth. The fog was oblong, transparent, and six to eight inches long. It had numerous one-inch, three-dimensional, connecting octagon parts. This was a spirit, one I had never seen.

I just sat there and watched, but as the dog closed its mouth, I felt a pinch on the back, right side of my neck. At that instant, the dog's eyes lit up to a bright red, and he looked toward me. I heard a woman's voice boastfully say, 'Now I can bite.' Then I got scared . . . even though I knew by the way the spirit boasted that she was just showing off and did not intend to hurt me. As quickly as I could turn my car around on that small road, I did.

This was the first time I saw a spirit that had scared me. None of the other spirits I had seen had wanted to hurt anyone. However, it was more than evident that just the thought of hurting someone made this spirit happy.

When I got back on the interstate I drove and drove. I drove for about two hours, then I became exhausted; I couldn't drive anymore. I stopped on the side of the road, this main country road, and slept in my car.

The next night, as I was still driving south, I saw a shadowy black figure in the backseat of my car. When I would turn to look directly at it or look at it through my rearview mirror, I noticed the black shadow would pop down very quickly, and then I could no longer see it. I soon realized that since this dark spirit had shown off for me the night before, she now felt more secure and decided to show more of herself to me. She also began to communicate with me. She could read my thoughts and she answered me with her thoughts. I did not have to talk out loud. When I asked her, she told me her name was 'Sue.' But still, she just showed herself as a shadow, popping up and down quickly in my backseat.

At this time she only appeared at night, saying she liked the darkness. I had no idea what she meant by this, nor did I have any idea who I was talking to. After talking with her for a while I noticed her vocabulary seemed limited.

As we passed cars on the quiet road that night, she would say,

'I'm going to get him.' Then I knew she was gone because I felt her presence gone from my car; however, she shortly returned. Some times when she came back she would say, 'I'm back.' or 'I got him.' or even, 'I really got him.' She seemed cruel. Hearing her say these things and thinking she hurt people really upset me. I continued talking to her, but for hours I pleaded with her to leave people alone and please try to be good. This did not stop her. Mostly, amidst my pleas, she would answer me with, 'I can't help it.' I am not sure what this bad spirit did when she was gone, but I am sure she was having a good time with me.

Again, this spirit was more secure at night; this was the only time that she appeared or talked to me at first. I thought of what Bob's spirit had said to me when I had started my trip, "Sleep during the day, and travel at night." I think Bob wanted me to see her. He wanted me to know: It was time for me to see, but I was a little scared.

The second night that this shadowy spirit appeared, she did the same things she had done the first night. She continually left my car to 'Get him' and I continually pleaded, 'Leave them alone. Please be good.' Then I decided I would try something else to get her to be good. I said, 'If you're good you might get to Heaven.' I still didn't realize who I was talking to. Angrily she replied, 'That's not it.' It surprised me that she got angry with this . . . it made no sense to me. I continued trying to get her to be good, 'But you can go to Heaven if you're good.' Mad at me again, she replied, 'That's not it.'

Further into the night, amidst my innocent, but well-intended, coaxing of about two hours, I heard a man's voice very angrily say, 'That's not it.' His voice was not totally human. Because Sue was a bit angry with me that night, if she did answer me, the 'That's not it,' was her normal reply also. Finally, Sue said, 'That's not it. I'm a devil.'

Well . . . slow as I was at this, I began to put things together. I now realized why Sue's spirit was so cruel, and why she really seemed to enjoy even the mere *thought* of hurting people. I have to admit I began to get scared after she told me who she was. But then I figured, Well, she hadn't hurt me, so far. However, while I was still trying to sort this all out, I stopped my continuous efforts of trying to help her get to Heaven, and for a while I just kept quiet and drove.

Now, you have to realize how I am. The fact that Sue was a devil's spirit did take a good hour to really sink in. Then, I thought, Poor Sue is a devil. Her quiet was over . . . .

I started again . . . because I really did want to try and help her. This time, foolish as it may sound, I tried to change her, to convert her. Sympathetically I pleaded with her, 'Stop hurting people. Be good.' I even told her to pray. I said, 'You might see Heaven yet.' Really, from my heart, I tried to change and save this devil. (I must bring this up again, although you might realize it by now, I wasn't exactly educated in my religion. In fact, some people might say I was downright ignorant. But you know I had Faith. I believed in God and I believed in what little I knew about my religion.)

What I will write here is very sad. At one time during our talks I remember the devil Sue desperately saying, 'I want to go to Heaven.'

The next night, when Sue popped up again, I have to admit I was a bit scared. But as I talked to her spirit, I still tried to change and convert her. Of course, all the time I was trying to convert Sue, I was trying to convert her to thinking the way that I do, as I had been taught as a Catholic. (Believe me, when I look back on this, I still get a little embarrassed by my efforts. But you must realize, I really felt very much that I wanted to help her.)

Later in the night, the thought came into my mind, She might be here because she's getting another chance, a second chance. So I

told her, 'Maybe if you're good, this time you might be forgiven.' Well, during my onslaught of naiveness and goodness, she became very angry. Three times her anger was so intense that I could actually feel it.

She called us 'humans.' This devil said this with the most disgust and hate. I told her to leave us alone; naive me still did not realize why I couldn't change her. Sue complained that 'humans' had more than her. She said, 'It wasn't fair.' A little later Bob's spirit told me, "She had a lot more than you, Joyce. A *lot* more."

Something else I remember this devil saying: 'We only wanted what He had.' At the time this went right over my head. (I will refer to this later.)

I was to learn firsthand that it could not be done; we can't change the devil.

One rainy night I was driving on a winding, two-lane road in Pennsylvania and Sue was talking to me. I only saw her shadow pop up and down in my backseat, but I heard her clearly as we communicated with our thoughts. Then, when I looked into my rearview mirror, I saw a young girl sitting in my backseat. She was just behind me, but a little to my right, looking at me. This attractive girl was only about twenty-four years old or so; she had black eyes and beautiful black hair. She had slightly pointed ears and four large upper front teeth. Now, this is what I saw, whether the devil was playing tricks on me or not, I do not know.

I only looked at the girl for a second because I had to look back at the winding road, but I was not scared. Then, about three seconds later, my car skidded. I could not stop or control my car and it slid into a guardrail that curved around a corner. I did not have my seat belt on, so when I hit the guardrail the impact pushed me down and to the right.

Luckily, both of my hands were on the steering wheel and my first reflective response was to push myself away from the steering wheel, which broke some of the impact. However, my chest still hit the steering wheel with some force, leaving it sore for about three days afterward.

My face also hit the steering wheel, and my right hand that was holding the wheel. Consequently, my right thumbnail cut me above my upper right lip. The cut bled, and later scarred slightly. And my chin was sore for about three days, from hitting the steering wheel. However, I never lost consciousness; basically I was fine.

My car's steering wheel became loose. I could move it around freely for an area of about an inch; this is how hard my chest hit the wheel. (Later I was to find out that the steering column had to be replaced.) It's amazing that I just had aches and pains from the accident.

The car's passenger front headlight was broken and the whole right front side was smashed. The right side of the bumper almost hung to the ground, as well as tightly rubbing against the front right tire. If I did not have new tires on my car, I really think that the impact would have caused a flat tire. The bumper was a mess.

Strangely enough, my windshield was cracked. The crack looked like a large spider web, and the center of the crack was to the left of where I sat in my driver's seat. I never hit the windshield; I had no head injuries at all, only face and chest injuries. I was thrown to the right and thrown down, not left or up.

Right after the accident I heard Sue's devil spirit say, 'You're the first one that's ever seen me and lived.' Again, I can only tell what I saw and heard. I do not know what hit the windshield; I never hit the windshield.

✝Now, I do not know if spirits in this state of visibility, when we can see them as I could see this spirit that was in my backseat, if they are as totally solid as you and me. The spirit looked almost as solid as us, but not exactly. However, I do know there are different levels or stages for spirits, where they can be more or less visible and solid. I hope I have explained this well enough for you. I think spirits can, for the most part, control their level of visibility and solidness.

I think this spirit might have, at the time, lost control of her invisibility. Again, I do not know. But it really seems she did not want me to see her, and it really seems she wanted to kill me right after I saw her. I know what bothered her the most about my seeing her was that I saw her teeth. She was very conscious of them. A few times the next night she said, very ashamed, 'My teeth.' I told her not to worry. She was very pretty. And she was.✝

Back to the accident. After I realized I was OK, and as I was looking at my car, checking the bumper, a woman drove up to me. She said she was sitting at home when she heard the crash and she wanted to see if I needed help; she did help. She told me there was a garage about 100 yards down the road, which made me feel a lot better.

I had to drive slowly to the garage because my bumper was rubbing the right tire very badly. I really do not think I could have driven my car much further than the garage. It was about 2:00 a.m., and the garage was closed when I got there, so I stayed in their parking lot and waited for them to open. I must say, I rested very little in my car the remainder of that night.

When the garage opened, all the mechanic could do for me was cut away some of the bumper so that it would not rub the tire. I was very grateful. Then I was off again.

At the time, it had just begun to dawn on me that I might not be able to hide from my problems. I figured I had a problem with the spirit Sue, but I wasn't fully aware that devil spirits might be a big part of my life's chaos. However, I did begin to think, naively, that somehow I had to fight Sue; but I wondered how. I am ashamed to say, I did not think of God.

That day I did not see Sue. However, at night her shadow returned. Her devil's spirit was still in my backseat. I was scared, but I was more angry than scared, and I kept saying, 'Look at what you did. Leave me alone.' I talked much less with her after the car accident. When I told her to leave me alone, she said, 'No.' She was very angry with me because she said I was a saint and I was going to Heaven. Well, always having a good heart, but just being me, I didn't say anything in reply and I didn't think too much about it.

The night after the accident something else happened. I saw God's wonderful angel again. The pure white angel appeared right outside my car, flying beside me as I drove. Seeing this angel has always left me in amazement and awe. God's angel calmly said to Sue, who was in the backseat, "We have had a lot of complaints about you." I just drove my car, surprised at the passiveness of the word this calm angel chose to use—Complaints. Complaints to describe the reactions to this devil's terrible behavior! My mouth almost flew open after the angel calmly said this.

 Then the thought occurred to me that Sue had a lot to do with killing Bob, and probably many others. This thought, this realization, God allowed me. Also, I knew what had been after Bob in his life - devil's spirits. Things were now a lot clearer to me in regard to Bob's behavior. I now knew why he was scared, carefully weighing all of his actions and words; and why people seemed to be watching him.

Complaints . . . . Complaints!!! I again thought to myself. I was still amazed at this mild word and at how calmly this angel said it. Well, I managed to keep my mouth shut and I just watched and listened as I drove. In response, Sue's black, shadowy, not human but somewhat human-like figure, hopped up in my backseat. Her hands went above my head, ready to grab me. The devil's spirit said, 'Let me just kill one more.' God's angel said, "No. You will kill no more."

They both disappeared.

I sat thinking for a while—something that I had thought would never happen, does happen; angels and devils speak to each other. I had thought that they were worlds apart, as they are; but they are also, as we are also . . . all in the same world.

I had wanted my life to be my own, and I still had many questions.

You see, even though I had seen a lot, I still did not put everything together until later. Therefore, I was not going home yet . . . stubborn me kept driving my smashed car throughout the south. I have to admit, since my car's right headlight did not work, this made things a bit difficult; but I did not worry about it.

Then, one day I again thought about Bob's important warning to me after he had died, "Joyce, don't ever take your cross off." As I thought about this warning I became a bit more aware. I began to realize that if my cross, the cross of Jesus, could protect me, then God and the Holy Spirit would also. I knew I *needed*, and I also *wanted*, to read and study more about my religion, and to familiarize myself more with Jesus, Our Father, and the Holy Spirit.

I figured in order for me to concentrate I should find some place quiet. With a bit of effort, a few rights and lefts on the Kentucky country roads, I found The Retreat House. I stayed in this beautiful, peaceful abbey for three days.

My first day at the abbey I was very happy to find the library. There were shelves and aisles of books on God, the saints, etc., etc. I thought, Great! Then I noticed tapes, and I figured the tapes might be easier for me to begin with, so I got my own table and picked out at least ten tapes for myself. I was so excited to be in this library, surrounded by religious material.

As I was listening to the tapes, and not really grasping what I heard, I saw Bob's spirit. He was standing at the front end of an aisle of books. He said, "Joyce, read." Then his spirit left. I also knew that when he told me to read, he was telling me, "This is the aisle to choose your book from." Right away I stopped my tape, got up, and looked down the aisle.

At the front of the aisle were Bibles, shelves of books on the Bible, and then other religious books to the end of the aisle. I felt overwhelmed because there were so many books in the aisle. With all good intentions, I stood there for about five minutes just looking.

I was very worried. I knew I only had a few days of quiet in the abbey, so I did not want to waste any time. I wanted to read the right book. (Now, when I saw Bob's spirit, he was wearing a white gown. But because I was so worried about getting the right book, I hardly thought about it. Please realize that at that time I knew how important Bob's words were. I will go back to this later.)

I thought, Which book does Bob want me to read? I got a book from the aisle on saints. I remember reading that if you do not give your soul to the devil, he cannot take it. You know we are all God's children. Please stay with your Heavenly Father. He Loves you.

I know that the book I chose and my other choices those few days were good. But now I know the book Bob wanted me to read: the Bible.

About an hour after I had seen Bob's spirit, I saw Sue's spirit standing in front of the same aisle. I knew she did not want to be outdone by Bob as she said, 'It's here.' She knew.

I traveled more in the south, to Tennessee, I went. I still thought, or maybe I should say I was wishfully thinking, that I could lose my problems on the winding roads. Even though I believed God would protect me, I still did not completely realize what was going on, and I wanted to know exactly what was happening.

I was running out of cash, so on July 3, 1995, I opened an account in Virginia with a personal check. Knowing I had to wait for my out-of-state check to clear the Virginia bank, I went looking for a church, where I knew I would feel peaceful and could pray. I found a beautiful church, and since it was in a small and quiet town, the doors were always unlocked. However, I was sad to find out that the priest had gone for a week. I quietly prayed that morning and the rest of the day; then I decided to stay in the church that night.

. . . . .

When night came, I turned on the lights, lit the candles, and sat in a front pew close to the altar, as I prayed. I have to admit I was not too comfortable in this church at night.

Later that night I saw small bolts of lightning, which were six inches or so, flash just in front of me. The bolts were white, and although they looked pretty solid, I knew they were spiritual. The small bolts came quickly at my chest, and then suddenly they dropped down. When they dropped down it seemed as if they were deflected downward. None of them hit me. I was curious, but since I had no idea what was going on, I did not think too much about it. (I will mention these bolts later, and I will explain them more.)

Also, white spirit figures flew quickly about the church, many times flying right in front of me. These spirits were basically zooming by so fast that they looked like clouds zipping by. They were the same white color as God's angel, and I felt peaceful with them.

Behind the altar was a wall that had a doorway to a small, back room. From this doorway, a small, three feet or so, red, spiritual figure showed herself for just a second or two, as she peeked out to look at me. Her color red was the same, deep red that I had seen in the dog's eyes a little while back. I only saw her figure once and only partially, as she stood at the doorway holding the wall. I saw her from the chest up, and her right leg was also showing. The all-red figure was a human-like figure, but definitely not human, mostly animal. Needless to say, I didn't sleep that night.

. . . . .

In the morning things stopped, and I was exhausted. I went to the church's balcony and slept. It seems that the dark spirits are more active and daring during the night, and they do like to scare us. It also seems that at night our angels are working their hardest to protect us. This is amazing and wonderful. While we are sleeping so peacefully at night, our guardians are probably working their hardest.

✝As I just retyped this, I thought of the prayer, "Now I lay me down to sleep. I pray the Lord my soul to keep. If I shall die before I wake. I pray the Lord my soul to take." I know this is not a Catholic prayer, but a Protestant prayer. I wanted to put this here because it shows such Faith and love toward Our Lord.✝

That afternoon a deacon came to the church to pray. He prayed the rosary over and over again. As I watched him pray, I thought, I don't even remember how to pray the rosary. So I waited for him to finish praying, then I asked him to explain the rosary to me. He did, and he even offered me the extra set of beads he had. I prayed the rosary.

. . . . .

My second night in the church, I was a bit angry. I wanted these devils away from me. Again I turned on the lights and lit the candles, but this time I walked throughout the church and prayed aloud. I walked up and down the aisles, in every room, and even in the room behind the altar. I did not sit in my seat scared, as I had the night before. I saw the bolts and the white spirits flying quickly by, just as I had the night before. I realized that the white spirits flying so quickly in front of me were my guardians protecting me. They do have to move very fast. By 1:30 a.m., I was so tired that I slept in one of the church's front pews. I slept with one of the church's Bibles close to me.

When I woke-up I prayed again, and I prayed the rosary. Then I went to the bank and left the peaceful town and Virginia. It began to become a bit clearer to me that devil's spirits could be my problem, and from this awareness I knew that I had to think about how I could handle this.

I needed to get my car fixed, so although I spent another day traveling, I decided to go home.

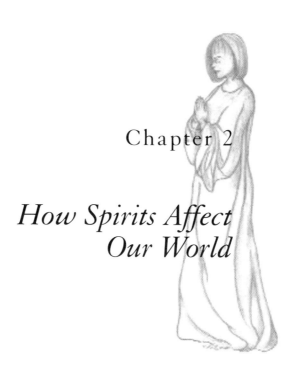

Chapter 2

How Spirits Affect Our World

† ON MY FIRST TRIP I HAD BEEN ALLOWED TO SEE EVEN more of the spirit world. I had seen that there is a very active spirit world of both good and evil on Earth with us—angels as well as devils. The spirits can see us, hear us, and even hear our thoughts, but most of us cannot see or hear them.

Although we do not know it, spirits do affect our lives, but only to the point where God allows them. For instance, Sue's devil spirit could have killed me, but God's angel did not let her. When my car was smashed, when God allowed this, the accident helped naive me become aware of just how bad the evil spirits can be. Also, this accident helped lead me back home.**†**

When I returned home one of the first things I did was take my car to the auto body shop for an estimate. When they took my car they told me it would just take two days to fix . . . it took five days. The front of my car was really damaged and the repair cost came close to two thousand dollars. Included in this price was a new front windshield.

While my car was being fixed I had some free time, and I found a couple of churches in the area that were left open all day. My trip and the spirits, God's angels, had certainly changed me. One of the churches that I prayed in was that of cloistered Dominican nuns. In their church, in back of the altar, was a beautiful wall that had windows on both the right and left sides. These windows were open only when the nuns, who were in the large room behind this wall, prayed aloud for all to hear.

On this day, after I had prayed for a while, the nuns opened the windows and I could see their room and hear them pray. As I listened to the nuns, I felt that a great and very holy older nun was praying behind this wall with them. I felt that another holy, but not so old, nun was praying there also. I prayed.

Then I felt a pull on the top of my head. I had felt this pull before, but since I didn't know what was going on, I didn't think too much about it. I continued praying with the nuns and watching one of the windows that was open. From behind this open window I saw a very beautiful, spiritual, orange/yellow oblong halo float out. I only saw a little more than half of the halo, as it did not go out any further from behind the window. Then I heard the older nun, the very holy nun, say to me, "This is yours." (I did not think of it until afterward, but I realize that this is one of the spiritual gifts God gives, and the devil's spirits want.) After the halo went back behind the wall, the very holy nun said to me, "They are beasts." I thought, She knows the devils also.

I can't help thinking that I should not have put this here, but it's related to other events in the book. This is when it happened.

I finally thought, I want and I really need a Bible. I thought a Bible might help answer some of my questions, advise me, and help me familiarize myself more with God's spirit world. So, who better to call? I called our church's priest and I asked him if I could borrow a Bible. The Bible was beautiful.

God's lights had brought about a change in me, but I was still very much uneducated and I had a way to go yet. Reading the Bible was to bring about an even bigger change in me, however, I didn't start to read the Bible until I was days into my second trip, which I will tell you about in a bit. Please have patience and continue reading.

Seeing Sue and other devil's spirits confused and scared me, so one day I decided to talk to my friend about some of the things I saw. I thought my friend might be able to give me some advice, as she had given me good advice on several other things in the past. She enjoys reading and retains much of what she reads.

As I was telling my friend about the devil's spirits I could see that she was beginning to get scared. She has known me since we were very young and she knew I was telling the truth. So I decided not to tell her too much, but I asked her, 'What should I do?' She said, 'Get a bottle with a spray nozzle and fill it with holy water.' Then she said, 'Use it.'

Now, what I had seen of the spirit world, and what I had actually put together about what I had seen, cleared up a very small amount of my questions. This was to be only the beginning of my journey. I still felt that someone or something, I wasn't sure which, was affecting my life, and I desperately wanted to run my own life. Also, as you can imagine, seeing just a bit of the spirit world now left many other things <u>unknown</u> to me. I needed more answers. . . .

. . . . .

One of the first things I knew I needed to do, was to be alone in a quiet place; to think without interruptions. I felt I could then find my heart's peace.

My hometown was now a busy city, and I thought this would

not do. So, I decided to go on another trip. Just like the first trip, I didn't make any definite plans before I left, although I knew that I had to at least decide in which direction I would travel. I had found that the southern states were pretty busy, so I decided to travel to the open spaces of the west.

I figured I would find quiet and solitude in the desert, as Jesus had done. Jesus, would again, help me in answering some of my questions.

THE SECOND TRIP

I LEFT FOR MY SECOND TRIP ON THE DAY THAT I GOT my car out of the auto body shop. It was a Friday, and as well as I can remember, it was the beginning of August. Although I had gotten my car back at 4:30 P.M., by 6:00 P.M. that evening I was driving on the highway. I was so anxious to leave, especially after the body shop had taken so many extra days to fix my car.

I soon realized that I should have checked my car more closely before I left on this trip. As I drove on the highway I noticed that the front wheels seemed to shake when I drove fast, and my steering column was still loose. However, I kept driving, not realizing how unsafe my car still was.

In the seat beside me, along with my road atlas, I now had my Bible. Although I had brought the Bible to read, I somehow also felt safer that I had it with me. I used the atlas quite frequently once I got off the highway and started to drive on the quiet routes, which was very shortly after I began my trip. As I drove west, I decided which routes to travel as I went along.

I was driving at night. It was my first night out. I knew Sue was in the backseat because I saw her dark figure; I saw her black shadowy

human-like figure. She appeared a few times, but only briefly, as I looked through the rearview mirror.

I drove with both of my hands on the steering wheel. My left hand was on the top of the steering wheel and my right hand on the side of the wheel.

I had been driving very peacefully for some time, when I heard Bob's spirit say, very quietly, "Let her see it." I saw a beautiful, illuminating blue, slightly turquoise, aura, begin to appear around both of my hands. I looked closer. The aura was so small at first, then, in only six to seven seconds, the light grew to about three-quarters of an inch. The aura was equally and evenly glowing and growing around both of my hands.

Then Sue popped up in the backseat. From her black form I could feel her anxiety and that she could not wait any longer. I felt the aura being pulled from me. I knew this devil's spirit was pulling the aura from me. I knew Sue was pulling. The aura and Sue disappeared.

✝I did not realize it at the time, but it seems that this devil's spirit turns visible and black; solid I will call it, to pull. It seems her spirit is stronger and can pull or take more from us, when she is in this more solid form. I will mention this black solid form and pulling, from time to time.✝

Dears, now back to this beautiful aura—another gift that God gives us. Of course, we can't see this spiritual gift, but the spirit world can see it. Unknown to us, the devil's spirits take this from us poor 'humans.' This is all that I know about the aura . . . but I do know that God gives us so much more than we realize, or see.

I drove almost continually on the small, winding routes for about a day and a half, then I became so exhausted, I knew I had to stop someplace to sleep. It was about 2:00 a.m., my second night out, when I turned down a small dirt road, parked my car, and soon fell asleep.

The next morning, when I woke up, I saw a huge bee flying around in my car by the back window. I remember thinking, That's a big bee, but being drowsy I just turned around and continued to rest . . . as you can tell I enjoy my sleep. A few minutes later I became curious. I thought I should lift both of my hands, palms out, toward the bee. I wanted to see if I could feel anything in my hands. Sure enough, there was a strong pulling feeling in the palm of my hand, but only from my left palm. I knew Sue's devil's spirit was in the bee, however, I was surprised that she was able to get her spirit into something as small as a bee. Of course, because of her pride, she had chosen the biggest bee I had ever seen.

In the palm of my hand, as I felt the pull, I could also somehow feel Sue's words as she said to me, 'OK. I'll change.' Then the pulling feeling went from my left palm into my right palm. I got angry with her. I wanted her out of my car and out of my life, so I looked for something to throw at the bug, but I couldn't find anything. Finally I found a napkin and I thought, I'll catch her in the napkin.

As I went after the bee it flew to the window by the driver's seat. So I sat back in my seat, and there on the glass, I trapped the bee in the napkin. When I tried to crush the bee, and I knew I had it, it disappeared. The bee soon reappeared by my left leg. Confused, I just sat for a second, and then I again tried to get her. I was unable to catch the bee, and it soon flew out of the small opening that I had left in the window.

Sadly, basically uneducated in my religion me, thought, I could not even crush her when she was in an animal. I wanted to be free of this evil spirit. At the time I was actually thinking that I could have crushed this devil's spirit, but I had lost my chance.

Then I felt even more sadness. I felt sad for all of the people this devil had hurt, and now for all of the people she would continue to hurt. I heard Sue's voice from the backseat. She said, 'You'll never get another chance again.' Her devil's spirit came back to taunt me.

From then on, when I slept in my car, I would leave my car windows open only very slightly. Of course, Sue could still come into my car in her spirit form, but she could only bring very small bugs in through the small window openings.

✝As I look back at this, I realize how little I knew. I now know spirits can enter any creature very quickly and easily, and leave any creature very quickly and easily. Therefore, when I tried to crush the bee, I would have done just that, crush the bee. Sue's devil's spirit would not have been hurt; her spirit would have just flown out of the poor bee.✝

Later that day, I thought back to the pulling feeling I had in my palms when Sue was in the bee. I wondered why this feeling was first in my left palm and then my right palm. Also, before this switch happened the devil said, 'OK, I'll change.' I thought, Several times I had heard of God's power being referred to as, the Right Hand of God. So I mentioned to Sue the power of God's Right Hand. She replied, 'We are the opposite.' I now realize that the devil's spirits are the opposite of all that God is.

Now I know Sue was only playing with me when she allowed me to feel this pulling feeling, first from my left palm and then from my right palm. Of course we can't tell where evil is by just a pulling feeling in either our right or left palms. And even if we could, remember, Sue could easily switch this pulling feeling to either palm.

✝The true way to know if evil is about, is by someone's words or, especially their actions. We do know when something is wrong or evil. Thank God.✝

One night as I was driving, I became angry because I knew Sue was still in the backseat. Without any forethought, I took my spray container of holy water and sprayed the holy water into the backseat area. (Remember my friend told me to get a spray container and fill it with holy water?) Instantly, I heard an unearthly scream from outside of my car's rear window. The scream was as if an animal, of sorts, was being burnt. I kept spraying. Then I heard Sue angrily say to me, 'Bitch.' I have to say this made me a little nervous. I thought, Now a devil's spirit is very angry with me. This is where my Faith helped. I kept on driving, and at times that night I kept on spraying the backseat of my car with holy water, which I kept very close to me.

At first I didn't realize why the scream came from outside of my car, then I knew that the holy water must have made this devil's spirit jump very fast, from my backseat, to the safer area outside the glass of my car's back window.

✝It is true that holy water burns the poor devils. And I would just like to add that it is our priests who bless this water to make it holy water.✝

It was about my fourth day out. I was driving on a very quiet and winding two-lane country road in Ohio. On the left side of the road I noticed a small church and I felt a strong desire to pray, so I stopped my car. As soon as I walked into the church a wonderful feeling of peace overtook me. I quietly prayed.

As I was leaving the church and opening the first set of doors into the hallway, I noticed the statue of a saint that was on my right. I don't know why I especially noticed this statue, in fact I must say that I cannot even remember who the statue was of, but I wanted to tell you this.

Off to the side of the hallway was the church's bathroom, which I used. As I poured the pitcher of water that was in the bathroom into the toilet to flush it, I knew I had succeeded in avoiding crowds and busy areas. (And definitely any cities.)

When I opened the door to step outside I noticed a priest standing on the other side of the narrow street. A woman that seemed very anxious was talking to the priest. However, he remained calm and he didn't seem to pay her too much mind. I wasn't sure why, but I walked toward the priest, not even sure of what I was going to say to him . . . then I asked him if there was a retreat in the area that I could stay at. He said he knew of one, but he needed to call them first to see if it was OK. We walked toward a building by the church and the woman followed us, but she said nothing.

I really admire the craftsmanship of old buildings, and as we sat in the priest's office I could not help but notice a beautiful old building down the road. The priest told me that the building had been a convent for a group of nuns (I'm sorry I can't remember their order); however, the nuns had moved from this building a long time ago. The priest said the building had been abandoned for years and years. He said after all this time the building had finally been sold and was being renovated. It was to become a motel or a bed-and-breakfast, or such. (I will tell you more about this building and these nuns later.) When the priest was done making his telephone calls he said he had found me a quiet place with some nuns. He gave me directions and I thanked him. I was on my way.

As I drove, I thought, This quiet time would give me the opportunity to read more about my religion and, as I read, if I had any questions, I could ask the nuns to help me. This is great. I wanted more knowledge. I knew I certainly needed it, and I wanted to strengthen my Faith.

. . . . .

When I arrived at the nun's hospital they kindly directed me to their convent area and gave me one of their quiet rooms. At my request, they also gave me plenty of religious material to read. In fact, I had more reading than I was to finish. (As I am writing this Bob's spirit said, in a very soft and saintly voice filled with compassion, "They were good to you." I know he has a great love for nuns.) The nuns were very good and helpful to me.

In the nun's hospital was a beautiful church, and at the Sunday mornings Masses many people came to worship.

. . . . .

For two or three days I spent most of my time quietly reading in my room. Then one morning I made friends with one of the nuns. Early that afternoon I again ran into this nun and I complimented her on their beautiful church. She told me that in this church, the monstrance with the exposed Eucharist was on the altar all day, and that she was on her way there to pray to Jesus. I had very limited knowledge of the monstrance, so this confused me. As I asked her questions I could see a look of surprise on her face. Then she told me she did have to go and pray now, but she would see me later on.

Later that day she did find me, and she gave me some literature on the monstrance and exposed Eucharist. She tried her best to explain this to me. The nun also gave me a beautiful picture of the monstrance with Eucharist, which she told me to keep. (More about this picture later.) She told me that during the hours of the exposition of the Eucharist there were always two nuns praying to Jesus, so Jesus would have prayers offered to him. This touched my heart. She told me this was why she could not talk to me earlier that afternoon, because she was on her way to pray with the second nun.

After that I also tried to find time during the day to pray in front of the monstrance with the Eucharist, Jesus. I always humbly sat behind the nuns, which I thought was only proper.

. . . . .

A day or two later, I again talked to the nun who had so kindly taken the time to explain the monstrance to me. I told her about some of my experiences with spirits, telling her about both the good and the bad experiences. She told me about a priest she had met many years before, when he had come to the convent to speak to the nuns. This priest, (I'm sorry I can't recall his name) had written a book based on his religious experiences with exorcism. The book is, *Begone, Satin!,* published by Huntington, Ltd., Our Sunday Visitor, Inc. (1974). Sister suggested that I read this book. So together we

looked for the book in the hospital library, and finally we found it. I had never read anything about devils before. I had never even seen any movies about them. I had always avoided the subject. Strangely, my only knowledge of them was through my experiences.

The book told of how, through Faith and the Grace of God, this priest performed exorcisms for poor souls. The priest wrote his true experiences in this book and I thought he was very brave in his efforts to help. Reading his book, I realized just how hard it is to send a devil back to the Abyss.

> Remember the priest that directed me to this retreat? (Actually, to the nuns and their hospital.) Remember the beautiful building I noticed as I sat in that priest's office? The building that had been a convent? (Page 59) That building was where the priest I was reading about had performed an exorcism. The order of nuns from that convent, with their Faith and prayers, helped the priest.

Finally, after reading this book and thinking about the battles the priest had with devils, I realized more about Sue's devil spirit. Naive me finally realized that Sue wasn't here for a second chance. Then, as I remembered Sue saying, 'That's not it. We just wanted what He had.' I realized this devil *had* wanted what God, her Creator, had. She was one of the fallen angels. She was one who lost the battle in Heaven, one who lost their place in Heaven. She could not return.

I stayed with the nuns for a week, and then it was time to go. I must say, From my experiences there and from the following weeks that I traveled the central states, I was to realize that many of the people in that part of the country knew about devil spirits. I am glad to say, There must have been some very Faithful and brave religious people to help and guide them.

On the road again, and using my trusty atlas, it didn't take me long to get onto a quiet, country, farming road. I had been driving for about six hours when I saw a church. I felt that it was time to stop and pray.

When I stepped into the church I felt compassion in my heart for the nuns I had been with, the nuns who had tried to help me in my Faith; the nuns who pray for so many others. I walked to the front of the church.

When I knelt in front of the altar the feeling of compassion became so strong that it overtook my whole being. I prayed deeply for the nuns . . . almost crying.

Directly in front of me, in front of the altar, Bob's spirit began to appear. He was big. His spirit stood a little short of the tall church ceiling and in front of the altar. The first thing I immediately noticed about him was the immense look of kindness on his face. This gentle kindness was the greatest kindness you could ever imagine, Heaven's kindness.

He was wearing a long, dazzling white gown that was tied around his waist. The gown's long sleeves gradually became a little wider around his wrists. When I saw the kindness in his face and the white gown, I realized he had made it to Heaven. Now, Bob was standing straight, he had never stood completely straight, but had always carried himself submissively.

As I looked at his face, I felt I was also looking into Jesus' face. I don't know how to explain this, maybe Bob was letting me know who he was, maybe their spirits were one at the time. I don't know.

Then, from behind me, from the back of the church, I heard the devil Sue desperately yell, 'No.' God's saint disappeared from my sight, but I can't tell you how happy I was for him. He had made it!

I sat in one of the front pews to quietly pray. As I was praying, I thought Bob certainly seemed to have had a terrible time here on Earth, some people might even say he failed . . . but he most definitely did not. Now, through his courage, and as he was to teach me, "Faith and Love," he was a saint. No longer will I call him Bob, but most respectfully and lovingly, I will call him God's saint, or Saint Robert.

> Remember on my first trip, when I was in the abbey and I had seen Bob in a white gown? However, I was so completely worried about getting the right book to read, that at the time I didn't give too much thought to what he was wearing. (Page 48)

Now I had been awed at this vision of Bob . . . and his gown was not only white, it was dazzling. Bob did not stay in ordinary clothes; he had become a light of God's.

✝Finally . . . ordinary clothes. Remember I had seen my mother and brother's familiar spirits dressed in ordinary clothes, clothes like you and I wear? Well, from the vision above and from the things that I had seen previously, I presume that even though our spirits may receive some of God's peace after our meeting with Him, not until we are clothed in God's white gown and light are we Heavenly beings.✝

As I was praying, Sue popped up behind me. Her hands were above me as she threatened, 'I'm going to kill her.' Then I saw God's saint in front of the altar again. His face was incredibly sad. He had his right arm slightly raised as he pointed his right forefinger, and there, at the very tip of this finger, a large white star appeared. The bright white light was at least four inches, and possibly five inches, large.

The star disappeared from the saint. Then I saw Sue carrying the star in her hands, as she excitingly ran down the center aisle of the church, toward the door. They both disappeared. (I remember, at the time I didn't understand God's saint's compassion and enormous sadness. I did not understand this for a while afterwards.)

✝This was the first time I saw one of God's heavenly beings give light to a devil. Later I was to see this many more times. I now know that when the heavenly beings give light, which must be the light God gives them, that this is one of the ways they choose to lovingly and compassionately pacify the angry devils, and therefore keep the devils from being so cruel and destructive on Earth. So, the heavenly beings give their God-given light (which the devils deeply want) because of their love for all of God's creatures. What a wonderful love. I also now realize that God's saint was so incredibly sad because Sue was a fallen angel . . . she had chosen to do evil.✝

In the church I prayed for an hour before I left. In that time I heard God's saint say to me, "You will be our connection." Briefly and naively I thought, I'll tell people what Saint Robert and God's angel tell me. For months I never even thought about writing.

As I was driving I decided to try my newfound strength . . . or at least at the time I thought it was my strength. The strength I had found in the name of Jesus.

It was getting dark. I saw only a few other cars on this two-lane route that went through miles and miles of farming fields. I began to feel sad and sorry for the many poor souls who have done evil because of devil spirits. And I was feeling sorry for the poor people that the devils harass. So, I couldn't help it. When cars came toward me on the other side of the road, I would say, 'Jesus revoke.' I thought I might be able to help the poor people in the cars. I thought if there were devil spirits in or around these people, I might be able to help revoke them from the people.

Well, I said it as I looked at a man that was driving alone in a truck. Shortly after he drove by me, a strong breeze came through my car from the passenger side of the car. The wind blew over the top of my head and as I looked over to the closed passenger window I thought, How could this be? After this breeze went by me I heard a man's spirit voice angrily say, 'I'll get you for that. He was mine.' At that, I saw God's white angel fly down in front of my car. She said, "Now she just wanted to help him. Is that all right?" The spirit answered. He no longer sounded angry, but very nervous. He said, 'OK.' The angel disappeared and I did not hear from the other spirit again.

✝Dear's, say "Jesus . . ." Talk to him. I don't mean to be repetitive, but this works. Call on and honor our powerful Lord, Jesus. Jesus loves you.✝

It was about 4:30 p.m., a nice day. I was driving on a two-lane country road. I saw a black limousine driving toward me on the opposite side of the road. As the limo drove passed me, I curiously looked into the window of the passenger seat. There, in the backseat, was the man that I had noticed . . . from the gentle awareness, so long ago in my hometown.

> Remember the man I told you I noticed in the twenty-four hour restaurant, the man who had sat two booths behind me? Then, after I left the restaurant I again noticed him outside with other men, but only he got into the backseat of a black limo? (Page 25)

As I looked at this man's face, I was stunned. I had never seen such an angry, evil face. When he saw me, he jumped from his seat, very much like an animal, almost up against the limo's closed glass window. He looked as if he wanted to kill me. (As I'm writing this God's angel said, "He is angry. He had a lot.") The man's face looked only half human, because the extremely angry devil's spirit that was in him was so strong, and so visible, that it almost overtook this man's human face. And both the visible spirit's face and the man's human face looked very angry. I was amazed that the devil's spirit almost completely overtook this man's human body.

Shortly after I drove past this limo, God's angel, Donna, said, "That was Satan."

As I drove, I had to make many stops at convenience stores to get things I needed. I will tell you about one of these stops now. I will try to help you more.

Before I even walked into this convenience store I looked through the front glass door and the large front glass windows. I saw three people in the store. A man was standing halfway down the first aisle to my left; and two girls were behind the front counter at the register, to my right. The very second that I walked into the store I noticed the man's face change to a cold stare. Then he slowly lifted his left arm and hand, palm out, toward me. I could feel the pull as some of my energy left me.

Evidently, one of the girls at the register was a close friend with this man, and when she saw what he did she angrily walked over to him. I continued to pick up what I had to buy. Just as she got to him I noticed his face went back to normal and he put his arm down. The next second she said to him, demanding an answer, 'Why did you do that to that poor girl?' He <u>innocently</u> responded by saying, 'I didn't do anything.' I could see the poor man truly didn't remember what he had just done, and he certainly didn't know why he was being yelled at. I felt so sorry for him.

I felt I had to try and come to the aid of these two victims, so I tried to explain as I paid for my merchandise. I told the girl that was still at the register, so all three of them could hear, 'It wasn't him. There was a devil's spirit in him. He really doesn't remember.' I left the store. I don't know if this helped them or not, but I do hope it did.

✝From this I realized that some of the time, when these devil spirits are in us, we can't control what we do, and we may not even remember what we did. Devil's spirits seem to have the ability to, at times, overtake our whole being. But I also know that at other times, we do know what evil we are doing, but we are weak and uncaring. Please do not allow yourselves to be cruel. Ask for God's help.✝

As I drove I watched the farmers working in the fields. Many of them drove heavy machinery and I was surprised to see that they usually worked alone. I thought, Do these farmers see the devil spirits also? God's saint said, "They're working in the fields alone all the time here. They see them."

I thought, Well, just as Sue turns solid and pops up around me,

to pull from me when I'm alone, other devil spirits must also have done this in these isolated fields. The farmers who work alone in these fields must know.

Of course, as I was driving at night, Sue appeared. One night she continuously popped up in my backseat, she was very threatening to me and was very close behind me. Then at the same second I would hear my angel's voice. The angel would seem to be warning me, saying, "Joyce." I figured she wanted me to know Sue was there and just how evil this devil was, or maybe there was another reason. Whatever the reason, these warnings, which sometimes came with lightning in the sky, always made Sue disappear.

Also that night there were other times that Sue popped up very angry, more angry than threatening. These times she would look out of my front window, into the *very* distant sky, and say, 'Show me a sign.' Right after she said this lightning would flash in the clear sky . . . . After the lightning appeared Sue seemed satisfied, but sad, and then she disappeared for a while.

However, a little later she might again pop up, and this time, sadly ask for a sign. Immediately lightning would appear in the sky and Sue would disappear. At first I didn't realize what was going on. Then I thought, Well, God's helpers are watching and protecting me. God's helpers allowed me to see this for two nights, and for those two nights I saw Sue very threatening, angry, and sad, and a good amount of lightning.

✝When God's helpers showed their lightning, these powerful but humble creatures were showing their love. The lightning would not only protect me, but also quiet the devil Sue. Sue might have figured she had some control or just liked God's light, I don't know. However, I do know that this only briefly lessened her anger or sadness, which soon returned. (As I now retype this page I realize how sad this was. Remember, Sue was a fallen angel. She had known Heaven and God very well.)✝

God always seemed to keep things under control, and I continued to drive. Since I knew God's saint and angel were watching over me, I wasn't too scared, and Sue just popped up and down. But I know if God's lights didn't work so hard, this devil would have tried to get away with much more.

This day was hot. I had been driving on a fairly straight two-lane highway for a while. I was no longer in the farmlands, but still there was very little traffic or people around, and hardly any trees about at all. I was getting a little tired, so I turned down a dirt road, thinking, On this road I might be able to find a shady tree to park under and rest. Finally I saw a large tree, but it was off this dirt road and down a grassy road.

After I had parked under the tree and opened both of my car windows to try and cool off, at least twenty birds came and perched in the tree. Then I heard a voice say, "You did it." I thought, Finally, no one is around me pulling. Well, this was fine for about all of ten minutes, then I could feel the pulling again and the birds quickly flew away. However, I stayed and rested under the shady tree for about two hours.

When I started to drive away from the tree I saw small, only about two inches, light blue, circular spirits, floating very slowly and calmly about in the air. They were so peaceful. Amazingly, I could actually feel the respect each of these lights gave to each other and to each other's space. So although there were very many of them and they were all moving, they seemed equally spaced from one another.

As I looked at these peaceful, light blue spirits, I was so awed that I sat up in my seat. I put my face close to the windshield and I tried to get a better look, but foolishly I kept driving through them. I only saw them for about five second and I seemed to leave them behind me as I drove.

One night as I was driving, I looked out of my passenger window and I saw God's wonderful angel. The beautiful white angel flew right beside my car, steadily keeping up with me. I asked her what her name was, and she very calmly and slowly said, "Donna."

Quickly Sue's black form popped up in the backseat and she said, 'What a dumb name.' They both disappeared. (I know before this, before I had written that God's angel told me her name, I called her by her name . . . Donna. This is because, as I have corrected and retyped my book I just wanted to call this beautiful angel by her name. I have so much respect and love for her.)

Shortly afterward Donna was flying beside me on the driver's side. I asked her if she was my Guardian Angel. After about a four- or five-second pause, she calmly said, with a little thought, "UmmmmHummmm." She talked with amazing peace and goodness in her voice. Just to be around her or to listen to her voice put me at peace. I didn't ask her any more questions. I sensed from Donna that she knew I had no more questions. She disappeared. I know now, and I did realize then, that I should have been full of questions, but I wasn't—because I was so peaceful and calm.

When I told my friend about this, a good year after it happened; she told me that the name Donna means lady, or great lady. Donna is, and she continually proves to be, a great lady.

About a week after I had begun this second trip, I found a desert . . . my place of quiet. As I drove into this desert I saw wild deer and cattle ranches here and there. But being me, I kept driving further into the desert for more complete solitude. After I figured I was in the middle of nowhere, I parked my car. Then I thought, Peace and quiet at last! However, for this quiet I had to drive almost all the way across the country.

Well, I was sure I needed quiet and solitude, but as I sat there I thought, What do I do now? After I sat quietly for a few minutes I turned my head and looked over to my Bible. I settled down on my car seat, put my pillow on my lap, and my Bible on top of that. Then I opened the Bible. I was finally, for the first time, ready to read the Bible.

I began with the Gospels. Awesome. Amazing. Words could not describe my feelings as I read about Jesus. His life was so interesting and filled with so much goodness and love. I became involved in every word and just wanted to keep reading. I had no idea how much I would read. I read from those first minutes that I had found my solitude until dark that first night. Then I read almost every morning until darkness at night for as long as I was in that desert. For days I sat in solitude and read. When it was too dark to read, I prayed. I fell asleep at night knowing that Jesus is Divine . . . and He loves us. I had, for me, found my peace . . .

✝In reading the Bible and opening my heart to Jesus, I was to regain my inner strength—God's given strength.✝

I will tell you what happened during this time of solitude. When I read the Bible and Jesus' words, Sue seldom bothered me. But I will never forget the first time she tried to bother me . . . .

I had been sitting on the passenger seat for some time, reading the Gospels. Then, from the corner of my eye, I saw Sue. Her relatively solid looking black figure was walking through the desert. As she walked toward me she looked at me very angrily. This devil's spirit was totally black and void of any color, or light.

Shortly afterward I saw God's white angel quickly fly down in between us. The angel said, "Now you know you can't bother her while she's reading the Bible." They both disappeared. It was awesome. God's angels, our guardians, are so beautiful, and they protect us with such love. After seeing this I felt so calm, and very safe. I turned my attention back to the Bible and continued reading. It was only about 2:00 in the afternoon and I still had plenty of time in the day to read.

✝I now realize that God, through His angel, was giving me time to do what I had freely chosen to do: Read the Bible and move closer to Him. God sends an angel to each and every one of us, and these angels do love and protect us. Dears, how hard Heaven works for us. Please thank God and His Guardian angels.✝

I wanted to stay in the quiet that had taken me so long to find. So at night I slept in my car, right where I was, in the middle of nowhere. Just before the sun went down I would see Sue's small shadowy black figure. At this time she would appear outside of my car, to my right. She would quickly pop up, and when I turned directly toward her, she would shrink down. I just looked. She said nothing but just watched me. It seemed she was trying to get my attention, or scare me; however, after a while she did very little of either.

Also, before nightfall, I would put religious pictures, rosaries, etc., in my car windows. Most nights it was completely black outside and I wanted to scare away any devil spirits that might be prowling about outside of my car. I put the picture of the monstrance and Eucharist up against the passenger side back window.

> Remember the picture the nun gave me at the convent, the picture of the monstrance and Eucharist? The picture that she had told me to keep? (Page 60)

Early one night, not even twenty minutes after it had turned dark, I heard a horrifying, unearthly, animal-like yell outside of my car. The yell came from in front of the picture of the monstrance and Eucharist. I knew a poor devil's spirit had walked up to my car and saw this Holy Picture.

At night I tried to think about God. I was still so excited, His angel had told me her name—Donna. How I now loved God and His lights so much; my Faith was growing. I slept with my Bible in my arms—to both keep it close to me and protect me. The Bible and

Jesus' words were expanding my knowledge, helping my love grow, and strengthening my Faith. How deeply Jesus loves his Father and us. I was beginning to really know Jesus, the Teacher and Our Savior.

One morning Sue was exceptionally annoying; and she started the very minute that I had woken up. Flying bugs continually found my one open car window. Now mind you, I was in the middle of the desert, where I had hardly seen any bugs at all, much less flying ones. Then Sue started to pop up and down in the back-seat. She did not wait for nighttime. Each time she popped up, she did it solely for the purpose of saying things like, 'I hate you' or 'I'm going to kill you.' Etc., etc. . . . I must say, She was able to keep this up at a pretty steady pace for almost three hours.

Finally, I asked her why she was such a pain that morning. She said, 'You walked in the clouds with him.' Well, I thought, Sue was like this from the time that I had woken up, so something must have happened last night. I tried hard to remember the nighttime, but I could not remember anything. (Remember I went to sleep at sunset.) I thought, Well, I'll try to remember last night's dreams; something might come back to me in the form of a dream. However, I hardly ever remember my dreams and I still couldn't remember anything from the night.

. . . . .

In reference to the above, I would like to put this here, although it happened two days later:

I was quietly reading in my car when I saw a vision. I saw God's saint in his long, white gown. He was walking so very, very slowly on a cloud, more slowly and more peacefully than I have ever seen anyone walk. I could barely see his feet as he walked, because with each step he took his bare feet sunk into the soft, white cloud. He was alone and he looked so deeply sad. Although I did not see myself, very vaguely, I felt my spirit was to his right and above his spirit. I was going toward him and I knew God's angel was leading my way. I also realized my spirit was small next to the angel, and really small next to this saint's spirit. Then the vision and the awareness left me.

After the vision, I knew that Sue had acted up a few mornings before because I had walked in the clouds with him. I realized that I had done this, but forgotten. However, God allowed me to keep the above memory of that night. In a vision.

✝I must tell you, I didn't know then but I know now (years later), that the devil's spirits can erase parts of, or even complete events, that are stored in our memories. Let me explain with an example. Several times I have seen spirits appear to people around me. Of course, these people would look excited or scared, depending on whether they had seen a light or dark spirit. But then these people's faces would quickly turn blank and they would not remember anything about what they had seen.

One of these times I sadly thought, When will people know about the spirit world? When will they see and remember? Saint Robert said, "When it's time they will." Then I thought, Since we are not able to see or remember seeing spirits, we are now more apt to use our free will to choose good or evil, as I'm sure Our Father in Heaven wants us to do; as He watches us. Then God's saint said to me, "You will be in it." I knew that I would be in my spirit form and helping God when the time comes for the people of Earth to be able to see, and remember seeing, God's spirits.✝

I know the above covers several time frames; I hope I have explained this well enough for you.

. . . . .

Back to that annoying morning of Sue acting up and the flying bugs. I do have my shortcomings, and later that morning Sue had gotten me to my shortest. After I had seen her pop up for the umteenth time, I said to her, 'I can see why He did that to you . . . all you do is bother people. . . . Leave me alone.' Well . . . ! Her black shadow lurched up furiously in the backseat, and behind me. She held her arms up and her fingers were stretched out and long, she was ready to grab me.

My Guardian Angel's white spirit quickly swooped down outside of my car to my right. There she stood. She said, "She told you to leave her alone." God's angel moved just her right pointing finger—ever so slightly. With this Sue's angry devil's spirit quickly went out of my backseat, through the trunk of my car and then down the dusty road. I watched her spirit as it seemed to form a ball of tumbleweed tossing in the desert, and I thought, Well, here we are in the desert and she looks like something from the desert, tumbleweed.

I turned to God's angel and asked her, 'Who told you to keep me alive?' She replied quietly and simply, "God." She stood and waited for 2 or 3 seconds; I knew she was waiting to see if I had any more questions. I also knew that she realized I really had to think about what she had just said. She disappeared. I can't even begin to tell you how important I felt. I kept thinking, God told her to keep *me* alive! God noticed *me*!

✝Our Guardian Angels are awesome . . . I must say this again. What a sight God's Heavenly beings are. I know I cannot even begin to imagine what would happen to us, 'humans' as the devil spirits call us, without our Guardian Angels to protect us. These pure white and powerful lights are sent lovingly to all of us from God. Please pray with them, and thank God for them.

Importantly, do not be afraid. Please realize our guardians' work hard to keep us alive here on Earth until our time comes. We are all so important to, and loved so much, by God. **God is the one who will decide when we will die here on Earth. We will not die until it is our time. Trust God. He will know when it is the best time for each of His children to meet Him.**✝

When I have learned all I am to learn here, and have done all I am to do here, I pray I will accept my time.

.....

Well, after God's angel had quieted things down I concentrated on reading the Bible. I became so interested and so involved in my reading that I didn't pay any attention to anything else for many hours . . .

Later that afternoon, Sue started to pop up in my backseat again, however, she did this in a very quiet and brief manner. She didn't like being ignored, and she certainly didn't want to be outdone—especially by an angel. As I read, at three different times, but just for a second, Sue's black figure would pop up slightly then down in my backseat. She wasn't cruel or frightening then, and when she popped up it was only long enough for her to say to me, as I was reading, 'That's true.' I must say, I do think God's angel was very close by and watching us.

Although the sun was out every day and I had no shade from the very first day that I found this isolated desert, surprisingly enough, I was comfortable. During the day there was always a beautiful cool breeze, so even though I sat in my car with the windows only opened slightly, I was fine. The days were comfortable and the nights were cool. I slept only using one blanket.

This particular morning, after I woke up and got myself together and comfortable, I put my pillow on my lap; I was ready to read. I picked up my Bible and opened it to where I had stopped reading from the day before, at my bookmark. Then out from the Bible flew Donna's white angel spirit. This angel's spirit was only about one inch, but how gorgeous she was, her tiny white wings fluttered so quickly as she flew out of the Bible. As I watched her wings fluttering I heard Donna say softly, and *very helpfully* to me, "This is the place."

She quickly disappeared after she had flown out of the Bible and had helped me, but I knew her tiny pure spirit had grown, very quickly, to her larger size. I read, and read, and read some more.

Dears, your guardian spirits can change size. There is so much God's spiritual lights can do for us. I will tell you more . . .

I continued to read quietly most of that day, with just one interruption.

It was about 4:00 or so in the afternoon. I was sitting in the car reading, but for a few brief seconds my attention was taken from my reading. I noticed a shadow that went over the front window of my car. Since this shadow appeared a couple of times I stopped reading and looked out of the front window, waiting for the shadow to reappear. As I watched, I saw that this time the shadow went across the car hood. Although the shadow was about one to two feet long, I didn't think too much about it. I thought that a large bird must have been flying high overhead.

A bit later I noticed that when the shadow appeared over the hood of my car, it disappeared while it was on the car hood. I thought this was very unusual. How could this be? After I saw this happen two times, I got curious. I thought, I want to get a glimpse of the bird flying over my car. So when the shadow came across my car hood again, I very quickly got out of the car to look. I was surprised, as I looked into the clear sky. There was nothing. Not even a cloud was around for miles.

About an hour later, when I looked up from my reading, I saw a completely black figure appear in the distant sky. I only saw the figure for a second or two as it flew toward a hill, and then disappeared from my clear sight before reaching the hill. His spirit became invisible. When I saw his spirit in the sky I noticed that his outstretched wings were jagged on the bottom. I didn't see his wings move. I sensed his wings could not move, and they really seemed too small for his body. He had a lion's head, but he did not have a lion's mane, and he had a lion's tail and back legs. But he was thin and his spirit looked weak in this black form.

I began to put things together. I thought, I was in solitude and there were no other humans or even animals, so to speak, out here. (I know I have mentioned this before, but . . . .) Since the devil's spirits could not find an earthly body to enter, they evidently choose to, or had to, turn solid and visible, if only for a second or two, into their own devil's black form to pull from me, or to pull from anything that God has given life and light to.

Hence, the shadow over my car that quickly disappeared. By the time I looked up, the bad spirit no longer needed to be visible, so nothing was to be seen. The devil's spirit very quickly pulled, then disappeared. I will mention this lion-like devil's spirit later. He did not try to, nor did he, threaten or hurt me. Seeing him made me nervous for a little while, but then I was left with curiosity.

> Remember when Sue showed herself to me on my first trip? Remember I heard a man's voice, not a totally human voice, come to Sue's aid? He said, 'That's not it.' (Page 41)

In the desert, as I thought back to the first trip, I knew that this lion-like black spirit was Sue's companion. I had finally seen him.

✝The devil's spirits pull and steal from us, some—but I'm guessing, I should probably actually say, many—of God's gifts to us. I have seen just a very small part of what it takes God to keep us alive here on Earth. With so many dark spirits, I do think that Our Father has to shower us with His Light very often, if not continually.✝

One evening, as I sat reading quietly, I thought about Michael the Archangel. Then, although I did not see Donna, I felt her presence behind my car. She said, I must say a bit excited, "You will see him." I could tell by this angel's voice that she does so admire that God would create such a creature. I wondered when I would see him and what he would look like.

It was just starting to get dark and I thought, Tonight, I would really like to be around some other people. I was getting a little lonely and a bit scared in the dark, so I figured I would go into town and sleep there.

After driving for a while on the winding, bumpy, dusty road, I could finally see the town in the distance. However, I knew this road would wind even more before I would be on the paved route, and then it would still take me at least another twenty minutes to get into town. I passed an old station wagon that was coming towards me, the first car I had seen all day. A good-looking man was driving. He was alone. After he passed me I curiously looked into my rearview mirror. I was amazed—I saw a huge, circular, brilliant, orange/yellow light, which was even bigger than the car that had just passed me. This light seemed to be turning around and slowly coming towards me. I also heard a noise. (Later, as I thought back, I realized that the noise was from the car tires moving over the dusty road.) Out there, in the middle of nowhere, this all really scared me. Brother, did I step on the gas!

The brilliant, round light seemed to follow me for about fifty feet—then I noticed the orange/yellow light rise, very slowly at first, into the sky. As I drove fast, just about as fast as that terrible road would permit, I kept looking behind me at the light. This light then seemed to become the moon that was slowly rising into the sky. Looking at the moon, the same color and shape of the light that had followed my car, I thought, Is this really the moon? It was. There were no other lights in the sky. I was still scared; I knew that this light had just been right behind me.

After I had driven off the dusty road and started driving on the paved road my knees finally stopped shaking. So I slowed the car down to almost a complete stop to look at the moon. The moon was fully in the sky then, and still the same color and shape of the light that had been behind me in the desert, the beautiful orange/yellow color.

When I got into town I parked my car and looked at the moon again. The moon was white. I looked about the sky, and looked, and looked again. I thought, What happened to the orange/yellow color the moon had been? The moon I saw rise slowly into the sky.

As I was wondering about all of this, a white dove flew to a nearby tree and just stayed there on a branch. I thought, They have white doves in this small town that is surrounded by a desert? I had to get a closer look. I got out of my car and stood under the tree that the dove was in. Was this really a white dove, here? Sure enough, it was. As I looked at the dove I heard a man's voice quietly say, "I'll talk to him." I realized this spirit knew I was scared. I continued to look at the dove, and then it flew away. I went to sleep, no longer scared, but confused.

Days later I heard the same man's voice, the quiet voice that seemed to come from the white dove. He said, "He knows he shouldn't have come to you that way."

I woke up early that morning, and I figured since I was in town I would stop to get gas. I always tried to keep my gas tank as full as possible, because I really didn't want to run out of gas on the desert roads that all tended to look the same. Now, I had made brief visits to this town previously, but usually only very early in the morning or late at night. The town was very small and only had about 300 people living there, but I liked this. I really still enjoyed the quiet.

The owner of the only gas station/convenience store in town worked from the opening to the closing of his store, 5:00 a.m. to 10:00 p.m. He worked alone, and we usually talked, so we were on friendly terms. He was very nice. I also remember a restaurant in town that made good salads with a very different, spicy dressing, and served in a taco shell. More about this later.

It was early. In fact, I was at the gas station just before its opening time of 5:00 a.m. After I had pumped my gas I asked the owner if I could use his bathroom that was in the back of the store. He had let me use this bathroom before, and he also let me use it this day. As I came out of the bathroom I picked up a gallon of water from the shelves by the back of the store. Then I walked down the aisle toward the register to pay for my gas and water.

As I walked toward the front of the store, I saw Sue's devil's spirit. Her totally black spirit was walking along the back of the front counter, toward the store owner. He was standing at the end of the front counter behind the cash register. As she walked closer to the owner, her black spirit got as tall as, but thinner, than him.

I kept walking toward the owner because I had to pay for my merchandise. I was almost to the register when **Sue's black devil spirit walked very easily, with no effort at all, into the man.** The second her dark spirit walked into his body, I could no longer see her, but I noticed that his eyes looked bloodshot.

Immediately, the owner, who had just kindly let me use his bathroom, looked at me furiously. Through his bloodshot eyes he looked at me as if he wanted to jump over the counter and kill me. Then, he angrily yelled at me. Because of what I had just seen . . . I knew it wasn't his choice, or actually even him, yelling at me, but it was the choice of the very angry devil's spirit that was in him. I

knew this angry spirit was almost totally controlling this man. (I think the control the devil has on a person depends on the devil, the person, and the circumstances.)

✝I must say, God certainly let me know this devil's spirit was in the owner of the store. Thank God. He let me see just how easy it is for the devil's spirits to walk into people.✝

After I had paid for my merchandise and was walking toward the door, I remembered that previously, very briefly, I had talked to the owner of the store about devil's spirits. As I opened the door to leave I wanted to help him, so I said to him, 'She was in you.' Then I became aware that he knew what I meant. He realized a devil's spirit had made him so angry.

Unlike the other time, when I had realized a devil's spirit was in a man (as I was driving west and had stopped in a much busier convenience store, Page 66), this time, I knew the person was aware that a devil's spirit had been in him. I thought, Good.

. . . . .

After leaving the convenience store I headed back to my solitude. Away from the town and onto the dusty roads I went. As I was driving back I thought about my first meetings with Sue. I remembered when I had first seen her spirit she would fly and turn red. Now, after days of my reading the Bible and praying, Sue was black and walked about. She seemed weaker now, and definitely angrier. It also seemed that when this devil's spirit was weak, her eyes turned bloodshot. I thought, My continuous reading of the Bible and praying might somehow have weakened her. Or maybe it was just that she couldn't bother me or pull from me when I read the Bible and prayed; when I got closer to God. I'm not sure. Dears, look to God. Through Him we can overcome all. Even the evil spirits must stand back when we talk to Him.

✝Now, these are just my thoughts as I retype this. Please do not get mad at your neighbor if he is cruel or seems uncaring. Please be very patient. Try to pray for him. Pray that if there are any evil spirits in or around him, they will leave him alone. This is important for me to tell you. This is important for you to understand. Please, especially understand this when interacting with your loved ones: Be patient, calm, and pray for them. Remember how easily devil's spirits can enter humans, bringing their anger and hate with them, into the person.

Also, it seems to me that evil spirits may be able to see seconds or even minutes into the future, although I'm not too sure about this. I know they can hear our thoughts, and it could be that they hear these thoughts and not see the future. God and His lights can see infinitely into the future. Please be strong. Go to and stay with God. Do not be tricked.✝

OK. I know I took the long way about, but back to the desert. After driving for some time I stopped. I was content . . . seemingly no one was around to interfere with the quiet. I read. I read the Bible, picking up from where I had left off.

Later that morning Sue was annoying, again. I knew this devil was really getting tired of the solitude, of only being around God's saint, God's angel, and me reading the Bible. My first thought was, She is full of tricks and irritating. However, in reality, I think she was trying to hurt me and I knew God's angel was working hard to protect me.

I looked up . . . and there was God's wonderful angel, Donna, standing outside of my car, to my right. Her whole body was white and she wore a long, pure white gown; she was beautiful. I could not see her wings. Donna said, "We're going to need help." (I must say, to me, the angels seem to be keeping very modern in their speech and appearance.) Right after she said this, she put her hands together in prayer and she slightly and humbly lowered her head. Instantly, I saw a white spiritual light come from the sky. It went straight to this beautiful white angel, and it shone as tall as Donna, going from the top of her head to the bottom of her feet. This white

light was continual, and I could sense and see that it was alive. It never stopped glowing down from Heaven, however, although it was continual . . . it seemed to surround the angel, and after it reached this white angel it stopped and went no further.

The angel stood there and did not move or lift her head. I could not hear what Donna said, but I knew this angel was humbly and lovingly talking to Our Father in Heaven. As she communicated, a white aura appeared and surrounded the angel's whole body; it was about two inches and it shined brightly, equally and evenly, all around the angel as she prayed. Now, the aura was brighter than the light from Heaven, but it somehow seemed that the aura was a part of, and together with, this light. (This is the drawing on the cover.)

✝Watching God's angel, I thought, **This is how to pray . . . Humbly and Full of Love**. Love for God, Our Father, and love for all.✝ A minute later, it all disappeared. I thought, Geez, there she was a beautiful and powerful angel, and what humility she showed to her Creator . . . sure enough, He answered her.

After that Sue wasn't so annoying to me.

Later that day I heard Donna say, "He was *very* good, but he was slow." I think when she said this, she then had her second helper from God, someone faster than her first helper that day.

As I drove on the desert's dirt road I noticed a fairly large majestic bird ahead of me, which stood perched on a wooden fence beside the road. The bird was a bit larger than a crow and looked very impressive. Before I drove by the bird, I sensed pride coming from it, and I then heard Sue boastfully say, 'I am beautiful.' I knew Sue's devil spirit was in the bird.

Although the wooden fence was right alongside the road I was driving on, the bird did not fly away as I drove by, it just stood there, seemingly so proud. I said nothing, because I felt sadness in my heart. I knew this bird's body did not belong to this devil's spirit. How Sue's spirit loved to show off; because of this I had first come to know about her. This fault would betray her, not only once, but other times also.

There were other times that birds flew close by me and I would hear Sue's devil spirit say, 'Do you blame me? I love to fly.' Or 'Wouldn't you do it if you could?' I would try to have compassion, and I would try to say nothing. Sue's spirit loved to enter birds and fly.

One day, after reading until late morning, I realized that I was short of money and I would have to go and look for a bank. Well, on this trip I had found out that with my bankcard I could get money from any bank machine or ATM machine I came across . (What a discovery!)

Since I had not seen a bank machine in the small town, I got out my atlas again. I figured I would have to get onto the highway and drive about fifty miles or so to get to the closest small city, where I thought I should be able to find an ATM machine.

After getting onto the highway and driving for at least thirty minutes, I suddenly saw God's angel, Donna, flying beside my car. This beautiful white angel flew just outside of my passenger window and she kept right up with me. I watched the road, but I kept turning my head to look at the angel. She looked straight ahead as we traveled, watching the road with me. But I also knew that she was watching me and I realized she knew I was watching her.

She was so awesome. Then my curiosity got the best of me . . . I drove faster, and she flew faster. As she flew faster, her white spirit looked more like a white streak, but I have to say, She was steadily in the same place beside my car, and me. Then I slowed the car down.

I could see her spirit for only about fifteen minutes. We said nothing, but just traveled peacefully. I felt good and very safe. She let me see her. God let me see her.

On the way back from the bank, I saw Sue pop up in my backseat and pull my energy. But this time I saw her throw the energy to the right of the highway, into the woods. When I saw the faint white spiritual matter that she threw in the woods, I became very worried. I thought, All this spiritual matter is being thrown away. What is this devil up to?

A little while later I saw another heavenly spirit of beautiful white. The spirit was flying toward me, but off to the right side of the highway. The same side that Sue had been throwing the white spiritual matter into. First, I must tell you about this heavenly spirit's dress. I don't know if you remember the older style of dress or habit for nuns—some nuns still wear this style. Over their long dress the nuns would have an apron, of sorts, down the front, full length of their dress. This apron would go from the top of their dress to the bottom, and it would be about one to two feet wide.

This beautiful white spirit had on this same style habit and apron. As she flew, she held the bottom sides of her apron, a hand on each side. She was using her dress's apron to collect the spiritual matter that the devil Sue had thrown onto the side of the road, and I could see the faint white matter being collected from the woods into the apron. The angelic spirit's face looked a bit worried and a little drawn. However, I could tell she was not drawn because she was tired, but because she had been working hard, and she was *really* trying very hard to do a good job.

✝From this, I presume that God's helpers collect any lost light that had been given to us from God, and probably give it back to us, or maybe they save it for us until later. Or, even a little of both, I'm not sure. But, don't you recover from being tired or ill? Don't worry, God's lights work so diligently.✝

After I had driven off of the highway and onto the main route, I headed back to my quiet. However, as I noticed several dirt roads that went into the desert I began to get a little curious, so I decided to explore another road. Off the paved road and down another dusty dirt road I went. Not too far down this road I found myself in a valley. Looking about I could see no one was around, so I parked my car. I thought, This is fine.

When it started to get late, I figured this valley would be a good place to rest and sleep for the night. Just before dark, Sue's shadow started to pop up behind the rocks in the valley. I prayed and rested in my car as it became dark.

Later, and the feeling came upon me slowly, I began to feel the presence of God's angel, but I could not see her. Then I heard God's saint say, "Joyce, tell your mother you forgive her."

I just sat quietly in my car for at least two minutes. I had to get enough strength to forgive . . . and then I became aware that it takes a lot of strength to forgive.

Finally . . . I answered this saint. In a weak and tired voice, because forgiving took most of my strength, I very quietly said, 'I forgive my mother.' Instantly, as I was saying this, I felt a weight lift from my heart. I was amazed at this feeling. This burden . . . this sin on my heart, was also forgiven. I'm sorry I can't tell you the rest of the conversation between God's saint, angel and me. But, the part I will tell you is important for you; Forgive and you will be forgiven.

✝Remember Our Lord's Prayer: **"Our Father . . . forgive us our trespasses, as we forgive those who trespass against us . . . ."** (Here I have to say, and as I thought at the time above, God's saint has always given me such good advice and guidance. Even though he says so little, using few words, he has always said so much.)✝

Also, later that evening, Donna told me, "There is something you have to do." As I quietly sat in her presence and peace, I never asked her what it is I am to do.

≈

At times, when I think about or talk about Bob or Donna, I have called, Bob, 'My saint,' and Donna, 'My angel.' I know that I have some selfish feelings here, but mostly I feel adoration and love when

I say this. I realize they are God's lights, and a few times Donna has reminded me of this. When I would say, 'Donna, my angel' Donna would so sweetly and purely say to me, "We're God's." However, I am sure they know, as I am sure God knows, what love is in my heart when I say, 'My saint' or 'My angel.'

I will try to refer to Saint Robert as God's saint and to Donna as God's angel, throughout this book, as they would like me to . . . as they *are* God's. (When you see God's heavenly lights and know their pureness, you will love them, and love God who created such goodness. I will pray that you will all see the angels and saints in His Heaven.)

On my last two days in the desert, again I thought about Jesus. I knew that when he prayed in the solitude of the desert, he also fasted. I decided to fast. In my car I had two, one-gallon containers of water, a loaf of white bread, and a few other snacks. I decided to fast by only drinking my water and eating my bread. A few times during these days, as I was eating the bread, I heard Sue's friend, the male devil spirit say, 'Bread, I hate bread.' Dears, the physical substance of the Eucharist is bread, and when we fast it is suggested that we fast by drinking no more than water and eating no more than bread.

Also, I must say something else about my last two days of reading the Bible and praying. I wasn't hungry at all. And surprisingly, even though I was sitting in my car in the sun, I wasn't even thirsty. I had to make myself drink water and eat a slice or two of bread each day.

Now I know what Jesus meant in the Gospel of John, Chapter 6:35 when Jesus said to them, "I am the bread of life; whoever comes to me will never hunger, and whoever believes in me will never thirst."

My last day in the desert I thought I should get my car completely fixed and safe; the steering wheel was still loose, and this bothered me. I thought I should return my car to the auto body shop that had originally fixed it, as they would be the ones who would best know the car. So I began to figure that to fix my car, maybe I'd go home, but I think at this time I was also really getting homesick.

That afternoon I drove toward the highway and home. With all the peace I had felt and as close as I had gotten to God's lights, I almost thought I was in control of my life. Then I remembered the turmoil and troubles I had before the trip. (You must realize that I still did not fully and completely realize what was going on in the world around me, and in my life.) As I drove closer to the highway and remembered this turmoil I thought, Well, maybe I'll try one last deserted road. Maybe on that road I'll be able to completely rid myself of my troubles and these bad spirits. As much as I had seen, I still didn't put everything together.

Thinking of looking for that last deserted area, I slowly drove onto the road that entered the highway. There, as I looked at a blue van driving on the highway, I heard a man's voice. I stopped my car when I heard him say to me, with a little bitterness in his voice, 'That's why she liked you.'

> I remembered myself as a young girl, in junior high school; I saw a vision of myself in my old bedroom. In the vision I was kneeling before my picture of Our Blessed Mother and I was saying my evening prayers, the prayers I said every night before going to bed. I also felt the pure, overwhelming innocence I remember I had in my heart back then . . .

As I was sitting in my car, I wanted so much, and I tried so hard, to hold onto this beautiful innocence I remember I had . . . but I couldn't. The vision and the feeling were gone. I thought the beautiful picture of Our Blessed Mary, which meant so much to me, was also gone.

I drove onto the highway.

In my search for another peaceful area I ventured off the high-

way a few times, but I couldn't find the quiet I was looking for. On the last exit I drove off of, I found a small,
deserted dirt road that wound around steep hills.
However, the hills were in a wooded area and I didn't
like that; I preferred the peace and quiet of the desert.

Since it was starting to get dark and I was starting to get tired,
as I drove around the narrow and winding hilly road I looked for a
safe place to rest. Sue popped up in my backseat. She said to Donna,
'I'll make her drive over the cliff.' I can't tell you how much this
devil wanted to kill me. God's angel Donna replied, **"Then I'll turn
back time."** (Just now, as I'm writing this, Sue said to me, 'They
can.') As I kept driving around that small road, looking over the
cliffs, I was so amazed by God's Guardian Angel's power—she was
going to turn back time! She could turn back time! I thought,
Donna was going to do what God had told her to do: keep me alive.

That night, when I parked my car on the narrow road to sleep,
I didn't worry as I looked about the hilly area. I peacefully fell
asleep. In the morning I headed for home.

✝Another thing I would like to tell you, that night as I rested in
my car, the devil Sue sadly said, 'We can go slow, but not as slow as
them.' I vaguely thought about traveling through time. I know that
in their peace, the angels do seem to move and talk very slowly.✝

I tried to take the back roads home, avoiding cities and traffic as
much as I possibly could. I drove for miles and miles on two-lane,
winding roads through farming areas, where I saw very few cars
and rarely did I see any people on the farms.

One day as I was driving, I just broke down and started to cry
and cry. I thought, Why does all this have to happen to me? Why
doesn't the end of all this turmoil and pain just come now, for me,
and for all of us, The Final Judgment? How can we bear pain any
longer?

Finally I calmed down and almost completely stopped crying,
except for a few sobs now and then. I drove around a curve in the

road and I saw another farm, but on this farm I saw two people. I saw a man who was standing beside a child that looked about ten years old. I could sense a great togetherness shared between the two, and with this feeling I supposed the two were father and son. (As I typed this, the sun came out from behind the clouds, and I heard God's saint say, "That is what keeps the sun out." At first I thought, father and son? Then I realized love is what he meant.)

The two stood beside each other on the large wheel of a huge bin. The bin looked big enough to be a belly dumper compartment of a train, and there was a long funnel dumping corn into the bin. I saw the cornstalks around the farm, so I figured that the corn going into the bin must have been from this farm.

The man radiated with contentment, but mostly self-esteem, as he watched the corn filling the huge bin to the top. He looked to the child, and as he talked I could sense and hear him softly say to the child, 'We did fine.' I could see love was there. The child innocently looked back at the man and I could see his questioning and wondering, How will this help us?

The feeling between the two touched my heart. Then I heard God's saint say, with a bit of surprise and astonishment, even in this saint's voice, "He is full of compassion." I just drove quietly, and then thought, Even the saints are amazed at the tremendous amount of compassion God has. My questions were answered. I gathered up my strength and totally stopped crying.

✝I thought, God's compassion and Love is so great for His children. He even quietly lets Himself be ignored, but still He allows His Loving Light to shine on Earth. God Loves us so much. He will not bring about our final destruction; we are the only ones who can do that to ourselves.✝

Later that day, I was amazed at all God had let me see and feel. I asked God's saint, 'Why did God let me see all this?' With a very caring voice he answered, "He wanted to save you." And now I know, in return, I must try from my heart to help God save you.

Finally . . . I realized where my problems were coming from, the devil's spirits. I realized where our problems are coming from, the devil's spirits.

On my way home God's saint said, "We will go slow with you." Again I became aware of his patience and love. I realized God's saint and angel are going at a steady but slow pace, as they teach me about God, His spirit world, and our world.

I started praying the rosary a lot; even as I was driving I would pray. I would have the steering wheel in my left hand and the rosary beads in my right hand. I had chosen to be closer to God, and this choice strengthened my Faith. I felt strong and safe.

Once when I was driving and finished praying the rosary, but before I had blessed myself, I asked in desperation, 'Jesus, please help me see the spirit that is harassing me so. Please. So that maybe, I might be able to fight it better. Please.' I looked up. One of the birds flying overhead had a red spirit that was the same size and shape as the bird; however, this spirit was flying one or two inches behind the bird. The red spirit was the same red color that I had seen the devil's spirit Sue turn to twice before. I could see the red devil's spirit was having a very hard time keeping up with the bird as it flew, and therefore the spirit was visible to me as it flew behind the bird.

My plea was granted. I knew where Sue's spirit was as she desperately tried to fly with God's bird. From then on, when I needed it, and many a times, I have an extra sense that helps me know where Sue or evil is. Although I cannot always (and usually don't) see the evil spirits, this sense does help me.

Early one evening God's saint said to me, "Now you can hear them." As I soon did . . .

This night I slept in my car on a small dirt road in a quiet woods, where I had chosen to rest. (In the quiet.) The next morning when I woke up, I heard a sad, empty, unhuman moaning sound coming from the woods to my left. The sadness in the moan was enormous, but even stronger than this, I heard a total emptiness, a void in the moan. It is hard to explain, but I heard the sound of emptiness.

This terrible moan never hesitated or stopped, it just continued steadily for at least five minutes. Realizing that the creature making this sound didn't have to breathe, I knew this was the empty, agonizing moan of a devil's spirit. I wasn't sure what to do. I just kept looking and looking about the woods for anything unusual, but there was nothing different about these woods. When I started my car to leave, the moaning finally stopped; however, as I slowly drove, I was still looking about the woods.

I had not driven for more than ten to fifteen feet on the dirt road when I saw a spiritual creature. He stood in the woods to my left, but his spirit was suspended about two feet about the ground in the woods. He was only about two feet tall. He had hair that was about two inches long all over his oval-shaped body, and his head was a small circle with the same hair everywhere also. He had one circular eye in the center of his head. This is what this poor agonizing creature looked like. This is what I saw.

As this spirit looked at me, I looked into its eye and I saw its eye was the color orange/yellow. My first thought was this is the same color I had seen before in my halo. Then I thought, Now as this spirit's eye is this color, there is no more moaning. I continued to drive onto the main route.

I was driving, about mid-afternoon, and for many miles I had seen hardly any cars on this very quiet, two-lane road. When I saw a black limousine driving toward me, I immediately thought, This limo reminds me of the one I had seen as I was driving west. Then

I thought, Even the road I was driving on reminds me of the same country road that I had seen the black limousine on.

As we passed each other I looked into the back passenger window. I saw the man I had seen at the twenty-four hour restaurant back home, and then again in the limo as I drove west.

When I saw that his face was only about one foot away from the limo's glass window, I realized that he must have been sitting up in his seat. He sat peering, very animal-like, out of the back window at me. His face showed much evil and anger; however, I could see that he was calmer than the last time I had seen him in his limousine. This time the devil's spirit's face did not show through and with the man's face.

After I drove past the limousine Donna said, "He's better now."

One night, after driving on a very barren and deserted road for some time, I began to get tired. Up ahead I saw some cliffs that were on both sides of the road and I thought the change of scenery, or any scenery at all, was a welcome sight. I stopped my car by the cliffs to rest for a while.

After resting for about five to ten minutes, I heard the sound of animal hoofs as they hit the side of the steep rocks of the cliffs. By the sounds I could tell that the hoofed animal was coming straight down the sheer cliffs. I thought, How could this be? Then I knew a devil's spirit was coming closer to me. I looked about and looked harder still, but at night with just the moon's light, I couldn't see anything moving. I began to get scared because I knew what was out there. Then I heard God's saint very calmly say, "They're curious." Geez, I remember thinking, I wish I could have been as calm as him.

I was glad to hear this saint's voice. As always, just the sound of his voice calmed me. However, a few minutes later I turned on the car and continued on my way. My rest was over.

. . . . .

What I'm going to write on this page happened a while after my return home. However, I would like to tell you now about the second time I heard these same animal hoof sounds.

I was at home alone and sitting at my kitchen table, when I heard the animal hoof sounds. I could tell from the sounds of the hoofs that this spiritual, animal-like creature, quickly ran behind me to the back door of my kitchen and then down the back steps. As this hoofed devil's spirit was running away, I heard him say to Sue, 'God sees everything.' He was scared. I knew he realized Sue was wrong in some of the things she did, and he knew God knew. Although I was glad for this devil's spirit because he knew Sue was wrong and he was leaving, I was also scared for him. I knew Sue immediately went after him for leaving. I asked God's saint to help him, but he said he couldn't.

However, days later, God's saint did tell me that this devil's spirit was back where he had been before. I knew this hoofed spirit was back on the cliffs.

✝Dears, this is important, and please remember—**God does see everything.**✝

Another night, I was driving into a town and I took a left turn at an intersection. Saint Robert said, "Joyce, look." I turned around, and since there were no buildings on either side of the street behind me, I could see the two cars that were a bit in back of me. The first car and driver had driven through the intersection and the car behind it was driving past the intersection. Well . . . the second car was a spiritual car, and the only person in the two-seater sports car, the driver, was also a spirit. This spirit seemed to be following the man in the car in front of him, who had a dazed look on his face. I could not believe it, a spiritual car!! A spiritual car?!! I looked and looked again. I also remember that as I was looking at the second car, I briefly thought, This car and driver is following the car in front of it at a steady rate.

Then I noticed a restaurant on the corner of the street I was on and I stopped my car . . . it was time to stop. However, I just sat in my car for about five minutes, saying to myself, and at times even saying out loud, 'I can't believe it.' Finally, I stopping saying this and I got out of my car to go into the restaurant.

In the restaurant, as I sat quietly drinking my soda and looking at the people, I thought, These people don't see this. They don't know, but God's saint told me to look, and there it was—a spiritual car and driver. I sat in the restaurant for at least fifteen minutes, still thinking, They don't see this . . . but there it was. Then I left.

HOME

HOME AT LAST, AND AT THE AUTO BODY SHOP, AGAIN. After my car was checked they told me that it needed a new steering column. Of course it took days and days to fix my car.

My first night back, after the month or so of my second trip, I slept at my friend's house. I felt uncomfortable telling her or anyone else that I could see and talk to God's spirit world, so I told her very little about my second trip. That night, as we lay in bed calmly talking, a tiny bright star blinked brightly in the room. The white light was only about half an inch, and as this very beautiful light blinked I heard God's angel Donna say, "We're here." I peacefully and quietly told my friend, 'They're here.' She just listened and we continued to talk, but I knew Donna was telling me that, "She's here with me. I'm OK."

. . . . .

When I had seen Donna's white angel spirit fly out of my Bible, I knew that she could change size and become very small. Now I began to put even more of what I had seen together. I realized that Donna's spirit could also become as small as a tiny, white star. I realized that the small, bright white stars I had seen were God's lights—they were angels and saints.

For those first several weeks after my return, I stayed at my friend's house. I have been a friend with this girl for many years, and I must say, At times she had to be nudged into doing her housecleaning. She was no different now. In the past her mother was usually the one who nudged her into cleaning, and a couple of times I helped them clean her home. I remember one day, at least ten years ago. On that day my visit to this friend's house turned into a cleaning day for me, after her mother volunteered my services. Years later, both of my friend's parents passed away.

Now, I was in my friend's dining room washing her hutch, cleaning. I was alone in the room and I became completely calm and involved in my work . . . then I saw my friend's mother's spirit. Her spirit was not dressed in white, nor was she in black; she was dressed in ordinary clothes. She said to me, 'You are doing that because you know that is what I would do.' Sue's devil's spirit popped up. My friend's mother's spirit slowly and sadly turned around and walked through what seemed to be a tunnel. The oblong, empty looking tunnel was just as big as she was. It all disappeared and I continued to clean.

Shortly after, I heard a young man's voice, the voice of a nineteen-year-old or so. He said, 'Go to it girls.' I felt this was the voice of my friend's father. I did not see him.

About an hour later I went into the kitchen where my friend was cleaning. I told her about the spirits; and I was glad to see that she wasn't scared. I said, 'Your father may have made it to Heaven and wanted to be nineteen again.'

She thought for a bit, and then she said, 'That sure sounds like him. He had always said that was the best time in his life.'

. . . . .

I don't want to scare you here, but remember I had just mentioned seeing an oblong tunnel? So here I would like to mention more about tunnels:

There were many nights when I missed the complete peace and quiet of the desert. So one night I figured I would just get into my car and look for a place where I might be able to find quiet again. When I'm alone it is easier for me to become completely at peace, and when I'm at peace it's easier for me to communicate with God's lights. I did find my solitude.

As I was resting in my car, I looked into my rearview mirror. I saw a black tunnel appear behind my car and a large and fairly strong looking black devil's spirit stepped out through the tunnel. He was the first strong devil I had seen. I calmly kept looking into my mirror. As he looked at me he said, in a completely cold voice, 'I came for you.' Then I got scared. Instantly, I heard God's angel Donna yell, very worried and very caring, "No." The tunnel and the devil both disappeared.

Dears, you don't know how much your angels do for you. They are always close to you—they have to be.

✝Now, about the tunnels. I do not think the tunnel I saw my friend's mother go through and this tunnel I saw the devil come from, were the same tunnels. Nor do I think the two tunnels were connected. I think these two tunnels lead to two different places. My friend's mother's tunnel was dark and almost black, but not as completely black as the devil's was. Also remember, my friend's mother was not black, her spirit was her human figure and she still had on ordinary clothes.

Months later, both my friend and I, and I let her bring this up, thought that her mother's spirit may have been in Purgatory.✝

I have grown to enjoy praying and the peace that it brings me, but I prefer to pray in quiet places. Down the street from where I was living is a church that was left open all day, so I would try to enjoy some quiet time alone in this church. However, many a times, in the middle of my prayers or rosary, a prayer group or even a Mass would start. We used to always kid about this, saying, 'I would go to an empty church looking for quiet, and usually I would end up in a church full of people.'

This day was no different . . . in the middle of my rosary the church became crowded and a Mass started. After the Mass, as the priest held the relic of a saint, he walked to the front of the middle aisle and invited everyone to kiss the relic. Of course I wanted to kiss the relic, so to the front of the church I went. Also, on my coat I had a pin of the cup and Eucharist, and for a few days I had wanted to ask the priest to bless my new pin. This seemed like a good time.

When my place in line came, I kissed the relic and then I asked the priest to bless my pin. The second **the priest lifted his right hand to bless** my pin, a black devil's spirit figure ran from behind me. Although this spirit was totally black, I could still see that he had a look of absolute fright on his face as he ran toward the church's door. His spirit disappeared before he reached the door.

A few days later I went to talk to this priest because, although I knew no one else saw the devil's spirit, I thought the priest should know what happened the second he had raised his right hand. He replied, with much care in his voice, "Receive the Eucharist as much as possible."

✝I must tell you, spirits are everywhere, but God lets me see them. He gave me this gift and I wish to share it with you—please have your religious articles blessed. Have your home, you, and your family blessed.✝

One day I was actually alone in this church for at least two full hours . . . I enjoyed the quiet as I prayed. I sat to the far right of the front of the church, in front of a large statue of Mary holding Jesus after he had been taken down from the cross, The Pietà. I was feeling very deeply the passion of Our Lord and the sorrows of his Blessed Mother . . . then I felt that I was not to go to the left side of the church. Shortly after I heard a voice say, "Don't go over there." I sat where I was and quietly continued to pray.

At least ten minutes later I heard a familiar man's voice say, 'Just let me see her.' Although I knew the voice, I couldn't place who it belonged to. However, I knew the voice was from someone that I had known very long ago, someone from my hometown.

Still praying, I was looking straight ahead, and then from the corner of my eye I saw a tunnel appear; it appeared on the left side of the church. A man in ordinary clothes came through the tunnel and stood in front of it for a second. I knew he was being allowed to see me, and I him. Then it all disappeared. I was not able to recognize who this man was. I knew for some reason I was not allowed. (God's angel just said, "Yes.")

Right after the vision disappeared, I heard this man's voice. He said, just a little stubbornly and seemingly from a very, very long distance away, 'That will last me another one hundred years.' I strongly felt that this man was very alone, and in Purgatory. Here God let me know that there is a Purgatory. I felt that when we are in Purgatory, it just seems to linger on . . . and on, for us who go there. And the souls there feel much emptiness and loneliness.

I knew God's helpers wanted to have this man see me praying, and praying in front of this statue. I knew they wanted to help his poor soul—to have him pray.

Days later God's saint said, "It helped him a little." I knew our friend was now praying some.

Following is a wonderful, loving prayer. Would you please say it, from your heart?

"Oh, my Jesus, forgive us our sins. Save us from the fires of Hell. Lead all souls to Heaven, especially those in most need of thy Mercy."

I will mention this prayer later, and explain the way that God let me become more aware of how loving, powerful, and meaningful this prayer is.

This prayer was given to us through our most Blessed Mother, Mary. The children of Fàtima were told to say this prayer after the mysteries of the rosary, or five times when saying the rosary. This prayer *does come* from a Mother's love.

Previously, I did not date everything precisely as to the dates things occurred on. Please excuse me. This is because at the time, I did not think I would be writing about my visions. I had never really thought I would be writing a book. Also, I have to say, I had tried my best to remember everything in the exact order things happened.

From here on, I have tried to write the exact dates on which all of my experiences occurred. From here on I have written my visions and experiences down as quickly as I could after I had experienced them.

Chapter 3

My First Vision of the Future

OCTOBER 1995

As I was driving my car I noticed a woman across the road in a van. I noticed her because she had a devil's spirit in her, which was using this woman's body to help it pull energy from a man driving the car in front of her. Sadly I turned to look at the road in front of me. I felt so bad for the man. I thought, He looks so tired. I heard Saint Robert's voice as he calmly said, "Joyce, they know they're going to Hell." Then I felt so sorry for the poor devil's spirits.

✝I would just like to add this here. I do not know if this woman realized a devil's spirit was in her or not. Remember, sometimes we know when a devil's spirit is in us and sometimes we do not realize when a devil's spirit is, or even was, in us. (Remember the men I had noticed at both convenience stores?) However, please try to not be like the woman who was following the poor, tired man in the car. Try to have compassion for each other. God quietly watches His children, but He knows.

Please do not give up the enormous amount of love and gifts God has waiting for you. . . . Do not give up so much for so little.✝

NOVEMBER 1995

One day I said to Donna, 'What do you do in Heaven?' I was thinking they might get tired of the continual Peace in Heaven. God's angel replied, "We *love* music." I could sense a love for the music from musical instruments, and then a love for singing. Well now, and this is just my own idea—I imagined great concerts in Heaven with angels just everywhere.

One of the churches that I like to pray in is a beautiful church of cloistered Dominican nuns; a church that has the exposition of the Holy Eucharist all day.

Today I prayed and talked for a while with Jesus in this church. Then, as I was walking down the center aisle to leave, I saw Donna's white spirit fly over my head. God's angel said, "I'm so proud of you."

When we are good we bring much joy and loving pride to our Guardian Angel. Wouldn't you like your guardian to feel joy and pride for you? Don't they deserve it? Don't you both deserve it? This is just my opinion, but I think that when we meet God, our guardians may present to Him some of their pride, or sorrow and tears, that they have felt for us over the years. In God's justice, what do you think He will do with what is in our Guardian Angel's spirit—which comes from our life?

DECEMBER 1995

I was sitting peacefully at home on the couch watching TV—E.W.T.N. (Eternal World Television Network, a Catholic broadcast station with prayers, Masses, church events, news, etc.). Then God allowed me, for a few, very amazing seconds, to feel pure love. It was wonderful! This love was the strongest in my heart, then it radiated out to fill my whole body . . . and it was so strong and overwhelming that love became the only thing my body was aware of.

Then God's sweet angel Donna sadly said, "This is how much

you should love." When she said this, along with my knowing how much we should love, I also realized how much He wants to give us—the pure love God wants us to have. However, strangely, as Donna told me this, I felt her sadness. I thought for a few minutes . . . then I realized that our angels know, although this should be the pure love we feel, we do not feel this. We do not love as we should—our hearts do not feel the love God wants us to feel.

✝Again, I was made aware of a spiritual gift our Loving Father wants His children to have, to feel, for now and for eternity. The angel Donna, through the Grace of God, wanted me to know, and We want you to know . . . Our Father, Our Creator, wants our hearts to feel pure love.✝

DECEMBER 2, 1995

I've written most of today, but as it got later in the day and darker outside, I decided it was time to go home. I'm at a peaceful monastery in their small, quiet, public church. In this monastery there are only three or four religious people still living here, one of whom works very hard to keep the monastery and the grounds around the buildings very beautiful. This is one of the places where I like to write, where I find peace, on the monastery's quiet grounds or in their church.

The stained glass windows of this church are small, so when it starts to get dark outside it gets even darker inside. When it gets dark I usually leave the church, or I only write for a little while, using the monastery's lights and electricity.

I saw no one else in the church today, so I thought before I leave I should shut off the lights. Although the light switch is on the side-wall that is in the middle of the church and I know it will be dark in the church after I shut off the lights, I'm not too worried. I figure that enough light should come in from the stained glass windows and the front door to help guide me to this door.

After I shut off the lights I hear an animal growl, of sorts, in the far corner of the church. I was scared. I just stood still, looking in the direction the angry growl came from, but from the little bit of light that came in from outside, I couldn't see anything unusual. I started walking. As I was walking down the middle aisle, half facing the door and half facing the direction the growl had come from, I heard Saint Robert talk to me. His calm voice came from behind me. Very close to me, God's saint said, "More Faith, Joyce." I did not see him, but I knew he was standing right behind me. I thought of God, His Wisdom, His Power and His Love for us. I was no longer scared. I turned and walked in the dark toward the light of the door.

✝Many times, remembering these few powerful words of this saint has helped me. More Faith. **Faith gives us strength.**✝

DECEMBER 17, 1995

Today I had been writing in the quiet monastery church again. As I started to pack up my papers to leave, from behind the closed door on the side of the church I hear three roars. These roars were like those of a lion, but I could hear a slight human sound in them. There was a pause . . . then I heard a man's voice, not a totally human voice, agonizingly say, 'Why?'

> I thought back to the black spirit that I had seen flying in the desert, close to the hill. Remember the black spirit that had the head of a lion, but no lion's mane? (Page 77)

When I heard these roars, I knew they came from the lion-like devil's spirit that I had seen in the desert, Sue's companion. I knew he was behind this door. I knew that although he had some humanity in him, he was not human. He did scare me, then I remembered the last time they scared me in this same church, and I remembered Saint Robert calmly saying, "More Faith, Joyce." I called on my Faith . . . as my saint, God's saint, had reminded me to do. Calmly I finished packing my papers, and as I walked out of the church, I was then sad. I thought, This devil's spirit must have been, like Sue, one of God's angels that had fallen . How beautiful they must have been.

✝Dears, please do not someday say this same desperate, Why? Thank your Creator and love your neighbor. As was said so beautifully in the Bible—Matthew, Chapter 22: 36-40—'Teacher, which commandment in the law is the greatest? He said to him, "You shall love the Lord, your God, with all your heart, with all your soul, and with all your mind. This is the greatest and the first commandment. The second is like it. You shall love your neighbor as yourself. The whole law and prophets depend on these two commandments.' "✝

1996

JANUARY 1996

It's the middle of January and I finally have more free time. I'm not working two jobs as I had been in the months before Christmas. Today, in just the last hour, God's white spirits have zoomed quickly by me three times, as they tell me, "Write."

When they have zoomed in front of me they have flown down, and I know what they mean . . . every day, every minute, people die and then their spirits will meet God. These beautiful lights of God want all souls to rise up, to become a part of Heaven, and not to fall down to Hell. They are so worried for our spirits. (As I wrote this I was thinking, God's spirits are working so hard to allow me to write for you.)

I must tell you something else that also happened during the month of January. Several times, as Donna flew by me, this angel said . . . so good and so grateful, "God made me." I was so touched by her goodness and gratefulness.

✝God made us, too. I can't help but think of what just a little bit of gratefulness might do to help us become good children.✝

JANUARY 10, 1996

Last night, as I was comfortably lying down and almost asleep, I saw my Guardian Angel's white spirit. As her tiny spirit, which at the time was no bigger than an inch and a half, flew onto my thigh I saw her white wings flutter. When Donna's spirit touched my thigh I could no longer see her; however, I could feel her warmth and I knew God's light was still there . . . I said to her, 'The lights of God are always welcome to sleep with me.' This angel replied, "We all sleep with them." How blessed each one of us is.

. . . . .

I have seen one other angel on one other person. He was a priest. Even though I was watching him on TV, I could still see his angel on his right upper chest, and when I saw this, my Guardian Angel Donna told me, "This is his angel's favorite place."

JANUARY 13, 1996

At around 7:00 p.m. I was at home watching TV. Our dog walked into the room to go to the next room, the bedroom, which is also her bedroom. From the room the dog had come from, a black shadowy spirit came flying very fast and hit the dog in the rear. Quickly, she spun around to face her attacker, but now neither of us could see the black spirit. She turned and continued to walk into the bedroom. I must say, it seems a devil's spirit does not like our old and peaceful dog.

FEBRUARY 1996

This month several things happened that I was unable
to write the exact dates on, but they are important:

One time, when I heard someone say something very
cruel to someone, of course hurting that person's feelings, I heard
a kind spirit say, "Donna is crying." Then I felt God's angel's great
compassion and sadness, and I also felt like crying. I knew that at
that time, somehow, this angel's spirit was touching my spirit.

Another time, when Saint Robert talked about the battle that had
gone on in Heaven, he said, "We can't have this happen again." Of
course, God does not want another war in Heaven.

Saint Robert told me, "We must have Peace." And I knew he
meant, Heaven must have peace. This I can totally understand.
God, the saints' and angels' home, our home in Heaven . . . must
have Peace.

✝This is just my own wording—but I think this is why we first
come here to Earth. Here we use our God-given free will and
choose for ourselves; good and peace, or evil. After we make our
choices here on Earth, our spirits will go accordingly to a peaceful
Heaven, or elsewhere. Here we decide our fate . . . so, our time on
Earth will separate the wheat from the shaft. Make loving and compassionate choices here, for **God will not allow another battle in
Heaven. Heaven must have, and will hold, its Peace.**✝

Over the past few months there were times when I would ask
Donna to do things for me that were selfish or not giving, loving
things. She would reply, "I can only keep you alive." God has given
me time—time to learn.

Finally, one day Donna very happily said to me, "I can do more for you now." I think I have learned to be less selfish and more loving and patient.

FEBRUARY 15, 1996

I really do like my work and the people I work with. However, at times Sue's devil spirit does go into the new girl that sits beside me, and then Sue tries to irritate me. I'm sorry to say that sometimes she succeeds and I become angry.

Today has not been an easy day for me and I did lose my patience. But, I know my Guardian Angel and Saint Robert are right with me and this makes things more bearable. At the end of my workday, as I'm leaving the office, I can hear the new girl and another girl as they talk and laugh about God and religion. I know the new girl is weak and she is being controlled somewhat by the devil's spirit, Sue, that is in her.

There are two other people whom I have never seen before sitting at the two desks by the exit door. As I walk by them I notice a heavenly, sad look, suddenly show on their faces. I know Donna and Saint Robert's spirits are in them. Then I heard Donna's voice as she sadly and compassionately said, "You do not know what pain they will go through." With this I felt some of the angel's compassion—and I felt sorry for the two girls who were laughing.

✝It did not make much sense to me months ago, but I can see more clearly why God's lights are so sad for those of us who are cruel or uncaring . . . . Of course God's lights are sad for the person the cruelty is directed toward, but they are even sadder for the poor person who is cruel. They are sad for the choice this person makes—therefore, they are sad for their sins.✝

MARCH 2, 1996

It's snowing today. When I looked out the window I saw God's angel Donna fly by quickly. She was so happy. She said, "We are proud of this." I knew it was the snow that she was so proud of. Donna said, "It's white." A second later, "God made it." I'm sad today because I haven't seen people being very compassionate toward one another, but I replied, 'It's beautiful. White is beautiful.'

MARCH 3, 1996

At the conclusion of writing today, I slowly left the monastery's quiet, little church and I walked down the sidewalk toward my car. Donna's white angel spirit, coming from above and behind me, flew over my head, and very humbly she said, "You wrote about me."

I quietly said, 'This will be everybody's favorite part.'

Donna replied, "She knows." Then I saw a glimpse of Sue's devil spirit sitting up in the backseat of my car, she looked very anxious and angry. However, I was full of Faith as I got into my car and drove home.

✝Remember, although evil spirits are about, you have a Guardian Angel from God with you. Please try not to be frightened by evil, but turn to God and prayer.✝

MARCH 8, 1996

I was wearing a turtleneck top, and I had my chain and crucifix on the top of this turtleneck. As I was getting ready to take a shower my crucifix accidentally came off with my top. Right after this I saw a tiny, no bigger than an inch, white angel's spirit wings fluttering as she flew off of my chest.

As I noticed this, I felt a tiny, heavenly presence leave my chest from the same place that the angel had flown from—this is the best I can do to explain this feeling. Immediately, I put my crucifix back around my neck, remembering Bob telling me so long ago, "Joyce, don't ever take your cross off." After I put my crucifix back on, I did not see the angel come back to me, but I did pray that she would return.

MARCH 9, 1996

I was thinking about Michael the Archangel, wondering what he looks like, etc. In the next room, the dining room, I saw a white spirit, not float or even zoom about, but I saw a white spirit flash down, as a very powerful bolt of lightning. God's angel Donna said, "This is him. God had to make him like that." I was allowed a glimpse of Michael the Fighter.

MARCH 28, 1996

I knew God's lights were with me at work. I could feel a heavenly sadness, pity, and compassion for the poor devil's spirits. God's angel Donna said, "God created them also." Then Donna let me feel a portion of how sad God is for the fallen spirits. Although I knew this feeling was only a very small amount of His compassion, it was a tremendous sadness, even more intense and greater than any sadness I had ever felt from God's helpers. . . . The angel sadly continued, reminding me once more, as she had before, "They are also His creatures."

I try to remember this and other things Donna has told me. I try very hard to feel compassion, and not feel anger toward all of God's creatures. As God's saint said to me many times, about many things, "It's not easy."

MARCH 29, 1996

A little bit before 3:00 p.m., the Hour of Mercy, I was sitting in my living room and I started to thank Jesus for his loving passion on the Cross. Then, for about two or three seconds, the sky outside turned almost as black as night. As I looked out of the window, God's angel said, "That's how it was." God let me know just how dark the sky became when His son, Jesus, died on the cross at 3:00.

Later that day I thought about Jesus again. Sue, as this devil is, and not wanting to be outdone, said, 'He is true.' The spirit world does know Jesus. And so shall you.

APRIL 14, 1996 —MERCY SUNDAY

Today is Mercy Sunday. On February 22, 1931 our Lord and Savior, Jesus Christ, appeared to a simple nun, bringing with Him a wonderful message of Mercy for all mankind. Sister Faustina tells us as one of His signs of forgiving Love, whoever will go to confession and Holy Communion on the first Sunday after Easter will receive complete forgiveness of sin and punishment. Mankind will not enjoy peace until it turns with confidence to my mercy. This first Sunday after Easter is Mercy Sunday. (Quoted from a National Shrine handout.)

I've been looking forward to Mercy Sunday and going to Mass on this day for a while. Since I don't live too far from the National Shrine of the Divine Mercy, at the Marion Helper's Center in Stockbridge, Massachusetts, I had planned on going to their Mass. Being me, I left the house at 8:30 a.m. to go to the first Mass, which started at 10:30 in the morning.

They expected a large crowd at the Shrine, so there were several parking lots available for the cars, then free shuttle busses to the Marion Center. After I parked my car in a lot, I headed for a bus. At the bus stop, and on the bus, people were very relaxed and friendly toward one another, but after getting off the bus I walked slower than the others. I really did want to be peaceful and quiet today. I had come to pray and thank Jesus.

Since I had arrived early for the day I was able to get into the church with little trouble from crowds. I prayed, and then I walked to the front of the church to bow down in front of the altar before leaving. As I approached the altar I could feel a heavenly presence, which felt stronger the closer I walked to the altar. I wanted to tell everyone, He's here!

It was a beautiful day and the Masses were to be held outside on a large field. At the first Mass, the 10:30 a.m. Mass, I was glad to see that the field was just full of people. As the priest was saying Mass I looked to the right of the altar, to the distant hills. Since it had rained a lot the night before, there was a thick fog in the forest on the hills. For a second, during the Mass, I saw the huge white spirit of a heavenly man in the fog. I could only see his spirit from the waist up, but he had such a good and holy look on his face as he looked down upon us celebrating Mass. I thought, Jesus is so lovingly watching us.

As I left the Mass I noticed an even larger crowd of people coming in for the next service. It was uplifting to see such Faith. However, now there were long lines everywhere; especially at the entrance to the church, where I had wanted to go and pray the rosary. I noticed a tent set about seventy-five yards from the church that didn't look too crowded and had many entrances, it seemed very accessible. When I walked into the tent I was surprised, in the center of the tent was the exposed Eucharist. I prayed the rosary.

In the tent there was a man with a microphone who was preaching. When he was done talking, the people started to sing. No one seemed to be putting much heart into their singing. I thought, Thank Him! I sang loud, louder than the others, than everyone sang a little louder. Alleluia! Alleluia! Alleluia! I kept thinking, Praise Him. And I felt sorry for their poor souls. I thought, Heaven is waiting. Sing.

At the end of the songs, as I stood in front of the Eucharist, I heard Saint Robert's voice. He said, "Joyce, your pride." I wasn't aware of it; I knelt on the ground and put my head down. In humility, I thanked Jesus. God's saint had let me know previously that my pride is one of my faults. Today he reminded me again . . . in front of the Eucharist. I wondered if anyone else had heard God's saint's voice. When I was done praying I left the tent and the grounds. I felt good, I felt clean inside.

That night I wanted to be in a quiet place, so I drove to the monastery. After I had parked my car I realized that I had to get something from the trunk, and after I had gotten it, I closed the trunk and got back into my driver's seat. Well, I have rosary beads hanging from the rearview mirror of my front window. I now noticed that the beads were twisted just above the crucifix, and I knew that the beads were not twisted before I had gotten out of the car. As I looked at the twisted beads I heard an evil voice say, 'We hate him.' I got a little nervous, but I remembered what I had learned today, "Jesus, I Trust in you." I put the beads right.

I looked out of my car's rear window and I saw a black devil's spirit run by, and not too far from my car. I then looked into my car's backseat and got my catechism book, planning to leave this book open and on my dashboard; opened to a page with a very holy picture. I wanted to find a picture of Jesus to protect me, a picture the devil's spirits would avoid. I flipped through the book. On the last page I saw the vision of a cross that I had seen in the book. The cross flashed on the white, blank last page. I heard God's saint say, "That one. We're here." I looked back in the book for the picture of the cross I had just seen flash on the last page. When I found this picture, I left the book opened to this page, on the dashboard of my car. I rested in quiet.

APRIL 22, 1996

Last night I watched E.W.T.N. on TV, and I saw a beautiful story about a saint. This poor girl was born blind, hunchbacked, and one leg was shorter than the other. Her wealthy parents were ashamed of her and when she was a young child, they had her locked in a single room for years. The room was sealed except for one opening; a small window that opened to the church this room had been built next to. Throughout most of this girl's youth her only communication came from the church's priest. He tried to keep her spirits up and he told her how much God loved her. She became very thankful to God for His Love, her life, and everything in her life . . . the things in and about her one room. She thanked God for her parents. She always thanked and praised God, her Faith grew and she became very holy.

This morning, as I was washing up in my bathroom I sadly said, 'God how could parents do that to their child?' I heard Saint Robert say, "Joyce, you almost did." At that instant I saw a vision of myself. I was pregnant and sitting in my gynecologist's office, the doctor sat looking at me from behind his desk. The vision only lasted for a few seconds and then it was gone, but as I stood very still in my bathroom—I remembered.

I remembered I was thirty-two years old, and at that time it wasn't advisable to have children after thirty. (Of course things have now changed, and thirty years old is not considered as risky an age to have children.) Because of my age, as the doctor sat at his desk, he told me that I could have the test, the amniocentesis, to see if my baby had Down's syndrome. However, the doctor said I would have to go to the hospital for the test, as the test would involve putting me under an anesthetic. Also, the doctor said he would not give me the test unless I signed papers before the test, authorizing him to take the child if the child had Down's syndrome.

Today, as I looked back at this, I was sad; sad because I told the doctor I had to think about it. Although I now know, at the time I did not fully realize why I had to think about this. I now realize I had to think about accepting my child if he wasn't just so. However, at my next doctor's appointment I said, 'No, no test.'

It was now time for God's saint to let me fully realize all of this. Instantly, I said, 'I'm sorry. I'm so sorry.' I kept going on and on about how sorry I was. I felt so ashamed. Quietly I heard my father say, 'Just listen.' Being me, and being totally ashamed, I kept saying, 'I'm sorry.' Then faintly, as if from very far away, I heard Saint Robert say, "You didn't." I knew, he knew, I didn't have the test. I didn't sign the papers.

Most of that day, at every chance I could, I prayed for forgiveness. Later in the day I heard Saint Robert say, I'm sure to pacify

me, "It's gone." I knew he meant that any sin I had from that time was gone. I did not decide to abandon my son because something may have been wrong with him. I would love my child no matter what.

After that I begged that any selfish feelings I had at that time, not be gone by hurting or burdening Jesus.

✝Well, I know I was not facing God here . . . but I felt, and I feel I can say, When we face God . . . you WILL know . . . and He WILL know . . . your life's trials, and your life's successes and failures.✝

APRIL 23, 1996—MY FIRST VISION OF THE FUTURE

This morning I got up as usual and started to get ready for work. First of all, I wanted to feed the dog and cats. After finishing with them I thought, Good, they are out of the way.

As I was running the water in the kitchen sink, cleaning the mess I had made, I noticed that the water slowly began to turn color. The water that was running from the faucet turned, not a deep red, but red. I just looked. I heard a man's voice say, "When the water runs red, then they will see." I thought of blood. I knew that when the water turns as red as blood, then we will see God's power. Then God will take back His torn World.

I looked slightly away from the running red water, but still I was looking into the sink. I saw another vision.

I saw myself floating high above the Earth, way above the clouds. I could only see a portion of the circular Earth and myself in this vision. I was wearing ordinary clothes, a dark skirt and a light blouse. As I stood in my kitchen, looking at myself in this vision, I could see I was crying so very hard. I knew I was crying in this vision because, as I looked down at the Earth, I was filled with a very deep sadness. A sadness that was brought about because of all the destruction and pain I saw going on below. I knew I was also crying because I thought I was so high above the Earth. I did not want to leave Earth; I wanted to stay and help.

Then, as I stood in my kitchen, my attention was turned away from myself in the vision and toward poor Earth . . . and I began to get very scared for the horrors we will have on Earth . . . .

My feelings from the vision—sadness, sorrow, then fright—and my vision—were gone.

The rest of that morning I felt very upset and scared for the horrors Earth will have before God comes.

APRIL 28, 1996

For a while this morning I thought about to the vision of April 23rd, and I wondered where this vision had come from. Later in the morning I knew this vision had come from the Holy Spirit.

APRIL 29, 1996

Today I had another vision of the future.

In this vision I saw what looked like the shadow of a man. Although the shadowy figure was completely black, I thought, Is this a shadow or a man? The thin and frail man's figure looked so tired. Although he was walking forward, he seemed to have no purpose, walking with no reason or intent.

He looked down and his head and shoulders were so bent over that he seemed almost dead.

The background of the vision was gloomy and all gray; all of the buildings in this background, and there were a lot of them, were almost completely tumbled down and full of destruction. I could tell that many of the buildings were at one time very tall.

Saint Robert said, "Joyce, this is how they will look." I knew the figure that looked like a shadow, was not a shadow, but a man, void of God's Light.

✝Dears, we will go through a lot before God comes. This will not be God's choice but our own. God will not bring about destruction . . . our lack of Faith and love will.✝

MAY 1996

I was at home watching TV and our dog was lying peacefully on the floor in front of me. Suddenly, I saw a white spiritual lightning bolt hit the dog in her chest. This bolt was about a foot, or even longer, and it seemed to come from nowhere. When the bolt hit the dog she yelled with pain, and then her head fell to the floor. She seemed to sleep. Although I was worried for her, I sat on the couch and just watched. Short of a minute later she put her head up and she seemed OK.

This lightning bolt today was just the same as the small lightning bolts I had seen flash in front of me in the church in Virginia. (Although this bolt was a bit bigger.)

> Remember the church I stayed at in the quiet town in Virginia? That night I had seen white spirits flying about so quickly, and lightning bolts that were so close in front of me, but the bolts never struck me? Remember the bolts were suddenly deflected down? (Page 47 and 48)

Today, as I watched our dog with her head on the floor, I knew the lightning bolts I had seen a while ago in Virginia were meant to hurt me. However, all of the lightning bolts that had come at me, at my chest, were suddenly deflected down. None of them hit me.

I also knew my Guardian Angels were protecting me that night. They must have been deflecting these lightning bolts down, away from me, as their white spirits had rushed and zoomed about so quickly. I thought, What a battle must have gone on that night! I have read that there is a spiritual war going on here; on Earth. A very active war. I realized that I had been allowed to have seen some of this war. What a fight God's lights go through for us.

This war is between God, His good spirits, and Satan and his evil spirits. I can see more and more that this war is going on every minute of our lives, whether we are awake or asleep. Please try to realize just how much God and His helpers Love us.

†God and His lights do not have to fight this war on Earth, nor do they have to fight any other battles. They have already won their war in Heaven. However, they choose to go through and fight this war—for us. **Dears, the time we have on Earth is given to us, and fought for us . . . by God and His lights.** This is our God-given time to be saved, *solely* . . . because of Their Love.

Many times God's saint said to me, **"Use your time wisely."†**

MAY 9, 1996

I went to the family clerk's office in my hometown today. While I was there I particularly noticed one man out of all of the other people there. Let me try to explain why. Somehow I felt that there was a peace about him and even that he had a peaceful smile on his face. However, when I looked directly at him, he wasn't smiling, but I continually felt his peace. (Now that I look back on this, his presence of peace seemed to be the same peaceful presence I had noticed in Bob.) I knew no one else was paying him much mind. The young man was nice looking, and he had long, straight hair, that almost came to his shoulders. He had on modern clothes, but to me he looked out of place. To me he looked as if, or, I should say I felt as if, he had come from a different time.

Later, as I was walking to my car, I noticed this same man across the street. We were both on Main Street and walking in the same direction. Then I turned my head and looked into a large glass storefront window that was on my right side and, for that second, I saw the reflection in this window of God's angel Donna and another Guardian Angel. These tall, long, white-gowned spirits were walking beside me, and very close beside me, one on each side.

I was walking very fast and I could see their white spirits rushing to stay close to me. . . . Walking quickly, I passed the large window and this vision.

I looked across the street. The man I had noticed turned the corner and walked down a side street. Because of the building on the corner I could no longer see him. My thought was, He's gone. I can't say for sure, but I felt that the man I had noticed, the man that seemed to be from another time, had somehow let me see God's wonderful guardians.

MAY 13, 1996

As I prayed from my prayer book, *The Pietà*, I compassionately and humbly bowed my head down, touching my forehead to the opened book. From inside of me I felt a great compassion, and I could feel the words, "God gives us Gifts." I knew the compassion I felt inside of me was just, a bit, of God's Heavenly compassion. God has such compassion, and as a Loving Father, He wants to give to all of His children. Please be a loving and good child. Allow Him to give you the gifts He so wants to give.

MAY 15, 1996

As I was saying the "Our Father . . . " in my daily prayers, I felt a Fatherly Love. Today I was allowed to feel some of the Fatherly Love God feels toward us, His children. God is our compassionate and Loving Father.

I hope that someday, every one of us will feel Our Father's Love.

MAY 17, 1996

I was watching a wildlife program on TV that was showing a deer running in slow motion. I was amazed at the deer's beauty. As I sat watching, in awe, I was hoping that the scene would never end. I heard God's angel Donna say, "God's always looking at them." I knew God, also, admiringly and Lovingly looks at His creatures. Donna paused for a second, then she continued, "He'll make more after."

MAY 18, 1996

There have been many times that I worried about God's wonderful spirits that are around me, because I know that the devil spirits are forever around them. This morning I was really worried about God's guardians (as turned around as this may seem). I don't want them hurt in any way.

Just before I closed my jar of cream makeup I saw a tiny white star light up for a bit in the jar. I twisted the cover shut and then I turned and looked toward the sink. I saw a tiny white spirit and I heard a pure voice say, "Don't worry. We get out." God's lights don't want me to worry, and this did help put me at ease.

Now I knew that the tiny white stars and the white spirits can be one and the same.

MAY 19, 1996

Today is Sunday. After attending Mass I went home. Right after I got home I saw Donna's white angel spirit, and I heard, "After church is when you are the most pure." I knew this wonderful light meant this not just for me, but also for all of us.

Later I thought, I'm getting old. I heard Donna reply with a very excited, "Yes." I must tell you, I was set back a bit and I had to think about this one. To you and I old age means aches and pains and that we are getting close to death, but God's angel was so happy!

After I stopped thinking about my aches and pains, I thought, These wonderful beings are waiting. When our bodies die and our spirits leave our bodies, our wait and the angels' and saints' wait, will be over. We, as spirits, will meet the spirit world, and God our Father. I will pray that when God and His lights' wait is over . . . when our wait is over . . . this will be a wonderful time for us all.

. . . . .

That night, as I lay in bed and saw our dog walk
by to go to the next room. I felt an emptiness. I knew
Sue's devil spirit was in the dog. As she walked by the open
window she stopped in front of it, then she desperately said, 'Feed
me.' Through the window came a round white spiritual object that
went into the dog's left side, into her lower neck by her upper chest.
She then continued to walk into the kitchen, where I heard her
drink some water from the dog's dish.

On her way back, as our dog walked by me, Sue said, 'I'm
better.' When she spoke I saw a small white spirit above her head. I
heard Donna say, "You have seen what not many have."

MAY 25, 1996

As I was walking into my kitchen I felt a tiny pull on my right
shoulder, it felt as if something, that was very delicate, was being
pulled off of this shoulder. I turned and saw a small white spirit that
was seemingly being pulled outside, through the window. When I
looked out this back window I noticed a black car stopped on the
next street, then the car and driver quickly went down the street. I
turned back and thought, They took Donna. Saint Robert said,
"They have no respect for what is God's." I could not help but sadly
think, Poor Donna.

A little later I sat back on the couch. Still worried for Donna, I
started to cry . . . but I heard, "Don't worry. She's OK. She's a
spirit."

MAY 27, 1996

I was looking through one of my books. As I stopped to look at
a picture of the Blessed Mother Mary, I thought of what I had heard
a priest say in a sermon. He said, "One day Jesus looked in Heaven
and there were some unfamiliar faces. Jesus said, 'I know I did not
let them in Heaven. How did they get here?' An angel said of Jesus'
loving mother, 'Your Mother leaves the back door open.' " Well

then, the priest continued, telling us that we should pray through Our Blessed Mother Mary.

Still lovingly looking at Our Blessed Mother's picture, I then thought to myself, Heaven can't leave the back door open. Heaven can't have disorder. Please, not like Earth. Not again. I thought, I could not bear the same sorrows in Heaven as I did here on Earth. None of us could. Donna's tiny white spirit flew out of the book I was looking at. She said, as Saint Robert had told me before, "We must have Peace." I knew Heaven would hold its Peace.

MAY 30, 1996

I seldom watch the news, but tonight I did. When I saw something on the news that I thought would surely lead to trouble in the future, I sadly said, 'Why?' The angel Donna replied, "It's theirs." My dear sweet angel was reminding me that this Earth is God's creation, however the devil is here and very busy. We live with turmoil; our lack of love and Faith has given evil much control. But I must say, Through it all, God still manages to allow us time . . . and tries to guide us to Him.

I remembered what God's saint had said a while back about the future of the world, "It's inevitable." I know hate destroys . . . .

JUNE 1996

One night, a severe rainstorm suddenly started outside. I could hear loud thunder. Sue's devil spirit, who was evidently in my sister's dog, frantically said, 'You don't know, it's going to come quick.' At that I heard a man's voice angrily say, 'Don't tell her anything.' The dog put her tail between her legs and her head down. Sue's scared devil's spirit, which was in the dog, went into the bathroom to hide under our old bathtub.

This was one of the few times I had seen Sue show she was afraid. A powerful storm, God's power, is one of the few things the devil spirits seem to be afraid of.

I thought, Sue must mean God's judgment will come very quickly to Earth; The Final Judgment. This made me think about a Mass where the priest had read the passage in the Bible: "God's wrath will come like a thief in the night." I thought, Sue and the devils know this very well.

Since this night Saint Robert had told me, "They will fall quickly. You will see." Or, he has said several times to me, "They will fall." I thought, At these times, he must have also been saying this as a warning to the devils, to help control them. I know the poor souls will fall quickly into Hell, into darkness; and I know on that day all of Heaven will cry very sadly for them.

Hard as it is, and believe me I do know it is hard, please try to be patient (but not foolish,) with these poor devil's spirits. They know they are going to Hell, and although they do not know the time, they know God will be quick.

JUNE 1, 1996

I was watching the noon Mass on E.W.T.N., and then I turned my head and looked out the window. I saw a white spirit in a white gown. He stood about two feet tall, and he had some places in him where there was a orange/yellow light. I knew he was God's light. He stood, suspended in midair, looking directly at me. The look on this beautiful, pure spirit's face was of a wonderful, total curiosity. Almost right after this spirit appeared, a bird that was in a tree close to the spirit, angrily chirped again and again. The spirit disappeared from my view. I knew Sue's devil spirit was in this bird and I thought, I have seen another of God's spirits. This must have made her very angry.

✝Dears, I think God would like us to see His lights, but the evil spirits stop much of this. A few times I have heard God's saint tell the devil spirits, "Please do not show yourselves, and we will not show ourselves." God's lights know we would be very frightened if we were to see such evil spirits.

Also, I know the devils threaten to bring much destruction and pain to us and to Earth if we see God's lights. I am sure evil thinks that if we could see God's angels and saints we would be amazed and we might be swayed to be good. The devils want to destroy our souls. (And they are very jealous of God's lights.)

And I think that if we could see God's helpers, their peace and light would bring about a change in us. However, I feel this change would not be permanent in some of us . . . no matter what, inevitably, in time, some of us would choose to be good, and some of us would choose to be bad. So, with God's army of Guardian Angels and saints here, they quietly and wisely wait for us to freely choose. He wants us to decide here on Earth and on our own, as we or our spirits would, in any event, choose to be good or otherwise. ✝

Back to the noon Mass. At the end of the Mass I watched a nun play her musical instrument. God's saint said, "She will play in Heaven." A pause, "Tell her when you see her."

. . . . .

I had been typing on the computer in the nearby library, however the library closed at 4:00 p.m., so I headed home. On the way home I noticed the familiar church that is close to my friend's home. Although I had intended on going to the Sunday morning Mass (tomorrow's Mass), as I drove closer to the church I had the desire to go to this church and this Mass. I stopped . . .

During the Mass I saw a white spirit fly above the altar. I could not tell who the spirit was; I just saw a large white spirit and no features. Then I heard Saint Robert say, as he has said so many times before to me, "We will not leave you."

. . . . .

I was at home and it was getting late and dark, it was 8:00 p.m., so I decided to close some of the windows and pull down the shades. I like my privacy. As I sat back down on the couch I began to feel sad and I started to cry. I said, 'God.' I heard Saint Robert say, "We

will give you Peace." I know what I have been allowed to write in this book is some of the things, a few of the things, that God's loving spirits would like to say to us all.

JUNE 2, 1996

I was at home in my living room and writing. It was 7:30 p.m., the TV was on and our dog was sitting on the floor in front of me. I left my writing for a minute to get something to drink in the kitchen. When I came back into the living room I noticed a commercial on TV with Smokey the Bear; a forest was burning in front of his picture. Smokey the Bear had tears running down his face and I thought, A forest fire is very destructive and sad. Well, our dog, who has never shown any interest at all in TV, was now watching this. I could see in the dog's eyes emptiness, hate, and an excitement as she watched the burning forest. I knew Sue's devil spirit was in the dog. The angel Donna said, "They would destroy it all if they could. We have to work very hard."

Later, I started to think about something that happened while Bob was alive. I wanted to write about it, about Bob. But I heard his voice. He said, "No, Joyce. This is your gift."

JUNE 3, 1996

This morning I woke up a little past midnight, about 12:10 a.m. I will write what I saw, but I have to admit that as I'm writing this, I'm still a bit scared. First, please let me tell you, I have almost completed writing about my experiences of last summer. Also, I know I now have at least two of God's helpers with me, but I have known that someday Saint Michael will come to help us. I know someday I will see Michael the Archangel, as Donna had said I would. I will see Saint Michael fight. (God's saint just sadly said to me, "Yes, you will, Joyce. Many times." You see, God's lights do not feel joy in their victories, but sorrow; sorrow for the poor dark spirits who choose to hate.)

Back to this morning and after I had woken up. I briefly saw two black devil spirits. Although I could only vaguely see the spirits, I knew these spirits were not human. The taller and bulkier spirit stood in the far corner of my room. I knew this spirit was Satan. He is one of the few devils I have seen that does not look weak. Next to the tall, black spirit I saw another smaller and weaker, angry devil spirit. He was standing in a very crouched animal-like position, as he stood over and looked at the papers of my writings that were on the floor in front of him.

I heard God's angel Donna say, "They are here." The spirits disappeared. I waited for a while, then, scared but curious, I got out of bed and walked into the living room. As I looked into the doorway of a dark and empty bedroom, I saw two small devil's eyes shining in the doorway. Angrily the devil looked at me. This is all I could see of the black spirit in the darkness.

I got back into bed, and then I heard an amazingly strong man's voice supportively say to me, "We will not leave you." His voice was the strongest voice I have ever heard—God's Spirit's strength. I heard Donna say to me, "Are you staying with us?" Quietly I said, 'Yes.' I have to admit I was scared, but from God's helpers I felt that Saint Michael would come to help in the nick of time.

A bit later I heard an angel say to me, "You must have Faith." Then Donna told me, "You must keep working." Minutes of quiet . . . an angel said, "Michael has been here." More quiet. Then, "Now they (the devils) think they have bigger fish to fry." I knew Satan was after others, and I knew Saint Michael must be close behind him.

After all this was over I turned on the TV. The midnight Mass was still on E.W.T.N. and I wrote. I was still a bit shaky and scared, even after I had finished writing this, at about 12:30 a.m. Then God's angel Donna said, "They are mad. You must live."

†Now back to when the angel Donna said I must keep working. I know she meant keep working on writing, but I also knew she meant, keep working. Donna has much respect for our work.

At the end of the day when I have worked very hard, more than once this angel has proudly said to me, with a sigh in her voice, "We worked hard today."✝

JUNE 5, 1996

I have to admit I'm a little nervous and angry today. So many people pull from each other, there is so much uncaring. I can't believe . . . I have a hard time believing this. Even I, who has been allowed to have seen so much and have even seen devil spirits, at times I wonder, Why *are* people doing this? Devil's spirits controlling people? Of course, God and His lights have continually tried to let me know that the evil spirits can influence people to do bad things. We must remember, Don't be uncaring toward each other, and be patient.

Well, as I left the pharmacy and walked to my car, I still felt angry. Then I looked up to the blue sky and saw a large white cloud in which I could see Saint Robert's spirit. He looked so calm. Although his spirit was only showing from the waist up, his spirit was as big as the large cloud. I could hear him very calmly say, "Patience, Joyce." I knew he was right, and I tried to calm down. Again I heard my father's voice, as he said, "Listen to him."

JUNE 7, 1996

This morning, as I calmly woke up, I knew that when I die and my spirit leaves my body, my heart will be able to love with the strength and pureness that God's angel Donna had let me feel in December of 1995.

I remembered when I was allowed to feel my heart's love.

Also, I realized that many of the things that Donna and Saint Robert tell me and show me fit together with, or build upon, past experiences and visions; and many of my spiritual experiences Faithfully follow the Bible. God has such Wisdom in His perfect plan for us.

JUNE 8, 1996

As I sat on the couch watching TV, I felt a wound just under my rib cage. This thin, about three-inch cut was on my right side. I heard Donna say, "He had a wound there." I knew this angel was talking about a spirit that was then with us. I knew this spirit was Jesus . . . but I still feel and humbly say, I don't think I am important enough for Jesus to notice me.

JUNE 10, 1996

If I am at home at 11:30 a.m., I will pray my rosary with the 11:30 rosary time on E.W.T.N. Today, as I finished praying the rosary, I realized, as I have realized before, that the prayer of Saint Michael the Archangel is very strong. When I had begun this prayer I heard a devil's agonizing scream down the street. It wasn't a totally human sound. I wondered if anyone else heard the scream.

✝**Please do not forget this prayer before completing your rosary, and please pray this prayer with much humility . . . as God would like you to. Don't forget; we are all God's creatures.** (Donna has patiently tried to teach us this.)✝

. . . . .

The angel Donna told me today, "They're getting mad. We let you see the spirit world, and a lot of it." I replied to this angel, 'I have Faith.' I thought, I know I have not seen a tremendous amount of spirits, but I have seen a lot of the spirit world . . . enough to realize that God the Father, Jesus, and the Holy Spirit, Our Blessed Mother, the saints, angels and devils are real; Heaven, Hell and Purgatory do exist.

JUNE 11, 1996

I was thinking about my father and the love he had for his mother. Even though his mother died long ago, I remember that his eyes always lit up whenever he talked about her. He held a tremendous love for her. I asked Donna if my father had seen his mother in Heaven. The angel replied, "That is what he really wanted." As she said this, I felt my heart filling to the top . . . this great feeling was as if my heart's wish was fulfilled.

✝You will love your Guardian Angel, and his or her ways . . . .✝

JUNE 12, 1996

I was washing some clothes by hand in the kitchen sink. As I was scrubbing the clothes with soap, the water was running needlessly. And on top of this, I was not using a basin or a stopper to catch the running water. God's saint said, "Don't waste it, Joyce. It's time." God's helpers want you to know this. As our water flows . . . so does our time on Earth go. Please use God's gift of water wisely and do not to waste it.

This was the first time, but there were to be many other times, when God's lights would tell me of their concern for water being wasted. There would even be times when I saw faucets leaking just slightly and I could feel God's lights worrying.

JUNE 14, 1996

Today, Sunday, is Father's Day. Although my father has passed away I decided to go to his church. The church he went to almost every Sunday. (By the way, as I am writing this Saint Robert flew peacefully by and he said, "This is important.") After Mass I visited my father's grave and there I thanked him. I thought my father's name was Peter, and he was one of the rocks who had shown me how to be Faithful and strong.

Then I went to the Dominican nun's church to sit in front of the exposed Eucharist and say my prayers. I thanked God, Our Father, on this day, "Our Father who art in Heaven . . . " Near the end of my prayers, as I was saying the "Hail Mary," I felt a *very, very* strong gentleness, if you will, and also a humbleness in my heart. I knew I was feeling a great gentleness and humbleness. I also felt a youthfulness and innocence, but the first and strongest feeling was from the gentleness; it was overwhelming.

My Guardian Angel Donna said, "Her heart is very gentle." I knew God, through my angel, was letting me feel Our Blessed Mother Mary's heart. In awe, I thought, **Mary is the Queen of Heaven . . . yet she is the most humble and gentle**. I also felt in my own heart an admiration, respect, and finally a total, and totally willing, submission, to the Queen of Heaven.

Donna said, "God made her like that." I realized, from the youthfulness and innocence I was allowed to feel, that Blessed Mary conceived Jesus solely through the power of the Holy Spirit, and that our virgin Mother in Heaven was always pure.

After the feeling left I was still in awe for about ten minutes. I was totally amazed at the gentleness of the heart I had felt. Then again, I thought, Is the Blessed Mary's heart really this gentle? I saw Donna's white spirit fly between the pews in front of me. The angel said, "It is." I thought, Now, this is surely the most amazing experience I will ever have here on Earth.

✝Dears, then I knew that in Heaven, along with seeing each other's wonderful spirits, we will also feel one another's radiating spirits. We shall be able to see, and feel, the spirits' pure love and hearts that are about us. And our own pure spirits will be seen, and felt, by those around us. Try to imagine just how wonderful this will be!✝

(When I had begun to correct my grammar and retype today, God's saint asked me to type five pages. This is the fifth page.)

JUNE 22, 1996

I was sick yesterday. So last night I decided to get into my car and rest quietly for the night at the old Monastery. In the morning, when I woke up in my car, I was rested and I felt better. (Since the time that I had slept so many nights in my car in the desert, I feel very comfortable sleeping in my car in the quiet.)

As I drove down the driveway of the Monastery toward the main street, I looked back. I could see behind me a large oval white spirit, and I heard Saint Robert say, "We're here." Very quietly I told him, 'I will come back.'

Just before I drove onto the main street Sue's black spirit popped up in my car's backseat. She was large and she was angry. As she popped up she said, 'I'm going to kill her.' Evidently she thought, Well, God's saint is back there so . . .

I saw two quick flashes of lightning come from where Saint Robert's white spirit had just appeared and I heard God's saint sternly say, "We told you, 'No.'" Sue disappeared.

> Remember, time and time again as I was driving west on my second trip I saw lightning flash in the sky? Then, as now, the bolts appeared in the clear skies, and those bolts then, were the same as the ones I had just seen. As always, when the bolts appeared, Sue disappeared. (Page 67)

As I was watching the 8:00 a.m. Mass on TV, I prayed for a spiritual receiving of the Eucharist. While I was saying the prayer I felt a pull on my heart. Angrily a devil said, 'They tried.' Then I felt a few more pulls on my heart. The devil continued, 'Can you hear me?' I sat quietly. The angry, dark spirits do not like it when you don't answer them.

✝But, as God's saint was to teach me later, during times of trial, you should try to turn your thoughts to God and His lights.✝

JUNE 23, 1996

When I woke up this morning, I heard the angel Donna say to me, "We will show you more. God said we can." I know that when the time is right, God's helpers will show me more of His wonders. I will learn more and I will write more.

. . . . .

I'm living at my sister's house now. She has two cats, both of which look like they were made to be cuddled. I can't help but pick them up. Now, although both of her cats love to be petted, they hate to be picked up. Whenever I do pick them up they get angry and try to get down.

Last week, after I put an angry cat down, Donna told me, "They have their dignity." I then realized that when I pick up these cats I do intrude on their dignity.

Today, as all week long, I treated the cats very respectfully. I have not picked up either of them, but I have just gently petted and fed them. Now, when they are around, they come to me, or when I walk by them they roll over to be petted. I realize they have their dignity.

✝In the afternoon, Donna said to me, "You did good." Then I felt a breath of peaceful heavenly air, what a beautiful scent. I am very glad I have learned this lesson. I am also very sure God's wonderful angels and God Himself, would be very pleased with all of us if we learned to extend this lesson to each and every one of His loved creatures. We all have our dignity.✝

JUNE 25, 1996

Just relaxing at home on the couch again. Although I wasn't eating, I could briefly taste a distinctively spicy salad dressing; the dressing I had only eaten in the restaurant of the little town by the desert. It has been over ten months since I have been there.

With this . . . I knew that someday I would return to the desert solitude and this town again. However, I knew that during my next visit to this desert I would see more evil and I would be much more scared than I was the first time. I also know that the next time in the desert, God's saint and the angel Donna will have to fight harder to protect me.

JULY 1, 1996

For the last couple of days I have been busy, so today I was just going to take it easy. As I was driving home I heard Saint Robert say, "Joyce, you should be writing." Then I saw Donna. Her white spirit was as small as it had been when I had seen her fly out of my Bible . . . again I saw her tiny wings fluttering. As this wonderful angel flew in front of my car, so very quietly and meekly, she said, "Yes."

At Donna's gentle, quiet, and meek manner I was almost tempted to giggle aloud. (I am still adjusting myself to seeing such meekness.) However, I did not want to giggle or laugh at the enormous Heavenly meekness, and seemingly helplessness; I wanted to giggle because I was filled with a tremendous love and adoration for this wonderful pure creature of God's.

Again I realized how loving God's helpers really are . . . . The rest of the day I spent writing for you, as God's powerful helpers, so quietly requested.

JULY 2, 1996

I was watching Mass on TV then I felt Saint Robert's presence. I said, 'Saint Robert, let me know what you know.' Sadly he replied, "If you knew, you would be very sad." I thought about it. Most of the time he is very, very sad.

The vision of a black spiritual cloud appeared in the room. Although the oblong cloud was no larger than two or three feet, I felt that this black cloud was huge. I knew that someday there would be an enormous (spiritual), black cloud over us. God's saint said, "It's going to be a black shadow, Joyce." I felt empty inside and I wondered what the future holds. The vision disappeared.

A little later a white spirit flew in front of me and I heard Saint Robert sadly say, "There's always more, Joyce." I asked to be told only things that would help people. I knew I had been heard and that God's helpers were happy with my response. I felt a breath of peaceful air.

JULY 3, 1996

Some of you might be thinking by now, It's great she wrote this book. But I want to say that I was the smallest part in writing this. It was teamwork that put this book together. The team of God and His beautiful lights, especially Saint Robert and the Guardian Angel Donna, and then me. I must say, Although I was the least humble of this team . . . I was really the most humble of all.

This team brought you this book.

. . . . .

It was 8:50 p.m. and just starting to get dark outside. As I looked out at the black cloudy sky I saw one white cloud among all the black clouds. I heard, "We're going to really open up the skies, Joyce." Then I saw a lightning bolt and I heard, "You'll see." But I realized that my spirit may not be here on Earth when this happens.

A few minutes later I saw a light flash in the sky outside. Then I heard a quiet voice, a voice that was a little happy and excited say, "There's more." I must say that the voice today that said, "There's more," was much happier than Saint Robert was yesterday, when he to said, "There's more."

JULY 6, 1996

I saw a white spirit zoom by. Saint Robert said, "I'm close." Shortly afterward one of the girls I work with walked by me. She looked very angry and I knew a devil's spirit was in her . . . but, I thought, I'm fine. I know God has sent His loving lights to protect me.

JULY 9, 1996

Tonight I decided to go out. There are several places I like to go to because I usually know a few people there. However, although I had wanted to go out, as I was driving in my car I thought to myself, I really don't want to go anywhere; and as I continued to drive in the rain I became so sad. I just drove around town for well over half an hour.

Still driving I thought, Geez, I'm so tired of fighting. I was so sad I started to cry. Then I heard a man's voice say, "Why are you crying?" I said, 'I'm lonely.' I thought, Sue usually seems to be close and making trouble for me. I am not having an easy time with this devil's spirit around me.

It stopped raining, and as I turned onto a straight road, Route 5, I noticed the moon. The moon was a beautiful orange/yellow color; the same orange/yellow color that I remembered the moon was as it rose in the desert some time back. I thought, How is the moon showing through all the black stormy clouds? The thick clouds blew about everywhere in the sky, but opened only in this one spot for the moon.

As I looked up at the moon again, I thought, It looks as if it's directly above the end of the road I'm on. The moon seemed to be hanging in the sky. I heard Saint Robert say, "It's right in front of you." I sensed that the moon, the light, was down the straight and direct road, and right in front of me. I became aware of the fact that Heaven is right in front of me, as well as being right in front of all of us.

Then the spirit said, "Don't look to the side." I knew we all should not look to the sides of the straight road God has left open for us to get to Heaven's light, rather we should look toward the beautiful light . . . . Please don't look to the side of the road. Please don't be sidetracked or tricked.

JULY 11, 1996

Again, most of the day, the devil spirits have been around me and pulling energy from me. I can usually feel the pull and I can tell from which direction the pull is coming from, so I know where the devil's spirits are, or were, but then I feel drained. When I look toward where the pull is coming from I usually see a person with their hands up, palms toward me. Or I sometimes see a person who has their mouth open and a half-conscious look on their face.

In the people with their mouths open, a few times I saw the

vague spirit of a devil's animal face, with its long snout mouth open. This devil's spirit face comes out of the person's mouth. From these devil's long snouts come a strong sucking and pulling, which pulls most of my energy, and even much of the air around me. These devils have a strong vacuum.

When these devil's spirits know I have caught them pulling or when they know I am looking at their spirit, they usually say, 'You can't have it' or they look so ashamed. I try to feel sad for them; although their spirits can enter human bodies, they know they are not human.

Later today, as I looked outside, I could vaguely see Saint Robert's spirit. He looked so sad; full of compassion and love, he said, "You don't know." Again I knew he was reminding me, as he and Donna have before—I don't know the pain the devil's spirits will go through.

From what little spare time I have had, and what little time I have had to learn about the saints, I have learned that whenever the saints were allowed to see even a glimpse of Hell, they could hardly bear it. Thinking about this and what God's saint had just reminded me of, I realized I should try to have more compassion and patience toward the devil's spirits. It is hard for me, but I think I'm getting better at it.

Now I'm feeling sad for the poor fallen spirits, so I asked God's saint, What should I do? I told Sue, 'I will try and not write anything too bad about you.' Then I saw her spirit briefly as she jumped about. She looked happy as she said, 'You're going to make me famous.'

JULY 12, 1996

As I was sitting at my desk at work I felt my energy being pulled. I knew the devil's spirits were about. Saint Robert said, "They just want what you have Joyce."

> I remembered back to when Sue and I were talking on my first trip. One of the things she said was, 'We only wanted what He had.' (Page 43)

Well, today, when God's saint talked to me, I realized why and how the fallen angels rebelled in Heaven.

Why . . . ? These angels did, as Sue had said, want what He (God) had.

How . . . ? I now realized from God's saint that these fallen angels not only took from other angels, but eventually they even wanted what God, their Creator and their Father in Heaven had.

✝Dears, please try to refrain from taking or pulling from another human, or from anything of God's. Think of what happened in Heaven . . . and then the great battle. Think of who ultimately lost this battle and think of *how much* they lost . . .✝

JULY 16, 1996

My father was born in this country and he lived his eighty-six years in the same city he was born in, his hometown. He was proud to be an American and he was proud of his city. I can still remember him sitting in his recliner and watching the local evening news whenever he could. From what I understood, my father's, father and mother were born in Northern Lebanon, the old country. Many deeply religious Catholics came from there. However, my father never had the opportunity to go there.

Again, I must say my father was a deeply religious man and I saw him show his Faith many times without any hesitation. My father's parents must have also been very religious people; there are so many old religious pictures, statues, and articles in my father's attic that belonged to his parents. Throughout my father's eighty plus years, I know he parted with many old and outdated things, but he always tried to hold onto these religious belongings. However, most of my life, I am sad to say, his religious articles were in our attic, as my mother's tendency was to keep up with the 'now' styles in home decor.

Today I'm downtown, so I went to the 5:00 p.m. Mass at our city chapel. The priest talked about his trip to Israel and his visit to Mt. Carmel. He said it was so exciting, as in that part of the world there was so much to see. The priest continued, saying that the sad part of his trip was to see that many of the little villages in the Mt. Carmel area are disappearing. He said the Arab Catholics are moving out because of the war, and he thought the loss of these old, small communities was a shame.

After Mass, as I was leaving the chapel, I walked past the center aisle and the altar. As I looked toward the altar I blessed myself. At that second I saw Saint Robert standing in front of the altar in his beautiful white gown. Although his spiritual white vision was vague, I still knew, both from his facial expression and from his voice, that he was favorably impressed as he said to me again, as he had said before, "You don't know who your family is."

JULY 17, 1996

I was sitting in my parked car and resting calmly on the quiet monastery grounds. No one was around and it was starting to get dark. I heard a sound, the sound was a chirp, but at the same time the sound made a spark noise. I had never heard a sound exactly like this before, so I turned my head and looked toward the sound. To my right and a little behind me, I saw suspended in the air, a two-inch white burst of energy with sparks of light coming out of it everywhere. This energy almost looked like a sparkler . . . but there this spirit was, floating in the air.

I knew this spirit was attracted to me because of something it saw in me, something spiritual. As this tiny burst of light made this noise, I also knew it was directing its attention toward me. I felt it was a little angry with me, almost complaining to me—it certainly got my attention. I just sat there and looked at it.

I thought, Although this spiritual burst looks very much like one of God's stars that I had seen previously, I certainly didn't get the same feeling from this burst that I had gotten from God's other stars. This star did not radiate with the peace and love I had felt from the angel Donna when she had shown herself to me as a star. I began to get scared. Then I saw the angel Donna right in front of my car. She looked at the small burst of light and calmly said, "Now

don't scare her." I knew the burst was then scared and it swiftly flew out of my car, to very quickly disappear. I think when the burst disappeared this was because it was traveling so fast.

JULY 19, 1996

I was reading *God's Word Today*, July 1996 Edition. The first, Daily Reading Guide, on page 7, was Psalm 8. It read:

> "We have been placed in the midway position. Just below the Heavenly beings, and above all other creatures on Earth."

I thought, How astonishing, we are! We do rule the Earth. But we *can rise* and become *even closer* to God and the heavenly beings. I thought, I want to tell everyone. I am so amazed at what I now know. I am so excited about telling everyone! I heard God's saint quietly say, "You will." A little later I saw a white spirit float gently and quietly by; I could hear the happiness in his voice as he quietly said, "Then you will die." I knew by him saying this he meant, ". . . and then you will have Peace." He was so happy for me; happy because of this wonderful time to come. The Heavenly beings know our Eternal Home and the happiness we will have there.

†God and His lights wait ever so patiently for us. I know it is hard for us to put death and happiness together, but Heaven will bring Peace and Happiness.†

JULY 22, 1996

I haven't been trying to convert the devil's spirit Sue lately, or anymore. But at times, I do say to her, 'Try to be good.' Several times when Sue was not bothering me God's saint had said to me, "Tell her she was good." (I think when he says this to me, Sue cannot hear him.) Sue really likes it when I say she's been good, and she usually says to God's helpers, 'Did you hear that?' Of course, she wants to make sure this was heard. Or, other times when Sue has not been bothering me and I tell her she has been good, she will say, 'Tell them.'

I know I should not get angry with Sue, but once in a while I still do. Those times when I am not patient, I may angrily say to her, 'Stop it.' After I had said this a few times Saint Robert said to me, "She can't" or "She doesn't really know." Even though at times I try to tell myself I understand this, I realize it is still very hard for me to totally understand. They don't really know? I know I should not get angry, but sometimes I still do.

Today God helped me more. I felt the devil's thoughts, I felt inside of their minds. It was only for a second, maybe two seconds.

My forehead and the front of my head felt as if it were blank. This part of my head felt solid, not alive. I had trouble thinking and I knew I could barely think sentences. (I knew I would barely be able to put enough words together to think a complete sentence.) I realized I would have trouble speaking. Then this feeling left.

God's saint said, "It happens when they go through the fires of Hell." He wanted me to know—they really don't know. Again, I think, They're not human. I still struggle with trying to be more patient with all of God's creatures. Thank God, He keeps trying to help me. Please also try to understand, and be patient.

JULY 27, 1996

I thought, There are so many people—and imagine, we all have Guardian Angels! This is so many angels. Then I began to think, Heaven must still have very many angels and saints there. Right? Geez. How big is Heaven?

God's saint that is with me knows how big Heaven is. A few times he said to me, "You're going to be amazed." I knew by the way that he said this that he was, and still is, awed by the sights and lights of Heaven. Also, when he said this to me, he was happy, because this loving saint knows we will be happy when we see the

vast and amazing Heaven. Remember Jesus' prayer, "Our Father who art in Heaven. . . . Thy Kingdom come . . . ."

I can even remember Sue mentioning that Heaven is a Kingdom.

JULY 28, 1996

I was shopping today in a large department store, and when I turned and noticed pads of note paper, I heard God's saint very softly say, "You're going to need more paper." I know I will.

JULY 29, 1996

Praying today I said, "Our Father . . . give us this day our daily bread . . . ." and at the word, bread, I felt a breath of heavenly air. As I breathed this wonderful air . . . I realized God's saint was telling me that a part of our daily bread is our daily breath.

AUGUST 2, 1996

Today, as I was getting out of the shower, I lost my balance and stumbled a bit. Right after, I briefly and vaguely saw a devil's black spirit appear in the bathroom. I felt a push and I fell even further, almost hitting my head on the bathroom sink. When I looked up I saw the black spirit shamefully put his head down and slowly walk to the back door. As he left he said to me, 'He was mad.' I knew God's saint had seen me stumble and I knew he had protected me from getting hurt. (The angel and saint God has sent me are so very good and strong.)

A little later the devil's spirit came back and told me he was sorry. I told him it was OK. I could not see God's saint at the time but I felt his presence in the room, by the side door, and I felt that this saint was still a little angry at the devil's spirit. I knew this devil could feel this also.

✝Please just take a minute to think about it. How many times must have, you been protected by God's heavenly helpers? I could dare to say, It is probably more times than you realize.✝

AUGUST 3, 1996

I have read, and I have been very impressed, with the booklet, *The Wonders of the Holy Name*, by Fr. Paul O'Sullivan O.P., (E.D.M.) Page 42 reads:

> You gain 300 days indulgence for the poor souls in Purgatory every time you say, Jesus.

Today, as I was getting out of my car, I noticed a card in my car that I had written the name of Jesus on. Thinking of the souls in Purgatory I said, 'Jesus, Jesus, Jesus.' I heard God's saint say, "Keep saying it, Joyce. There are a lot of them." I knew he was also thinking about the poor souls in Purgatory, and I knew he meant there are a great multitude of souls there. I briefly saw the black shadow of a devil's spirit. Then in her purity, the angel Donna said, "They tricked them." I continued saying, 'Jesus, Jesus, Jesus . . . .'

✝Dears, many of us *are* being tricked by the dark spirits. God has and continues to patiently Love you. He has given us so many good things and so many graces, but still some of His children ignore Him and blame Him for all of the wrongs in the world. **God does not spread evil and hate in the world.** Remember, evil spirits are about and can influence people. Please pray for strength and wisdom for yourself and for all.

Please think and use your time here and your free will to show your Father how good you can be and how deserving you are of Heaven; no matter what the obstacles.✝

AUGUST 13, 1996

I had decided to go to church and quietly pray today. I went to the church that has the exposition of the Eucharist all day; this

would be the first time I have been in this church in at least two weeks.

Before I sat in one of the back pews, as I was bowing down in the aisle and blessing myself, I heard, "What happened here." I sat in the pew. I felt a great sorrow, and although there were no other people in the church, I vaguely saw the images of four or five people, men and women, sitting scattered about in the pews in front of me.

I know some people come here, even in God's house, and they are dis-respectful. I knew this was what had hap-pened here. I heard God's saint say, "Joyce, you don't know." I felt so sad. Just the thought of Jesus being sad makes me very sad. I said, 'Please don't be sad. Let me take some of your pain.' I began to feel a sorrow in my heart. As I kneeled, looking at the Eucharist, tears came from the outside corner of my eyes. The tears ran down my cheeks, and my bottom lip quivered as I cried. (This is not the way that I cry. I have never cried like this before. My tears have always come from the inside corner of my eyes, and my lips have never quivered.)

Still looking at the Eucharist, I sadly said, 'I will take more of your sorrow. Please do not hurt.' I felt more sorrow and more tears. After a little while I heard, "It's gone." I knew Jesus and Mary were no longer so full of sorrow. The tears stopped and the sorrowful feeling was gone from my heart. I prayed.

(Just now, as I was retyping this, I realized that in my asking to take Jesus' and Mary's sorrow, I was granted a gift—the gift of my being able to take tears back from Our Heavenly Mother Mary . . . the tears that my sins had given her. You will see this later, on September 14, 1998, and as God's angel Donna was to say, "This is Good.")

Well, Sue was in the back of the church and I heard her devil's spirit say to Jesus, 'You and your big mouth.'

At the end of my prayers I thanked Jesus and Mary for letting me take some of their tears . . . and I prayed for strength for the people who had been in this church and had hurt them so.

AUGUST 25, 1996

I woke up from my sleep. It was 12:45 a.m. so I just lay in bed, still resting for a while. A white, oblong spirit, that was about one and a half feet long, appeared; within it, there were several, one-inch or so circular areas where there was no spiritual matter. I felt from this spirit that it was a life form, and I heard a very, very, very patient voice say, "We're time, and we're waiting."

This was the most patient voice I had ever heard. The spirit disappeared.

For at least ten minutes I just lay in bed, really puzzled. Although I tried and tried to figure out this vision, I couldn't. Then I thought, This might be my time tunnel that I go through when I die. I thought, As my time comes closer—the time for me to die— the tunnel entrance, the spirit of my time, must get larger. I saw a white spirit fly by and God's saint said, "You're right."

. . . . .

I know this is not relevant to the above, but I would like to tell you this. Many times I have been wrong and I have taken it upon myself to judge people. This is one of my faults that I am continu-

ally battling to overcome. †God's saint tells me and reminds me, "You cannot judge. This is up to God."†

SEPTEMBER 1, 1996

During today's Mass I received Jesus in the Eucharist, then I went back to my seat. As I sat down I noticed papers sticking out of my purse, the papers I had written some of my book notes on. When I went to push the papers safely back into my purse I heard Saint Robert say, "Write."

God's helpers are working so hard to help me get this book out to you; they do so want to help your souls. Although I haven't written for a while, this afternoon I plan to write.

SEPTEMBER 2, 1996

I was sitting very quietly at home, but I felt sad. Donna came into the house and she was also sad. With compassion in her voice, she said, "There is so much pain here." I knew this angel had just come in from being out and looking about at the world, and I knew she had been sent down from Heaven.

Still sad, I asked her the question, 'Will God finally end it?' She replied, "He said, 'No, it is not time.'" Humbly and submissively I said, 'He will know when.' Then I felt God's saint was happy for me, and he said, "Good, Joyce." I thought about him telling me before, "You must not question God." And I knew this saint was now very happy for me because even though I was sad . . . I did not question God.

SEPTEMBER 12, 1996

I woke up almost an hour and a half before my alarm was set to ring this morning. It was early, but I knew I wouldn't get back to sleep so I decided to go downstairs to use the bathroom. As I was walking down the stairs, just before the last step, I tripped and almost fell; however I caught the railing in time and didn't fall. I was so tired. In the bathroom I said, 'I really want to be in Heaven with Robert.' Donna's white spirit flew by and corrected me, she said, "Saint."

Although the sun was not up yet, before going upstairs I decided to pull up the shades in the living room windows. I do like the day's light to come in through the windows. Under one of the windows the dog lay on the floor.

As I began to walk back up the stairs, I heard a voice coming from him say, 'Why?' When I looked back at the dog, I briefly saw a faint glimmer in the dog's left eye. I turned and continued to walk up the stairs. Then I heard the same man's voice, but this time his voice was happy, as he said, 'We scared her.' This devil's spirit did scare me, but I did not want to show that I was scared, so as I walked up the stairs, I foolishly laughed and said to my sleeping roommate, 'Your dog just asked me why.'

When I lay back in bed I thought, Donna, what can I say when these devil spirits bother me? *I know I am wrong when I get angry with them, or when I am uncaring and I laugh.* I remembered that several times before God's saint had told me, "This is not funny." Donna then told me how to reply to them: "Leave me alone." I realize they may not decide to leave me alone or they may not be able to leave me alone; but I know that my being patient and just saying, 'Leave me alone,' will show more compassion, and also help me keep my soul from becoming hateful and cruel.

I told the angel Donna, 'Thank you so much. I know I did not act as good as I should have this morning.' This wonderful angel said, "Tell God." I tried very hard to deeply concentrate on God (although at the time I knew I did not have to concentrate that hard). I said, 'Thank you, God.' In reply I heard an amazingly Fatherly voice say, "You have a lot to learn." This older man's voice struck me as a much more Fatherly voice than that of even my earthly father.

Briefly, I saw Donna's tiny white star blink, as she so very softly, and so very lovingly said, **"Father."** It was so awesome to hear an

angel say, Father. This was the most tender I have ever heard her voice, and this angel's tender voice radiated with immense love. I knew whom we had been talking to, Our Father in Heaven, Our Creator.

I saw her star blink again, and so softly this angel said, "Ours."

✝As I sat here re-reading the above, I started to cry; thinking about this wonderful gift. Then I felt the tingling of a light everywhere inside of me, and I knew my guardian's spirit was in me. I kept saying, 'Thank you, God. Thank You . . . and Thank you for our angels, who so openly and lovingly share you, Father.'✝

SEPTEMBER 17, 1996

When I woke up this morning I thought about my cousin, whom I had called yesterday and made plans to see this afternoon. She has always been good to me and does try to give me good advice. I do love her and she is my favorite cousin. Now, although she is my cousin, being a daughter of my father's half brother, she is in her eighties and her husband is in his nineties.

As I lay in bed I really began to worry about her. I thought, Will her spirit go to Heaven? I briefly saw a tall, bright white-gowned spirit begin to appear in my room, then quickly vanish before completely appearing. Although this saintly figure didn't appear in his total brightness, I knew this man's spirit was Saint Robert. I knew he was in my room. After the vision vanished I heard this saint say, "She will be with us." I was so happy for my cousin. I thought, She will meet God's heavenly lights. I said to Saint Robert, 'I will really miss her; so many people will miss her.' He replied, "This is why she was here so long."

I thanked God's saint for telling me all this. He said, "We are here to serve." I thought, Serve! Serve? But you know, God lovingly sends His heavenly, strong, but humble spirits to help us. I do not like to say, serve us, but God's lights, with their humility and love, would . . . and, dears, they willingly and gladly—Serve us.

SEPTEMBER 18, 1996

When I finished my shower I opened the shower curtain. The whole bathroom was just filled with a heavy mist. (I have to say I do like to use plenty of hot water when I take my showers.) Briefly, in the mist filled room, I saw the angel Donna's pure white spirit. She looked right into my eyes, and so lovingly and supportively she said, "We're here." It was amazing to look into an angel's eyes. I remember thinking, There is such *purity* in her eyes—and her eyes are *free of any guilt.*

Later that day, after work, I got off the bus and walked down the street to go home. There were a lot of puddles on the sidewalk because for days it had been raining. As I was trying to avoid stepping in the puddles, I heard Saint Robert say, "The storms are done." (Let me explain a little more. For a couple of weeks we have had bad weather in the area. We have even had three to four mild tornados.)

Today, God's saint told me that this spell of bad weather has ended. I know there will be no more tornados in the area for now. He went on to say, "We had to warn them." Then, "They wanted to destroy a lot." I knew these storms were sent by God to warn and control the devil spirits—and to protect us.

> Remember the devil spirit Sue is very scared of storms, especially thunder and lightning storms? The devils know there will be a great storm the day God takes back His Earth and the devils fall into Hell. (See June 1996, Page 124)

SEPTEMBER 19, 1996

I was done shopping and waiting in the checkout line at the grocery store. Well, I couldn't help but hear the two women in the line behind me; they were speaking to each other very fluently in a foreign language, and they were going on and on. Both women had a very heavy accent. I thought, Gee, I bet they haven't been in this country very long. I bet they can't speak much, if any, English.

Then, in very clear and distinctive English, one of the women sarcastically said, 'So be it.' After this woman said this, in such clear English, I could see a look of surprise on her face. I knew she was more surprised than anyone that she had spoken in such clear English. I knew this clear spoken English in this very foreign woman, did not come from her, but for that brief second the devil's spirit Sue was in this woman. Sue was trying to irritate God's saint, who must have been very close by . . . . This saint who several times before had said to me, "So be it." Then I heard God's saint very sadly say, "They are going to destroy God's Earth."

OCTOBER 1996

Sue has told me plenty of times that she is going to kill me. I can remember these threats as far back as when Bob was alive.

> Remember these threats were never said aloud, but relayed through thoughts and facial expressions. However, at the time I never realized that this is the way spirits communicate, and these evil threats were actually coming from devil's spirits that were in humans. (Page 22)

God has shown me enough so that I know where hate and destruction come from. Now I understand where these threats were and are coming from. Thank God, I realize devil's spirits can enter human bodies and can sometimes take over our whole being. So, I realize why people close to me, and even people in my family, were sometimes selfish and uncaring. God let me know. Thank God.

✝My brother and mother passed away long before I realized this, and I still do not forgive myself for not having more patience and forgiveness toward them. Please have patience and forgiveness—especially patience and forgiveness toward the people you love and the people who love you. Please show your patience and love now, before these people pass away.✝

Today, I thought back to the time I had once said to a priest, 'God let me see the good spirits because the evil spirits were harassing me so much.' As I thought back to this time, Donna's white spirit flew by and corrected me. So sweetly and innocently she said, "You have to do something." I am so peaceful when God's lights are around me. I know they have told me this same thing before, but again in my peace, I did not ask what it is I am to do.

I think writing may be what I have to do, I am not completely sure . . . because I have not been told that this is my job. Writing may be just part of my task. However, I will write down what God lets me become aware of.

Another day I thought, I would really like to visit my cousin and even tell her about some of the things I have seen. Seeing God's lights has always been peaceful for me, but seeing the dark spirits is sometimes very upsetting. I called my favorite cousin, asking her how she was, and I was promptly invited to her home for supper.

As we sat in the kitchen I told her about some of the good and bad things I have seen. I could see she was beginning to get nervous, so I told her only a few more things about the good spirits. I told her about Bob. I knew her husband, who was in his nineties, had at times been in the next room, the dining room, and I knew he could hear us talking.

Later, when I was setting the dining room table for supper, my cousin's husband walked through the room. He said, 'We called him down from Heaven.' I knew he meant Bob. I said, 'Oh come on, things couldn't have been that bad.' He replied, upset and worried, 'You don't know.' He left the room . . . and I knew that was all he could tell me. Again, I thought, Either Bob or the spirit that was in him came from Heaven. He did have a peaceful, heavenly presence—I will never forget his loving and compassionate eyes.

Once again I realized just how closely the evil spirits were watching Bob, and how closely they watch anyone they know is good.

> Remember when I met Bob. The bartender, and then the man in my car's backseat, watched Bob very closely? Now I realize that there must have been devil spirits in these men, these men who really had no reason to watch Bob.

> Also, remember how the devil's spirits growled at the mere mention of Bob's name for months after he had died? Bob was very, very good, and the evil spirits knew this. Evil hates good, God, and His lights. (Page 17)

OCTOBER 3, 1996

As I was driving home I noticed a man who was washing a car in a driveway. In one hand he held a cloth, which he was scrubbing the car with, and in the other hand he held a garden hose. The water from the hose, which was set at a fairly high force, ran wastefully onto the driveway and into the road. I felt very sad seeing the large amount of water being wasted, and I knew this sadness was God's saint's sadness. I heard Saint Robert say, "Joyce, they don't know."

✝Please conserve water . . . water is so important, and it does coincide with our life and our time on Earth. God's lights are aware of this and they want you to also be aware.✝

I just felt the presence of God's angel, Donna . . . .
Now I know what angels are . . . . **Angels are love.**

OCTOBER 4, 1996

It was a bit past 4:30 and I had just gotten out of work. Although this was a bad time for traffic and driving was slow I was rushing, because in less than thirty minutes I had an appointment. I got stopped up at a rotary intersection behind a Mac truck, and we had to go through a blinking light to get off the rotary. I noticed a little room to the left of the truck, and worried about being late, I pulled between the truck and the space to the right of the rotary. Although I could barely see the traffic coming from my right side or the other side of the truck, when I thought traffic was clear I stepped on the gas.

From the right came a car, and I just barely missed hitting the car's backside. The driver of this car became angry, and he slowed his car down to look at me and let me know just how angry he was.

But in my rush I drove behind him and I was on my way. As I drove I heard God's saint say, "Say your rosary tonight." Still rushing I said, 'Yes, Saint Robert.'

I did say my rosary that night and God's saint told me something else, but I'm sorry to say that because I did not write it down right away, I later could not remember his exact words. I am sorry that I cannot write what this saint said.

✝I know many people will say, 'Well why did she write this if she can't remember what he said?' But I want to try and write everything exactly as it happened, and I would like to say, When we pray the rosary this is a wonderful thank you to Our Blessed Mother and God. And from our thank you, I am sure Our Father in Heaven will give us an even greater Thank You in return . . .✝

OCTOBER 16, 1996

For the past few nights I have been waking up from my sleep at 12:00 a.m. or a little past midnight. This morning I woke up at about 12:30 a.m.

I heard Saint Robert say, "There is more about twelve." Sue bitterly said, 'You would tell her.' God's saint continued, "When I tell you, you must write it down." I know that this will be very important, and I must write down what I am told as soon as I can, so I do not forget anything.

. . . . .

I try to keep paper and pens with me at all times. In amazement I once said to someone, 'My pens seem to multiply themselves. If I put one down, there seems to be two in its place.' However, my thirty or so original supply of pens came from my father's home, and I sometimes wonder if he knew I would write someday.

OCTOBER 17, 1996

Well, as I had done last night and other nights, at about midnight I woke up . . . tonight I woke up about four minutes past midnight. As I lay in bed I thought back to when Saint Robert had said, if he could, he would come to me at twelve o'clock. I knew he meant twelve noon or twelve midnight.

Still restless, I walked downstairs to the bathroom, and then I thought, I have to write, but what if I don't write? As I said this, I looked into the bathroom mirror and I saw a faint white light behind and about me. Although this light was white, and I knew it was a heavenly light, it was small. My first thought was, This heavenly light around me is not very bright. Then I knew that this is fair, and God is fair. If I choose not to use the gifts God has given me, the gifts that could help many others, then God will reward my spirit accordingly, and my spirit's light will shine accordingly. My spirit will shine, but not very brightly. Justifiably—I myself will set, or my choices will set, my eternal light.

In my heart I thought, I have to write, not for myself but to help others—and as I do write, from my heart. I wondered, How much will I write? How long will I write? And how will I ever be able to publish what I write?

OCTOBER 19, 1996

As I was driving home I noticed a woman walking her greyhound dog. I had only seen this type of dog on TV, so I couldn't help but glance over to the dog as I drove. The dog's legs were so thin, I thought, God, they are so delicate. God's saint replied, "Yes, God made them that way." When he said this, I also knew that God made greyhounds this way because He wanted to watch us, to see how we take care of such delicate creatures. But more, God does not want to only watch how we take care of these delicate dogs, but how we take care of all creatures, big and small, and how we take care of Earth.

✝God's wonderful saint had told me before, "Everything is for a purpose."✝

OCTOBER 20, 1996

As I lay in bed I thought, I want to do so many things while I'm here on Earth. I want to help God to help His children, and I hope I am here for a long time so I can accomplish a lot. I saw a white star shine for a second, and in that second I heard God's angel Donna say, "You will be." Then I saw about thirty to forty smaller white stars light up briefly. Donna said, "There are so many." I lay in bed for a while, trying to figure out what this angel meant, but I couldn't. I went to sleep.

OCTOBER 21, 1996

Today I was at my sister's house, sitting at her kitchen table and talking with her. However, I was thinking about when I was at my sister's house last week and we were sitting at the same table and talking:

> My sister has changed jobs a few times in just the last year, and if my father were alive he would be upset. He had always told us to stay with the same job. As my sister talked about her new job, I briefly felt my father's presence in me. I said, 'Now, stay with this one.' Right after this I became excited and I said to my sister, 'That was Dad.' She said nothing but just smiled a little. I knew my father's spirit was about.

Back to today. After I thought about what had happened last week, I thought about what happened two weeks ago:

> I was in my car driving, when I came to a four-way intersection and stopped for the red light. As I saw the green light to go, I noticed a man stopped in his car at the red light to my left and a man stopped at the red light to my right.
>
> The man stopped at the red light to my left started to move his hand to his head in the same mannerism that my father had used. Then I faintly felt my father's presence coming from this man. I also faintly heard from this man, as Donna and God's saint had said to me so many times before to comfort me, "We're here."
>
> Immediately the man in the other car, the car stopped to my right, angrily looked at and honked his horn at the man to my left. I knew the man in the car to my left was stopped and he wasn't doing anything wrong, so I thought, What is the problem? Then I knew that the man to my right must have had a devil's spirit in him and he had noticed that the man in the car to my left had my father's spirit in him and my father was comforting me.

Back to today and back to my puzzlement over what Donna said to me last night, October 20th: "There are so many." I know this explanation may seem complicated, and round about, but today as I thought about all of this, I figured out what Donna was trying to tell me last night.

I now realized (from their similarities) that the angel Donna had taught my father; my father, who two weeks ago had said to me, as Donna and Saint Robert had said to me so many times, "We're here." Also, I know that last night Donna was again teaching; teaching all of those tiny white stars—us (humans) who make it to Heaven . . . so many of us. God's wonderful angel Donna is not only a Guardian Angel, but also a teacher.

OCTOBER 31, 1996

I take the 7:15 a.m. bus to work now. Since the bus stop is very close to the church at the corner of my street, I leave home early so I can attend at least some of the 7:00 a.m. Mass before catching the bus for work.

This morning before Mass, as I knelt in front of the tabernacle, I thanked Jesus for opening the doors of his house to me. I saw a faint white spirit fly from the tabernacle. Still kneeling, I said, 'I hope we save thousands of souls today.' I saw the spirit again, he said, "There are that many angels." I knew he meant, that many angels—today.

I thought for a while about what had just happened. Then I thought, For each new soul there is a Guardian Angel sent to them, thousands of new souls and thousands of Guardian Angels each day, today. How wonderful! However, I also felt and knew this spirit meant, God sees we are protected and guided . . . we choose whether we are saved or not.

After I left the church I stood at the bus stop and waited for the bus. For a second I saw a heavenly white spiritual light. This light went straight from high in the sky to Earth, and I knew this light went straight from Heaven to Earth. My thought was, This heavenly light is similar to the light I saw go straight to God's angel Donna the day I saw her praying to Him in the desert. However, this light seemed very far away, maybe five to six miles. God's saint said, "We are always coming down, Joyce." I wondered who God was sending His heavenly helpers to this morning.

NOVEMBER 1996

I was driving home, and just as I was driving by a synagogue that was on my left, I felt a heavenly presence, which I knew was coming from inside the synagogue. I knew there was a holy spirit and there were angels inside this synagogue. So, I don't know if it is considered proper, but my first reaction was to bless myself. I did this out of respect.

From the right side of the road, to the right of me, I heard Saint Robert calmly say, very saintly, very humbly, and with *much* abiding respect in his voice, "But not me, Joyce." I was then sure Saint Robert is a Christian saint, and I also knew this saint of God's respects the beliefs of the people who attend this synagogue. Therefore, this humble saint would not enter the Jewish people's place of worship, out of respect, and he would only go to places of worship where he is welcomed—as I am sure all of God's gentle and humble lights are just as respectful to every religion, to their beliefs, and to their places of worship.

Now, I'm not exactly sure which one of God's saints, Saint Robert is, so I will continue to call this wonderful light Saint Robert, or God's saint. But, I do know that this saint knows Heaven and God very well, and he is very close to God.

NOVEMBER 1, 1996

As I was thinking back to my vision of April 23, 1996 (page 117), I began to realize more about this vision. I realized that when I saw myself high over the Earth, my body will have died; this vision of myself was just of my spirit.

I also realized that the greatest pain which will make my spirit cry so hard, will be sorrow. Sorrow, because I will think, Now, I will no longer be able to help the poor suffering people on Earth. I know as I will be so high above, I will want so desperately to help Earth, so far below. My desire to stay on Earth, to help, and thinking I can no longer help, will bring me a great sorrow—I will cry tremendously.

NOVEMBER 2, 1996

Today the president of the United States came to my hometown to support one of his fellow party members. Well, my cousin, my second favorite cousin, was excited about seeing the President, so we decided to wait in the crowds to maybe get a distant glimpse of Mr. President.

Surprisingly, we got a closer place to stand by the speakers than I thought we could possibly get. The president and his group were in front of city hall, on the top step, and although we were near the bottom step and to the far left of the politicians, we were in the front row and we could see and hear the speakers fairly well.

As the politicians began talking, the crowd became quiet. Shortly afterwards, I heard a man's voice, a voice which I knew was a spiritual voice say, 'All right. Now.' I was surprised. I was surprised at all the dark spirit cloud forms that rose from the crowd. The dark spirits hovered above the unaware crowd of people who stood attentively watching the politicians speak.

I thought, Gee, the poor politicians look so nervous. I wonder if they can see the dark spirits? Either way, I thought I should try to help, as the politicians looked very nervous. I thought, I have to help. I prayed. I saw Saint Robert's large, white-gowned spirit, standing at the far end of the crowd, just in front of a building. Then Donna's white angel spirit flew above the crowd— and as this wonderful, peaceful angel flew, the dark spirits shrunk down before her.

When all was done and I was walking back to my car I heard Saint Robert say, "This is an important lesson for you." I am not sure what the lesson was.

NOVEMBER 17, 1996

Last night I read some of Paul's writings from the Bible. After reading, I left the Bible on the table by me and then I went to sleep. (I am sorry to say, Last night was the first time in a long time that I have read anything from the Bible.)

This morning when I woke up I did my laundry and some housework, but after a while I was tired and I decided to lie down and rest. The Bible was still where I had left it the night before, on the same table. (I know what I have just written may not be directly connected with what I am to tell you, but for some reason I felt I had to write what I just did.) As I lay resting very quietly, I saw a

white spirit come in the window and I felt this spiritual presence enter me for a second. In that second I saw another vision of the future. This vision is very hard to explain:

I saw what I thought to be two women standing in front of the Monarch Building downtown, which is on the corner of Main Street and Boland Way. The two identical figures dressed the same and wore what seemed to be hats; both were equal in size, stature, and looks. Their faces were the same, but I especially noticed their chins, as they were somewhat elongated. In this vision I was looking at the figures, which almost seemed to be mechanical, from their sides. The two women were much taller and bigger than the other people walking about downtown on this sunny day. The majority of the people were of Spanish decent and the rest were Black.

The two equal and identical women stood facing each other, and they had their hands on the other's shoulders, as they stood, one foot in front of the other. Both seemed to stand their ground, angrily it seemed, but not viciously, as they pushed each other back and forth. However, their feet, legs, or anything below their waists, never moved.

No one walking on that busy Main Street paid any attention to the two women, who to me were seemingly fighting. Not one person tried to stop them or help them. I thought . . . I *desperately* thought, Why doesn't someone try to help them?

The vision was gone.

God's saint said, "Remember this . . ." I knew this was a vision of the future.

NOVEMBER 20, 1996

As I left for work this morning, walking out the front door, I noticed a man drive his car by my home and down the quiet street. I could not see who the driver was, but I heard a voice, a voice that I somehow knew was coming from the man driving this car. He said, "Don't stop trying to help them." My heart was touched by the immense compassion in his voice. I was sad this morning, then I thought, His timing is good. I did need a lift in my efforts to help.

NOVEMBER 29, 1996

Walking home from church I looked up at the dark, cloudy sky. I heard Saint Robert say, "It will be a cloudy day, Joyce. And it will be raining." (Thunderstorms in some places.) I knew the end of the Earth, as we know it, will come about on this type of a day. (See, June 1996, page 124. Sue, the devil, is afraid of storms; and some of the worst fires are started from lightning in thunderstorms. Also, see June 8, 2000 for more on lightning and its effects.)

Shortly afterward, for a second, I saw a poor dark devil's spirit standing about thirty feet or so in front of me. God's saint said, "They know." Again I thought of how scared Sue gets in thunderstorms. Feeling a bit angry, I thought, Huh, you bet they know. God's saint said, with much sadness in his voice, "This is a very sad thing I just told you." The immense compassion in this wonderful saint's voice made me feel very ashamed at my lack of compassion. I should have had more compassion and sorrow for these poor souls; and for the day they will fall.

DECEMBER 1996

I was not going to write the following, not until months after this happened did I decide to write it. So I am sorry, I don't have the exact date of this vision for you. However, this did occur in the winter of 1996. I will put it in December.

I was working one night in a nursing home. As I was coming back from my break I heard some other workers in a room, so I walked into the room to see if the girls needed help. I saw two girls standing by a resident who was lying in a bed. The workers had their backs to me. They were changing the bed sheets of the elderly woman resident.

In between the two workers, was a strongly visible spirit, who was wearing a black gown. The gown had a fairly large hood that went over the spirit's head. He also had his back to me, but as soon as I walked into the room the hooded spirit turned to look at me. I looked into the opening in the front of the large hood. There was no face, just darkness.

God's saint said, "This is death." Scared, I quickly turned and left the room.

(I must say, although this spirit was there that night, no one on the floor I was working on, and I don't think anyone in the building, died that night.)

✝Now, I must write this for the nursing homes: evil and death are everywhere. You will die when it is your time, no matter where you are. Also, I feel death will probably not be as lurking and prominent when it is our time. And I feel our time will come to each of us differently, (or as individually) as we are individuals. God will know when it is the best time for each one of us . . . when it is the best time to help save our soul.✝

DECEMBER 8, 1996

As I drove by a church in my old neighborhood I noticed that many cars were parked around the church, so I thought a Mass must be going on. Well, today is not Sunday and I knew this was not a time for a weekly scheduled Mass, but I figured, I'll go into the church and pray for a bit.

The Mass was for the Catholic Vietnamese people in the area. There were Vietnamese lectors, altar girls, and even a Vietnamese choir. The older Vietnamese people sat in the centers of the very front rows of the pews—they looked so proud and dignified as they seemed to lead the others who sat around and behind them.

As I stood during the Mass, Saint Robert's spirit came to me. He was crying as he said to me, "Joyce, you should feel their pride." I knew that God's saint could feel the pride in this small group, the pride for their Catholic belief—and I was struck by the strong, loving compassion I could feel he had for them. This saint's emotions were so strong they consumed me and I started to cry. The tears fell down my cheeks . . . coming from the outside corners of my eyes.

From God's saint, I could feel that the pride these Catholics had was not a selfish pride, but a binding, good pride. A pride that I knew would help them stay together and give each of them strength through each other. I could also feel their pride was for an accomplishment well fought for. I looked and noticed a paper beside me in the pew. Although I read some of this paper in the church, I finished reading most of it outside of the church. This is what was on the paper:

A SHORT HISTORY OF VIETNAMESE MARTYRS

The preaching of Christianity began in Vietnam in the early 16th century, with the priests of Dominic, Francis, Augustine, and most famous the Jesuits. These priests arrived in Vietnam by trading boats from Europe. By the 17th century there were already about 50,000 Catholics in Vietnam. At the time, Vietnam was run by a system of monarchical government ruled by a king who was seen as a son of god appointed by heaven. The main religions were Buddhism, Confucianism, and the worship of ancestors: these religions were very gentle and peaceful. During this period the missionaries spread the message of Jesus Christ without any trouble or obstacle. Later, however, a civil war erupted, and since the kings believed that Christianity was the cause, this led to the beginning of the forbidding to believe or follow this religion.

The period of persecution lasted for 30 years and the most difficult time of all was the reign of Nguyen at century 19th. The Nguyen kings feared foreigners. They thought the missionaries had come to conquer their land and to make the people upset, so they tried to shut Vietnam off from the world, including blocking new technologies and new ideas from the west. The king blamed the Catholics for all the riots in the community, and for threatening his power over the people. During this duration of oppression by the tyranny, 100,000 Catholics were killed by the sword.

Because of the king's law, the Vietnamese Catholics became fugitives. They were hunted from house to house, village to village like animals. Their houses and their possessions were burned, all was lost. If you could not run fast enough, you were subjected to imprisonment, burned alive, tortured, slashed. The lean bodies of Catholics shook and fell like the bamboo leaves and their blood painted the dark soil from North to South. The majority of believers wouldn't denounce their belief and so their fate was sealed. They were the ones that would not walk over the cross that lay on the ground under their feet to save their lives. Their faith was so strong that they would rather die than walk over the sacred cross to symbolize their unfaithfulness.

The killing of Christianity finally ended in 1888, when the army of France defeated Vietnam. On June 6, 1988, pope John Paul II chose one hundred and seventeen martyrs from the 30,000 who died to honor as saints. In the one hundred and seventeen martyrs, some were priest but the majority were the village people. At present, there are about 100 million Catholics in Vietnam.

Compared to other countries' histories of Christian persecution in the world, Vietnam is one of the most enduring countries that has gone through the ordeal. Vietnamese people are full of life, innocence, and simplicity, but they have amazing faith and lasting strength. One must bow their head in acknowledgment at this incredible strength and must praise their strong loyalty and devotion. These martyrs used love to cover the violence, and they chose death to live forever in heaven because they knew who their God really was. Their faithfulness brought them to highest glory in heaven.

(This short history was copied directly from the paper in the church.)

DECEMBER 18, 1996

This morning, as I got into my car and sat down I sighed a deep sigh. I thought, This is the type of sigh you have after you have been crying very hard and for a very long time. Then I knew God's saint had been sitting in my car driver's seat last night, and I knew he had been crying. He said, "You don't know what I've seen."

I did not know what he had seen, and he did not let me know, but I knew why he had been crying. I knew last night he had seen souls that were lost. I thought, We have to try and help them. He replied, "They have to decide." I took another sigh, not as deep as the first sigh. Then I thought, Good, God's saint is getting over his crying.

As I drove I said, 'God you have such good helpers.' A white spirit zoomed in front of my car window and I heard, "He knows their hearts."

DECEMBER 19, 1996

After saying my last prayers for the day, I wished well for the world and then I quietly lay in bed. I heard God speak again. I knew this older man's voice, that had a *very* Fatherly tone, was Him. He said, "You are a good daughter." As He talked His voice became fainter.

I sadly thought, The devil spirits are about and somehow interfering . . . and I really wanted to let God know that I had heard everything He had said. I said, 'Thank you. I heard you.' God's saint replied. He said, "He knows."

Now, He called me daughter; This Our Father. I remembered when even the wonderful angel Donna so lovingly called Him, our Creator, "Father."

DECEMBER 22, 1996

Today at Sunday Mass I began to think about my family and about how many times Sue had said to me, the damn Lebanese. I thought, as I had thought one other time and Sue quickly got very mad with me, How many in my family have been martyrs? A few rows in front of me a little girl turned around and bitterly said, 'Seven.' I knew the devil's spirit Sue was in this poor little girl.

The Bible reading in Mass was from the Gospels according to Luke, "The words of the angel Gabriel to Mary, 'Rejoice, O highly favored daughter . . . .'" At the word daughter I got so excited . . . just days before God had called me a good daughter. I thought, Our Father, God, Lovingly gives life to all of us, His sons and daughters—His Children.

DECEMBER 24, 1996

I worked late today. After finishing my first job I went to my second job. At my second job I continually stand and I'm not that young anymore, so this is hard on me. After work I was very tired.

On the way home I stopped by the church at the corner of my street. I was hoping to attend the evening Mass, but I was too late for the service. As I walked up the long center aisle of the empty church I heard the floor creak beneath me. When I had gotten up to the tabernacle I thought to myself, Well, now I have to get my creaky self down to kneel. Slowly, I knelt on a step in front of the tabernacle; there were flowers just everywhere around me. I prayed to Jesus and talked with Mother Mary. I thought, What a happy day Christmas Day must have been for Blessed Mary, on that beautiful day she held her child. Then I thanked God for letting me also become a mother.

The flowers were so beautiful; I couldn't help but touch them. Well, after I touched them they did not seem so beautiful to me. Saint Robert said, "Don't touch them." I prayed again and just looked at the flowers. From within myself I felt a wonderful admiration for the precious flowers, and I can even say I felt a love for them. God's saint said, "Do you understand?" I continued to pray, not sure of what he meant.

Well, I knew it wasn't going to be easy for me to get up from kneeling. I thought, Now I have to get my creaky body up. With a beautiful pure voice I heard Donna say, "We will help you." Although I barely felt them, two angels, one on each side, lifted under my arms to help me get up.

✝At the time, hearing the purity and goodness in Donna's voice impressed me so much, however, the thing I was most impressed by was the fact that the angels did not hesitate, even a bit, to help. Their complete and total unhesitant willingness to help is an awesome part of their purity.✝

I left the church still thinking about, but not knowing, what God's saint had meant when he had said, "Don't touch them."

DECEMBER 25, 1996

Christmas Day, what a wonderful day! And, because of the great Love God has for us, we have another day given to us.

I slept late this morning, so the earliest Mass I could attend was the 10:15 a.m. The church was full of people and it was a beautiful Mass. I must say, God's spirits were very active. There were many white spirits zooming above the crowd. As we read the Nicene Creed and said, "We believe in one holy Catholic and apostolic church . . . ." I began to cry. I knew the spirit of God's saint was in me and he was crying. I felt he was crying because he knows God, our Father, does so want His children to be one . . . one holy Catholic and apostolic church. Our divisions, and I tend to think our pride, is hurting God very deeply.

✝Again, Heaven let me know so I could tell you. This is a goal we can, and should, all strive for—One Holy Church. I think we could obtain this goal through Love.✝

DECEMBER 31, 1996

The end of another day at work. As I was getting ready to leave, one of the ladies from work started discussing the image of the Blessed Virgin in Florida. The woman also had the newspaper article and picture on the event. I read the newspaper she had. Maybe you heard about the image? The large image of our very humble Mother, that appeared, and still appears, on the huge glass wall of a tall Florida business building.

After I read the article and as I was walking back to my desk, I became a bit angry. I thought, Well, I'm skeptical about the image. But I soon realized my skepticism was actually a feeling of selfishness. I have to admit I was jealous at the thought of someone else seeing or talking to one of God's beautiful lights, except me. I wanted these beautiful lights to myself.

Thank God, I quickly realized this selfishness was wrong. I know Heaven's love is given to all. (As I wrote this a beautiful light-blue light lit up on my paper. I know Heaven is happy with what I have just written.) I accepted sharing, even sharing God's Saint Robert and Donna . . . as I then fully realized I will do someday.

After I sat back down at my work desk, I heard God's saint say, "We will be doing more." I knew that the image in Florida was real, and I knew that many more miracles are going to happen.

Later, I got so excited about God, the saints, and the events to come. I asked God's saint if I could be a part of all of this. He said, "Yes."

✝God is just waiting for you to ask Him to come to you; to let Him into your heart. Please let His Light, and His Love, glow brightly in your heart.

Let your life, your miracle, glow brightly.✝

Chapter 4

"We're Here . . . Don't Worry"

JANUARY 1, 1997

Today I prayed the prayer of my God-given Guardian Angel: "Angel of God, My Guardian Dear, to whom His love commits me here, ever this day be at my side, to light and guard, to rule and guide. Amen." There I sat in the Laundromat, with my prayer book opened and my head down in prayer.

I saw God's wonderful angel Donna . . . her white spirit knelt on the floor close to me, the angels forearms rested on my knees, her hands were folded together in prayer over my lap, and her head was bent down. She was so full of love and care as she humbly prayed, and I could hear her say to God, "Please help me keep her alive." The angel's pure white image disappeared from my sight. Then a tiny white star blinked in front of me and I heard, "You saw her." Dears, the love and care God gives us is enormous.

JANUARY 5, 1997

Remember back in 1993, when I was driving and I saw a large lightning bolt in the clear sky? Then I heard a voice

say, "This is yours." I knew the voice was talking to me and I was amazed, but I was also puzzled. (Page 23)

Today, as I was driving home and thinking, I'm able to see God's lights, I got so excited. Then I looked up at the clear sky and saw a large lightning bolt. I thought, This is the same bolt I had seen years ago. This is my lightning bolt. I heard God's Saint say, "Now, deserve it." I wondered, Will I be a fighter for God? Will this bolt be one of my weapons?

God's saint added, "And this." I knew the other gift this saint was reminding me I had was my gift of seeing and talking to spirits.

I do truly hope that I am deserving. May I use whatever God gives me, even the breath I am now taking, with the patience, wisdom, and love I have seen in His saints and angels.

. . . . .

Early this evening I was driving by our beautiful Forest Park. This park has an impressive display of lights around Christmastime called, Bright Nights. Since it was dark, the Christmas lights were on in the park and as I drove by the front entrance to the park and looked at the tiny white Christmas lights, I thought of God's helpers. The tiny white lights reminded me so much of what God's helpers look like when they blink so brightly and communicate with me . . . I got so excited. I thought, If everyone could only see God's stars! Saint Robert replied, "They will Joyce, through you."

JANUARY 10, 1997

I went to my son's school tonight to see the play he was in, *Inherit the Wind*, by Jerome Lawrence and Robert E. Lee. The play was based on a book with the same name, and the book was based on an actual court hearing in (I think) Hillsboro, North Carolina. This court case debated the teaching of evolution in schools. The prosecution did not want Darwinism taught in schools. (In actuality I know very little about this case, but I would like to write this.)

In court, the defense attorney attacked the Bible, and strongly attacked the passage that refers to God stopping the world from moving. The attorney based much of his case on this. He said it is impossible to stop the world, as I'm sure it is, scientifically. But for God . . . who He Himself created the world . . . I'm sure this is far from extraordinary.

The defense attorney won his case, but I feel he actually lost, as this poor man had no Faith. He looked at the Bible, purely, if I may say this, in a scientific way. God is Spiritual. God is Light. God is Life. God, our powerful Creator, is Our Father in Heaven.

> Remember, long ago, when Sue said she was going to make me drive over a cliff? Donna, my guardian, calmly responded with, "Then I'll turn back time." Sue did not respond. She knew, and I could feel that she knew, God's angel could turn back time. (Page 89)
>
> If God's angel can do this, can you imagine what God—the Creator of the angels—can do?

The Bible is correct: God can stop the world from moving. He can stop, or turn back time. But I think this is far from being His greatest ability. I *think* God's greatest ability may be the creation of life.

.....

Here I would like to put in these two quotes:

First, the night that Sue threatened to drive me over a cliff, she later sadly said, 'We can go slow, but not as slow as them.' (I felt this was to do with how God's lights travel through time.) I feel there is a lot more to know about time, and how we travel through it, then we will ever know until we are in God's spirit world.

Secondly, more than once God's saint had very calmly said to me, "It's only time." He has always said this as if time is something that is very easily overcome.

JANUARY 12, 1997

I was driving by a synagogue, the same synagogue I wrote about in November of 1996. I felt the same spirit inside the synagogue that I had before, then I heard this spirit say, "We are here, but we are not as strong as him." I knew he meant that Saint Robert is a much stronger heavenly light than they are.

Then I saw Donna's tiny light blink briefly inside of my car, in front of my odometer where I could not miss her. For some reason this angel's light was a beautiful light blue color now, and as she shown her light she said, "They're not."

I am telling you everything exactly as God allowed me to hear and feel. I have to say, The saint God allows me to talk to is strong and wise. I do not mean to upset anyone by this, but as the holy spirit in this synagogue meant to do, I too also wish to do—to help.

JANUARY 16, 1997

I've been working two jobs lately and I have also started night school, so for about two months now I have been so busy that I haven't written much.

Today I asked God's saint if something I had done, that was not very considerate, was OK. Sadly he said, "Yes." I was so ashamed; I realized that after all God has given me, I have been ignoring Him. I thought of when, several times in the past, God's saint said to me, "Don't forget me." I had forgotten God and His lights. I asked God to forgive me. The angel Donna lovingly said, "He will."

I plan on quitting my second job next week and getting my computer working again. I knew as I decided this, God's saint thought, Tell the people who read this you're sorry. So I will tell you, I am sorry. I should have been working hard—as God's lights do, to help our souls. Please be strong and faithful, always remembering to love—you are watched over by, protected by, and guided by, the purest of beings.

JANUARY 19, 1997

It was getting late, and as I was driving home I noticed the full moon was a bright orange/yellow color. When I turned my head to look at it a second time, I thought of the huge moon I had seen of this color in the desert, long ago. I remembered I was so scared of the light . . . I looked at the light again. I heard a man's voice say, "Next time, don't be afraid of me." I knew there would be a next time for me, a time while I am still on Earth, when I would see this fiery light of God's.

I really hope I will not be scared. I pray I will not be scared . . . I'm so excited. I wonder who this light is, and I wonder what the next time will bring.

JANUARY 1, 1997

This morning, as I drove to work, I thought, There are so many cars on the road. I thought, There are so many people. I saw one of God's white spirits zoom by and I heard, "Someday there will not be so many."

I am not definitely sure about this, but I think this spirit was trying to tell me that someday, something very destructive will happen on Earth, and this destruction will eliminate many people.

JANUARY 22, 1997

I had just been in one of the phone booths at work; we have three booths and I was in the middle one. Our telephone booths are older and fairly private. They have two full walls and they are up against a wall, so they have three full walls.

When I was on my call they put me on hold, so I had some time to think. I was worried and I thought, Please keep me alive. I do so want to finish my writing. Briefly, I saw Donna's white angel spirit. She was directly in front of one of the phone booth's sidewalls; there, her tall spirit stood, very close to me. Her wings were partially open and almost wrapped completely around me—protecting me.

JANUARY 24, 1997

I would like to mention again that God's saint had calmly said to me, "Don't forget me." Although this loving light said this to me several times in the past, he has never said it in a boastful or selfish manner. He has no desire to be known . . . he desires to help souls. Let me explain what took me a while to understand.

I know that by my remembering and thinking of this saint, all

he has taught me, and the God he represents—I, my soul, is brought closer to God our Father. With pure love, God's saint does not want me to forget him . . . for me.

✝I will try to write down everything God's lights say, so I will not forget them, and to help you not forget them. Also, I want to write so I can let you know, and hopefully feel, some of the beautiful Love that is in Heaven. This Love awaits all of us, if we so choose. Please don't forget God . . . please Love.✝

JANUARY 27, 1997

It has not been an easy day at work today. Sue was really angry. All in all, it didn't seem as if anyone was really having a good day. As I sat at my desk, typing, I heard Saint Robert say, "Time is ticking." Then for a few seconds I could hear a clock ticking . . . tick . . . tick . . . tick. He continued, "It can't go on like this." I knew no one else working in the room heard this, and I knew these were warnings to the devil spirits. As time ticks by, God's time to take back His Earth comes closer. Heaven does know our sufferings.

FEBRUARY 3, 1997

As I was driving I could not help but cry a bit. It had been very hard for me today and I was sad. The sky above was completely cloudy tonight, but between the clouds appeared an opening . . . and in this opening I saw the big, orange/yellow moon. I heard a man's voice say, "It won't hurt your eyes." I stopped crying. I knew God's Light, Heaven's Light, will not harm the eyes of us who freely choose to be compassionate and be with Him—to become a part of His Light.

FEBRUARY 12, 1997

Today is Ash Wednesday. Ashes to ashes, dust to dust. Today we are reminded that our physical bodies and our physical lives come from ashes and dust, and so they shall return, to ashes and dust. Our spiritual souls, which will live on forever, are what we should be concerned with.

I missed the morning Mass, so I decided to go to the 7:30 evening Mass. If I arrive at the church late, I will usually walk to the front doors of this church, which are actually at the back of the church, and then I can quietly take a seat in the back of the church without disturbing too many people.

However, I was about five minutes early for the service, so I went into the church through the side door by the altar. I knelt in front of the tabernacle. As I knelt I heard God's saint say, "Joyce, bow down." I'm sorry to say, It took me a few seconds before I humbled myself and prostrated in front of the tabernacle in the somewhat crowded church. I prayed.

Before the Mass started I quietly went to get a seat in the pews. The Bible reading today came from the book of the prophet Joel. ". . . Rend your hearts and not your garments and return to the Lord, your God . . . ." I knew my lesson was complete. I shamefully remembered my pride; one of my faults that God's saint reminded me of today, again. Just a little while ago he had told me to bow down; however, my pride had kept me from immediately prostrating myself before Jesus. This saint reminded me, Give the Lord your heart—wholeheartedly.

MARCH 3, 1997

I had just put my clothes in the Laundromat washing machine and sat down. The washing machines are in a row in the middle of the Laundromat, and there are aisles on either side. I sat in a chair down one of the aisles. On the other side of the washing machines, in front of the other aisle, stood a woman who was completely involved in talking to herself.

I heard God's saint say, "Joyce, stay calm." Well . . . I have heard him say this before, just before something terrible is about to happen. I sat still and tried to remain calm. About five to ten seconds later a huge black spirit rose from the lady that was talking to herself. I must say, The second the spirit rose from the woman she stopped talking to herself, but I could see that she was totally unaware of what was going on.

The large, black devil's spirit, angrily looked at me. I saw God's saint's white spirit fly very quickly and hit the black spirit. Upon impact I heard a bump sound, but not like any other bump sound I have ever heard before. Instantly, with this impact, the black spirit was pushed out one of the huge front glass windows.

I looked out the windows and noticed a man who was parked in a truck that was in front of the Laundromat. Then he drove away, and as he did, he turned his head around and I could see his face. Timidly, he looked at what seemed to be just an empty space in front of the Laundromat, but I knew Saint Robert's spirit was standing there in that space. The man's expression seemed to be clearly saying, 'Why did you do that?' (Remember spirits communicate very well using their facial expressions and thoughts.) I'm pretty sure the man driving away in the truck was where the large black spirit came from, and where it went back to. Spirits go very easily from body to body.

I was glad I was told to stay calm, but I must admit, after I finished writing this I became a bit nervous.

MARCH 10, 1997

Something happened to my car today and it will cost me about two hundred dollars to fix it. To me this is a lot of money. I was upset, so before going home I went to church to try and get my thoughts together.

There was no one else in the church. I was alone as I prayed. God's saint said, "It's just money. Think of your heart." God's wonderful saint was trying to tell me . . . our hearts are what is of real value. Do not let your heart be destroyed by greed or anger. I thought I should try to keep my heart as pure as I possibly can. I should pay the two hundred dollars, and not get angry—it would be wiser to lose money . . . than to lose or destroy some of our hearts.

MARCH 17, 1997

I was thinking, What will God have me do for Him? Will He have me combine all the religions into one religion? (As you can tell I got carried away here, but I want to let you know what God's saint said.) Saint Robert said, with much respect in his voice, "Someone else will do that." I felt this someone else would be a man.

. . . . .

When I pray the rosary, I pray for my family, friends, and for other people I know that I think may need help.

✝As I wrote the above sentence, I saw Donna's tiny star light up when I typed the word, family. I knew she was telling me . . . **we are all family. Dears, the angels are also a part of our family. Imagine!** More than once I have felt in my heart the love Donna, and I'm sure, all the angels have for us—it's tremendous and it's consuming. And the love within them is for each and every one of us.

As our family of angels lovingly watches, they love us and look at us as children. We are the part of this family that is still learning, and still making mistakes . . . . **So, we are all God's children . . . but as humans on Earth, we are the *children* of God's family (or the youngest children).**✝

I hope this is clear for you.

MARCH 19, 1997

I was in my room praying the rosary. My head was down and I was deep in prayer. As I said the "Our Father." I thought about God. I felt a gentle light, unlike any I had ever felt before, shine down upon my head, face, and on the top of my arms. I said, surprised, as I still thought about God, 'It's a light.' God's saint replied, "He is a Light."

MARCH 25, 1997

I was reading, *Jesus Teaches about the Works of Mercy*. Jesus speaks: "When the Son of Man comes in His glory, with all of the angels of Heaven, He will sit upon His royal throne, and all the nations will be assembled before Him . . . ." God's saint said, "Yes, Joyce, they will have to answer." I read further, "The King will say to those on His Right: Come, you have My Father's blessing . . . ."

APRIL 2, 1997

As I was driving, I heard Donna again say to me, "We're here."

I felt relieved. I have to admit, today I did need some support—this angel knows my heart. God's saint said, "Don't worry," as he has so lovingly said, so many times before to me.

APRIL 7, 1997

When I was driving to work this morning I noticed a bird, as it dove and certainly seemed to be attacking. I could not help but notice him because he dove just outside of my car, in front of my driver's side window.

I thought back to the time I had seen the angel Donna flying so protectively beside my car. I also remembered how much Sue's devil spirit likes to enter birds; how she likes to fly.

I knew Sue was in this bird and that she was angry. I thought, An angel's spirit must have been by my car this morning. (Just now, as I retype this, I heard a voice in me say, "Don't worry about me." I knew this was my angel's voice, and I know that our angels are so worried about the poor souls that sin and hurt their own souls, that these loving angels completely forget about themselves. But I want to tell you about this.) After the bird had flown away I was so worried for Donna, I said, 'Donna are you all right?' I saw a white spirit figure briefly appear in my car backseat. God's saint said, "She's OK."

✝Your heavenly lights go through so much for you . . . you don't know, you just can't imagine all they do for you. Please take some time right now to thank them and your Heavenly Father, God. They can hear you.✝

APRIL 16, 1997

I shut my eyes for a second, just to rest a bit. Then I felt a light on my eyelids . . . I opened my eyes up. God's saint said, "It will be really bright. Then you will open your eyes." I knew God's kind and loving saint was letting me know what it would be like when I am awakened from my death on Earth.

APRIL 18, 1997

I had a visitor today. I was sitting calmly at work in front of my desk, typing. First, everyone and everything, seemed to become very calm in the large room. Next, I could actually see the calmness settle, as a very vague, white, spiritual cloud set, from the top of the room to the bottom. However, everyone in the room kept working and talking to one another.

Then, everything in the room slowed down to an almost stillness; everyone seemed to be moving very slowly. I realized I was the only one in this large room that wasn't moving slowly. I knew I had a heavenly visitor and I knew who the visitor was. I felt the presence of the man I had seen long ago in the desert, the man who seemed to turn into the color of fire, the orange/yellow light that slowly rose into the sky. In the stillness, I knew this man's spirit was in the room. Although I did not see him, I heard him say to me, "You do not belong here. You belong in the desert." Then, as I knew he would, I felt him slowly leave.

I knew I was still typing, because I could see myself typing, just below me. Slowly everyone in the room started to move about and talk to one another at a normal pace, and then I knew that I was back at my desk, typing. (This may also have been an out-of-body experience.)

I got so excited because of the visitor we just had . . . I could not help but say, 'You don't know who was just here.' In their peace, which I felt everyone had for the next thirty seconds or so, everyone kept typing and talking calmly to one another. I continued to type.

MAY 5, 1997

The Shriners Circus is in town, so I asked my son if he wanted to go and see it. Well, he's a teenager now, so of course he said he wasn't interested in the circus. Being me, and since we had this Sunday afternoon free, I decided we would go to the circus.

In the circus tent we sat quietly and waited for the show to begin. Then, just a few minutes before the show was to start, I saw one of God's angels: her spirit was very large. This beautiful white spirit flew in through one end of the oblong tent and went out the other. She flew over the arena and the crowds. As this beautiful, loving wonder of God's flew calmly over the arena, she scattered what seemed like, white spiritual snowflakes, everywhere in the tent. I remember I was so amazed, not because she did this with practically no effort at all on her part—but because the white spiritual flakes were so evenly distributed all about the huge tent.

After she had flown out of the tent I looked around at the still unaware crowd of people. Everything was going on just as if nothing had happened. I knew no one else had seen this angel, but I was awed. An angel had just flown through this tent. God does send us so much more light then we realize.

†A bit later Saint Robert said, "Joyce, you don't know what they have done to them. And you don't know what they will do." I realize that the evil spirits have done many evil things to us 'humans' and I know they will do many more evil things to us.†

MAY 11, 1997

As I sat in the living room, I saw my sister's dog walk through the room. She had her head down. I knew Sue's poor devil's spirit was in the dog, who walked so slowly and seemingly so ashamed, through the room. (I had noticed that God has given the devil's spirits an awareness to know when they have done wrong. Not always, but sometimes, after they have done something wrong they immediately become aware they were wrong and their soul becomes very ashamed.)

Today, after Sue had walked through the room, I felt God's saint's presence. Then I could feel his Heavenly compassion and even the love he had for Sue. In feeling his love I was reminded, again, that God has compassion and Love for all, including the fallen spirits.

I knew by God's saint allowing me to feel His heavenly Love for

all, this saint was trying to help me become more patient and loving toward all of God's creatures also. I thanked him.

. . . . .

Much later that night, almost midnight, I was watching TV "Mysteries of the Bible." The program was almost over and it was showing well-known areas of sightings of Our Blessed Mother Mary. Included were the healing waters of Lourdes. The program showed people collecting this water in jars and children washing their faces with the running water. I became involved as they showed the water sparkle in the sun.

> I thought back. I remembered the cluster of thousands of tiny, bright white sparkling stars (God's Lights) I had seen hovering over a river. (A group of one. Page 26.) Now I realized some of the beauty I had been allowed to see.

✝As I continued to watch the water sparkle, God's saint said, "It's in there everywhere, Joyce. Tell them." (When I just typed this, very briefly, I saw a white spirit flash to my left and I heard God's saint again say, "Tell them.")

Here I must also tell you that many times God's saint has told me to drink water, and as I would drink, he would tell me to finish the cup of water I had. He would say, "Finish it." **I do believe God has given us much more in His water than we realize . . . or we can see.**✝

MAY 14, 1997

When I was driving tonight I looked across the river at the few tall buildings we have downtown, especially noticing one of them. On the top floor windows of this tall building, many times there are large letters, or symbols, pertaining to events or holidays that are occurring at the time. For example, around St. Patrick's Day there will be a large shamrock in the top windows. Around July 4th there will be a huge, JULY 4th, in the windows, etc.

As I looked at this building I had a vision of the word, PRAY in large letters on the top floor windows of this building. God's saint said, "This is when you know you succeeded."

(I now realize that not actually this word, but when people start praying, praying more—and praying more from their hearts, this is when we will have succeeded.)

MAY 15, 1997

I was remembering back to February of 1996, to the time I had been thinking about the terrible battle that must have happened in Heaven. Then God's helper had said, "We can't have this happen again."

✝Again, I think . . . this is why we have our time here on Earth. God, filled with His Love and Wisdom, allows us this time, and our free will to choose for ourselves. **Here on Earth, we choose good or evil.** I must emphasize the point that . . . **the choice is ours.**✝

JUNE 3, 1997

Well, I finally got home and I was glad. I thought, Now I can relax. As I put my purse down, the top of which was opened, out rolled an ink pen. God's saint said, "Write, Joyce." I wasn't sure what to write, so I sat down to pray the rosary. As I was saying my rosary I remembered something I had seen today . . . and I knew what to write:

At work, as I was typing at my computer, I heard someone behind me say, with a little bitterness and anger in her voice, 'She has to see it.' Then for a second, I saw a black devil's spirit standing behind my computer, to the left of it. He quickly threw the white lightning bolt that he had held up in his left hand, at me. Instantly, as the bolt left the devil's hand, I felt a sharp, quick pain on the left upper part of my chest. I said nothing, but then I knew the voice I had just heard had come from Sue. I knew she was mad because God's saint was to let me see what I had just seen.

Now, at home, as I was still saying my rosary and thinking of what had happened at work, I heard God's saint say, "Everything you see is for a reason." I knew what he meant; I knew I had seen the devil's spirit throw this bolt for a reason.

> I thought back to all the bolts that I had seen long ago, in the church in Virginia. (Page 49) The bolts that were deflected down as they came at my chest.

Today, this bolt the devil had held, was the same as the previous bolts I had seen. Well, even before today, I had realized that these bolts coming at us are meant to hurt us; as when one had hit our dog (May 1996, Page 119). But now . . . I also knew where these bolts were coming from.

JULY 11, 1997

As I walked into the ladies' room of the restaurant, I could not help but notice water leaking from the sink's faucet. Even though the faucet was shut tight, a lot of water was being wasted. God's angel Donna said, very worried, "They don't know. You have to tell them."

✝**Please, please, don't waste water.** So much does depend on it.✝

JULY 15, 1997

I was thinking, Will they believe me? Saint Robert, will they believe me? He answered, "You will tell them something about the Earth." I knew what I would be allowed to pass onto you would surprise you, and, as I had wished, what I am allowed to tell you, will also help you.

JULY 16, 1997

After I had finished writing a little, I thought, I'll say Blessed Mary's rosary. God's saint said, "Yes." As I heard this one-word reply I could also hear at the same time, this gentle saint's, "Yes, you can pray . . . but, your task is to write." Remember, when spirits communicate, especially God's helpers, so much more is radiated to you, much more than just the words you hear. The best that I can figure is, as we hear their words, the spirits of these magnificent beings, which are so filled with compassion and love, also touch our hearts and souls. Their enormously loving spirits just radiate.

JULY 28, 1997

It was a beautiful day. I was sitting on my front porch, eating supper. I thought, I like the name I had picked for my book, *God Sees Everything*. The name will remind people that God does see all, and He knows all. Then God's saint said, "That is not what we would have named it." I just sat quietly for a second. I thought, This is the name that I like. God's saint said, "*From the Heart*. It's yours Joyce." Donna added, "It's a gift." I started to cry. I know God and His saints and angels worked and fought so hard to help me with this book. This book was written with Heaven's efforts, but yet they give it to me.

I am so glad to give this gift to you.

JULY 29, 1997

I knew Sue's devil spirit was in the girl sitting beside me. Sue's spirit within the girl pulled from me, using the palm of her hand. Then she took this hand and rubbed what she had pulled onto her face. God's saint said, "It still hurts them, Joyce." I knew the fires of Hell still burn the poor devil's spirits somewhat, and I felt very sad for them. Saint Robert continued, he said, "You help a lot." I thought, If I can bring some relief to these poor souls, then this is good.

AUGUST 19, 1997

I was sitting in my car at the quiet monastery, just writing. I saw the vision of a great gray fog. Slowly it went from the left of the sky to the right, it just covered the sky. God's saint said, "It's coming."

Much later, as I was still writing, I looked up into the now blue sky. This time, I saw the vision of a rainbow. God's saint said, "You'll see it." This rainbow was beautiful and large—almost two times larger than any other rainbow I had ever seen. I knew I would someday see this rainbow in the blue sky, but I knew I would be a spirit when I see it.

I knew this large rainbow will signify the end of the gray sky, or the very bad Final Days.

AUGUST 20, 1997

I was in church, sitting in front of a statue of Our Blessed Mother and thinking of her. I remembered that Saint Robert had told me to, "Thank her." As I looked at the rosary in Our Blessed Mother's hands, I heard a woman's soft voice humbly say, "Say them before you write."

SEPTEMBER 1, 1997

I was resting peacefully, almost asleep, but my eyes were still open. I felt Saint Robert's presence, and he simply said, "They're watching." I knew with these words he also meant, Be good. They're watching you, Joyce. . . .

At that second, I saw the vision of a white cloud. Settled in this cloud were three rows of men. The men sat comfortably on white chairs that looked like they were a part of the soft white cloud. I didn't count the men, but thinking back, it seems that there were about seven men in each of the three rows. (I'm not sure.)

All of the men wore long, white robes with long sleeves. Most of the men had white beards of different lengths; maybe that was what made them seem older to me, but they certainly did not look old or tired. Most of the men looked straight ahead, only a few turned their heads slightly, as they seemed to be talking with one another, though I felt that they certainly did not have to turn their heads to talk with one another.

The vision was gone.

Shortly afterward, I felt a quick burning feeling around my ankle, then another. I heard Sue's devil spirit say, 'You saw the Elders.'

Later, God's saint softly said, "They cried for you." He added, "They know more than I do." I knew they cried for the sadness I will have on Earth.

SEPTEMBER 9, 1997

Today, I went to a church to visit and thank Jesus for the strength he has given me. As I prayed, my head gently turned toward a statue of the Blessed Mary and I heard God's saint again say, "Thank Her."

(Reading this years later, September of 2000, I shamefully looked back on some of my sins. I realize how grateful I am, and probably, we all should be, for the loving compassion of a mother—A Heavenly Mother.)

SEPTEMBER 15, 1997

I worked the 11:00 p.m. to 7:00 a.m. shift, but work is over now and it's Sunday morning, so I've decided to go to the 8:30 a.m. Mass. As I drove from work I noticed a deer lying close to the side of the road, on the lawn of someone's home. A man was standing beside the deer, kicking it. I figured the man wanted to see if it was still alive, however the deer didn't seem to move. Since I still had some time before the morning Mass, I decided to stop and see if the deer was alive also.

When I walked up to the man who was standing by the deer, I asked him if he had hit the deer with his car. He said, 'No. I just noticed it lying there.' But he also thought the deer had been hit by a car, as it was pretty well beat up. I was a little relieved when I saw that the deer had antlers, because I figured at least it wasn't a baby deer.

As I drove away I thought, I hope the deer died quickly and didn't have much pain. God's saint said, "Yes, Joyce. He never hurt anyone." I thought of the innocence animals have. He continued,

"Someday you can run with him." As I imagined this beautiful deer running, I remembered back.

> I remembered back to May 17, 1996 (Page 121), to the time I was watching TV and I saw a deer running in slow motion . . . I couldn't take my eyes off of the deer as I admired the beauty of this creature of God's. Then Donna said to me, "God's always looking at them." I was so amazed, I thought, *Even* God is looking at His creations and admiring their beauty. What Love God must have for His creatures.

Still driving, I thought about me running with the deer I had just seen, and then I thought, His antlers might hurt me. I saw Donna's white spirit to the right of my car. As her spirit flew through a telephone pole she looked at me and said, "We're spirits, Joyce. You don't understand yet." I thought, Well, when both the deer and I are spirits, his antlers can't hurt me.

I thought . . . But then I won't be able to touch him.

> I remembered back to December 24, 1996 (Page 167). I was praying in church, kneeling in front of the tabernacle. There were flowers beside me that were so beautiful, I touched them. After I had touched the flowers I did not have such admiration for them.
>
> Remember, I prayed and again the flowers looked very beautiful to me. God's saint said, "Do not touch them." As I looked at, but did not touch, the flowers, they became more awesome and precious to me. I could almost say I began to have a great love for them.
>
> Finally God's saint said, "Do you understand?" But I did not understand, and I left the church confused.

As I now remembered this, I thought, I finally know what God's saint meant when he told me, not to touch, but to only look at the flowers. God's saint was trying to show me how God and His spirits, who cannot touch, as we can, Love . . . and how great these spirits, can Love. I realized that as pure spirits watch and admire all of God's creations, their love grows, just as my love grew when I prayed and only looked at the flowers—just as my love will grow when I am a spirit. I was allowed to understand and feel the love of the spirits . . . . I felt a sigh as God's saint now said to me, "Yes." He realized I finally knew what he meant so long ago in church.

(Do not misunderstand; spirits do touch, but ever so gently and lovingly. Donna and Saint Robert have both held my hand, but only upon my request or when I had been so sad and I needed support.)

My thoughts went back to the deer and me running as spirits. I know our spirits will have admiration, respect, and most importantly, a great love for each other. As spirits, when we watch and admire all of God's creatures and creations, a great love will grow in our hearts, and within us, for all.

 Next, I remembered the time Donna told me to treat my sister's cats with dignity (June 23, 1996, Page 134). As I treated the cats more respectfully and gently, only touching them when they wanted to be petted, they became more affectionate towards me.

Our respect and gentle touch will allow others their dignity, and dignity will also allow love to grow between us. So, I thought, God watches and admires us, and also, His Spirits' Light, only touch us ever so gently, and this gentle touch, His Love, allows us our respect and dignity. Then I thought, When we are spirits and treat each other with dignity and touch each other only ever so gently, with God's Light, our love will grow and be enormous.

Although God's helpers really did most of the work here, this was very hard for me to explain and put together. I hope I have done a good job for you.

God's angel Donna has just given me a new word to use. She said, "Everything will <u>intertwine</u>." I have certainly seen this today.

OCTOBER 2, 1997

I was sitting at work and thinking about how terrible the great battle in Heaven must have been, angel against angel. I thought, What tremendous pain God's good angels must have had in their souls as they fought. Then I looked out a nearby window and I heard God's saint say, ever so sadly, ". . . and then they fell." At that instant I saw the vision of a white angel falling to Earth on his back. I knew he was falling swiftly, because his wings were helplessly blown upward beside him as he fell. The vision vanished just before the angel came into contact with the Earth. I was amazed that the angel that fell was white. I know the fallen angels are no longer white.

✝I thought, To this point in time, God's saint has never mentioned the sorrows he and the good angels must have had in Heaven before the battle; nor has he ever mentioned much about the terrible battle itself. The single, seemingly most remembered event God's saint has ever mentioned about this great battle was, ". . . and then they fell." His loving spirit is only filled with compassion and sorrow when he remembers the battle.✝

OCTOBER 12, 1997

As I drove to the shopping mall, I was thinking of Mary, the wonderful, meek Mother we all have in Heaven. Parking my car in the huge mall parking lot, I wondered what name I should most respectfully use when I talk to Mary, the Mother of Jesus. God's saint said, "Blessed Mother." The wonderful angel Donna said, "This is what we call her in Heaven." For hours afterward, I was just awed by the beauty of this wonderful name Heaven adores our loving mother with . . . Blessed Mother.

OCTOBER 14, 1997

This morning I thought, When will my writings ever end? It would be so nice to finish and publish a book. Then I realized, When God is done letting me know what He wants me to write, then my writings will end. Also, when my job is completed, I know my time here on Earth will end shortly afterward. But for now, I know I must decide when to finish this first book; at what point to stop writing and start publishing my visions. This, my first writings.

NOVEMBER 1997

Tonight I was doing my CNA work. I have a Certified Nurses' Assistant License and occasionally I do this work in nursing homes. I have mentioned this before. Well, this night I was assigned a one-on-one, to stay with one person all night. Usually this is done because the resident has had many problems and needs constant supervision.

The resident I am watching is sleeping now, and she has slept most of my 11:00 p.m. to 7:00 a.m. shift. This night has not been a bad night; however, I still have to record her whole night in fifteen-minute increments. Since the patient's bed is by the window, I had put my chair next to the window to settle down.

Early in the morning, as I looked out of the window into the far distance, high over the buildings and trees, I saw the vision of a tornado. I heard God's saint say, "It will come, Joyce." Although the tornado in this vision seemed far away, I knew it was very large.

Then, directly outside of the window, a strong wind picked up the leaves from the ground and swirled the leaves around in a five-foot or so, tall circle. This was the only wind that arose that whole night. With this whirlwind I heard a very pure and innocent voice say, "It will bring a great wind." I became concerned about the great tornado to come.

As I was driving home and worrying about the tornado, I asked God's saint, 'Why?' He replied, "God will punish Earth for their sins." I thought, When? He said, "We will tell you before."

NOVEMBER 6, 1997

I went to bed yesterday at 6:00 p.m., figuring I would just nap for a little while. Well, when I woke up at 4:00 a.m., I knew I had not realized just how tired I was. So much for my nap.

I usually don't get up until 5:00 a.m. to go to work, so as I laid in bed, wide awake, I figured I finally have an hour of free time. What should I do? Well, God and His helpers won this one. I went right to my computer to type for that hour.

On the way to work I felt myself start to cry. I realized God's saint's spirit was in me. He said, "She wrote today." I knew this saint was talking to God, and as he was saying this to God I also knew he was asking, Can I help her today? At the moment this saint said this, but just for a second, I saw a huge white spiritual form in the sky. I realized this saint had been heard, and answered.

Today was not a hard day for me. Thank God, and thank His saints.

NOVEMBER 7, 1997

About a week ago, I went to a coffee shop (a shop that I had never gone to before) and I bought a long needed coffee mug for myself. When I bought the mug, I noticed a passage from the Bible on the side of the cup; however, in my rush to get to work, I read it so quickly that it never really registered with me.

Well, today at work, a girl started to read the print on my coffee mug. I had not taken the time to read the passage on the mug since I had bought it, but because she was having trouble reading it, as she was born in another country, I took the cup and finished reading it for her. It read: Sing and make music in your heart to the Lord!— Ephesians 5:19 Even though I knew I had pronounced Ephesians wrong, I was now happy to have this cup.

Right after this, when I went on my break, I thought back to the times when God's saint had said to me, "We chose you." Now, I can assure you that they did choose this innocent, and barely educated in my religion, me. Never, ever, would I have imagined myself telling anyone about God and His lights . . . but what wonderful teachers God has sent to help and guide us.

NOVEMBER 27, 1997

Thanksgiving Day is almost over and my son and I are at home in our beds. We had spent the day at my sister's house, where I used much of my time to eat. Today is the first time, after two years, that I have gone to my sister's house. I have finally forgiven her, and I think we all had a good day. (Again you will see just how important forgiveness is for you, and to God.)

As I was in bed talking to my son, who was telling me to be quiet so he could sleep, I started to smell roses in the room. I said to my son, 'I know I don't have any roses in the room, but I can smell them.' I asked him if he could smell them. Again he reminded me of just how tired he was.

I could not see a spirit, but still smelling the roses, I thought of Our Blessed Mother Mary. Then I heard a very gentle woman's voice softly say, "You will also smell them." Being me, I got excited and I started to ask her questions instead of listening to her. I thought, 'Will my son go to Heaven?' Softly she said, "You will live together for a long time." She then said, "He loves you very much." I thought of the times that I could see a tremendous love in his eyes when he looked at me. I said, 'I know.' 'Thank you for letting me know what is going on.' I wanted very much to say, Thank you (I know God allowed me to know, but I felt I should thank her.), that I now realize there are devil's and angel's spirits involved in our lives here on Earth. I wanted to say, Thank you, for letting me know that many of the cruel things that are done, are done because of devil's spirits. She said, "We are proud of you."

As I lay in bed I could still smell the roses, but I could sense that some of this Gentle Lady's thoughts were elsewhere. She said, "I have to go now." I could vaguely sense that some very bad devil's spirits were on their way here. Then the rose smell was gone.

DECEMBER 4, 1997

I was working, looking at my computer and going through one customer's order after another. Then I came to an order and stopped for a second or two. The order was from a boys' home. I heard God's saint say, "This is what I want you to do." I thought, hmm . . . .God wants me to have a home for boys. (For abused and neglected children.) I was so happy. I love children. And then I worried. I thought, How will I ever get the boys?

I thought about a boys' home I had heard about out west, and I remembered hearing that children go to this home on their own to look for help . . . . I started to cry. As I am crying now as I write this.

DECEMBER 23, 1997

I'm doing some of my Christmas shopping today. I'm a bit late this year. I have had very little spare time because I have been working my full-time job, and also trying to get hours in for both of my part-time Christmas jobs. I'm shopping at the religious gift store downtown, where I have chosen to shop for a girl I work with. I am her secret Santa and I am glad to have her. I think she is the person at work who would benefit the most from a religious gift.

Right after buying her gift, a picture of the Blessed Mother caught my eye. I was amazed. The picture was exactly the same as the picture I had in my bedroom as a child, the picture I had kneeled and prayed before every evening before going to bed. However, along the way, as I had forgotten God and my religion, I had also lost track of this picture.

Now, here was this picture . . . and I couldn't help but buy the picture for myself. I heard a spirit's voice, a woman's voice very softly say, "This is your gift." She continued, "She will talk to you through this."

I put the picture of Our Blessed Mother on the wall behind my computer, where I can look at it as I type this book.

DECEMBER 24, 1997

Christmas Eve, and as usual I am working; I was scheduled to work until 10:30 p.m. As I was working I glanced over to the girl who was working across from me. In her fairly large belt buckle I saw, for a second, the vision of a lit candle. In that second I heard God's saint say, "You will see a candle tonight." When I saw this I remembered that this morning I had planned on going to the mid-night Christmas Mass, however, at work I had forgotten about this. I was very glad God's saint had reminded me about going to Mass.

At the midnight Mass the priest gave a sermon about a Jewish man who had cut off three of his fingers in an accident. The doctor told him that he had very little chance of these fingers being replaced on his hand, so that he would be able to use them again. The story continued. As it was, a nun in the area prayed for him; and to the surprise of everyone, after his operation all of the three fingers that had been operated on were fine. He was forever grateful.

As I listened to this story I received a message from God's saint. He wanted me to go to the Shriners Hospital again. (I am sorry I can't remember his exact words.) Also, as I looked over to the statue of Our Blessed Mother I heard, "We will be there."

I know I have to explain this more. Months ago I had visited the Shriners Hospital for Crippled Children and prayed for the children. But because of my busy schedule I have not been able to return to the hospital to pray since. Now, God's saint was telling me to please visit the hospital again and pray for the children.

DECEMBER 25, 1997

On Christmas morning, as I was still in bed, my thoughts were at the Shriners Hospital for Crippled Children. For years, I have asked God to bless me and let me heal others using His power. I knew I now had this gift. I said to God's saint, 'This is my Christmas present.' He said, "Yes." I replied, 'This is what I would have chosen.' He said, "I know."

DECEMBER 28, 1997

I was sitting at home and thinking about the sermon I had heard in church just days before; the sermon about a Jewish man who had accidentally cut off three of his fingers. (This terrible accident actually helped his soul.) I thought about another time when God's Saint Robert had mentioned the Jewish people. He had said, "They will be the ones you will have to convince. They will be your worst critics." Even as this saint had said this, I must say, I still felt the compassion he has for them. He has always shown compassion for them.

I thought more about God's saint's immense compassion for the Jewish people, and then I asked him 'Why?' God's saint replied, "Because they sinned. They knew." Then I also knew that this saint knew firsthand that the Jewish people knew Jesus was really The Son of God. Again I thought, Is Saint Robert, Jesus Christ or someone from Christ's time? God's saint said, "If you can help them, you will see how much better the world will get."

1998

JANUARY 11, 1998

I woke up early this morning, and since it was still dark outside I just lay in bed. After a little while I heard a car outside that quickly sped up and went down the street. I could tell the driver of the car was traveling fast, much faster in this residential area than the speed limit allows. Somehow, although I did not see a spirit, I knew the driver of the car had just left a devil's spirit in my room. I said, 'Out. You must leave us alone.' Then, just briefly, I saw the devil's spirit as he walked out of my room.

His black shadowy figure was so filled with sadness that his whole figure slouched and his head hung down. I could feel his empty soul and his sad thoughts, which echoed through to an enormously sad voice saying, 'Nobody wants me.'

JANUARY 19, 1998

I had a few spare minutes today and I actually had the chance to read the front page of yesterday's newspaper.

I read . . .

Abortion: The enduring debate

I read on . . .

When does human life begin?

I'm not exactly sure where the passage is in the Bible, or the exact wording of the passage, but I remember reading that God had told us, Life begins at the moment of conception. I would like to tell you the following:

I remember back to the exact second that I became a mother. As I lay in bed after intercourse, within ten to twenty minutes later (I can't remember the exact timing, it was a long time ago), I briefly felt a very small, beautiful new light inside of me. I find it hard to explain this light to you, but again I must tell you, it was the feeling of a beautiful light.

Right after feeling this light, my first thought was—life. I knew I was pregnant; I knew a brand new little life had begun in me.

This is another gift God gave me very, very long ago. I wish to share this gift with you. I felt the light of life begin—at conception.

FEBRUARY 15, 1998

Many times God's saint has said to me, "Write," or "Please write." Ever so patiently he waits for me to find some time, and so gently he reminds me to write. When he says this to me his voice is always filled with such love and concern for me—and for many.

This morning at work I had been at my computer typing. But now it's my break time and I have found some valuable time. I have written this.

MAY 1998

I was feeling rather lost today, however, as I looked at a man in a red shirt, God's saint said, "It will be a Cardinal that helps you." I wondered which Cardinal in the church will help me.

MAY 15, 1998

I was in a restaurant eating my lunch. (The restaurant whose placemat I had originally used to write this down on.) I became more aware of the job, and what an important outcome of our job is to be. God's helpers have reminded me so many times to write, write, and write. Well, I gladly write to help you become aware of the fact that we share this world of God's with a variety of spirits.

✝I hope my writing will help you realize **the dark spirits are usually trying to trick and deceive us, they want to destroy our souls and all of God's Earth**. Satan and his evil spirits would like us to think that other people, or even that God, causes evil. Please don't believe this.

Please realize, and I will remind you again and again, that the devil spirits are about. Please turn to God for strength and help. Several times I have even seen these evil spirits in people's bodies. Now when the devil's spirits are in these people, sometimes we still have some of our own awareness about us; however, I have seen the devil spirits enter people and overtake their whole being, their thoughts, and their actions.

When the devils enter us, many times their intention is to make us 'humans' act evil; sometimes causing trouble amongst us, or even trying to make us hurt one another. Please remember that people, your family, neighbors or friends, do not spontaneously or inten-tionally try to hurt you or others. **Praying can help us in weak times, as the evil spirits do not like to stay in a 'human' that is praying. Also, saying the powerful name of Jesus, and thinking about our Savior, does help. Please choose to love and forgive your brothers and sisters.**✝

In the past, there had been times when I have watched people and I thought, He is good or she is good. In reply, God's saint said to me, "They are all good." It took a long time for this to sink in, and for me to really realize what he was saying. Again, saying so little, he has said so much. Please realize, each of us is good. It is the evil spirits that cause much of the havoc. (At this time, I finally *fully* realized this.)

I know that all of this may not be easy for you to totally comprehend and sort out. Believe me; sometimes I still even have a hard time with this.

In the restaurant, as I thought about the job God has for us, I said, 'Saint Robert, these devil spirits will really be after me. Even now they tell me that I had better shut up.' Suddenly, I saw a bird come and fly just outside the glass door of the restaurant. Although the bird did not hit the glass door it flew frantically outside the door, seemingly trying to get into the restaurant. God's saint said, "They are after you now." I knew Sue's devil spirit was in the bird, and I know my guardians work hard.

JUNE 6, 1998

I was driving by the movie theaters and I looked at the large board in front that advertises the movies now playing. Along with the movies were the words, Angels have Wings. I thought . . . Yes, they do. I was thinking about God's beautiful angel Donna. At times I have seen her wings and at other times she has not shown them. I don't know why, this may just be her preference. I thought back to one night in particular . . . a night I had spent at the nun's convent, at the hospital in Ohio.

> I was in my room, in bed resting, when I sensed a dark spirit coming down the long hallway outside. I knew he was coming toward my room. I saw Donna's white spirit zoom by my bed toward the door, and I knew my Guardian Angel quickly went to stand in front of my room's door to face the dark spirit.

When the dark spirit saw the angel standing in front of my door, he stopped. He spoke to her with a voice of emptiness. He said, 'Let me see your wings.' I realized his emptiness was great because he knew what agony his inevitable future held for him; and when he said this I knew he was looking for a bit of relief from his pain, relief by seeing this angel's beautiful wings.

Before he finished saying his last word I knew Donna had let him see her white wings, which were not showing before. Then he said to her, 'You come with me.' I realized he was going to show her some of the pains he had gone through. She followed him, and this is all I was allowed to know.

As I lay in bed I was amazed; amazed because at the time, I thought, This powerful angel chose to humiliate herself by doing what he asked instead of just pushing the dark spirit aside. (This is what I thought at the time.)

Now I know, when Donna showed her wings this was an act of love by this angel, this light of God's. **Love is what yields these great and powerful beings to be so humble.**

Also, at the time I was amazed because Donna had shown her wings, even before the devil's spirit had finished asking her to see them.

But now I know, God's lights, along with having the ability to know our present thoughts, also know our future thoughts. (And, Donna just added this "Our future actions, also.")

JUNE 20, 1998

As I was getting out of the shower I felt a shove and for a second I lost my balance, but just a bit. That same second I heard a devil's spirit say, 'He always favored you.' The devil's voice was full of bitterness and jealousy. I thought, Gee, his voice sounds so much like that of a child who is very angry because another sibling is getting more attention than him.

God's saint also heard this. He replied, "He is, Joyce, but he knew what he had to do to get this attention."

I realized by the sound of this saint's voice, that he was very well aware of the fact that this other child *knew* what he should have done to please his Father. Even more . . . God's saint's voice let me know that we *all know* what we should do to please Our Father.

JULY 6, 1998

I was just laying on the floor and resting . . . I saw the vision of a small boy. He was walking down the sidewalk of a nice looking, quiet suburban street. In this vision it was a nice day and everything looked quiet and peaceful, except . . .

I could only see the backside of this child, but I could tell that he was around five or six years old. This child was alone and he walked so slowly, he almost seemed to be stunned, or in a daze. However, he continued to walk— seemingly aimlessly wandering down the empty street. I knew something very bad had just happened to this child. In a very sad and desperate voice, God's saint yelled to me, "Joyce." I knew the child needed help, and I knew this saint was calling on me to help him. The vision was gone.

Again, I thought, I do so hope to use the money I make from this book to start a home for children . . . as God's saint had said he wanted me to do.

JULY 14, 1998

I was about to drive by a church, a church that I had driven by many times on my way home. I thought, I would like to go into the church to pray, but I know that I can't because the church's doors are locked. I said to Jesus, 'I am sorry. I would go into your church to pray but your church is locked.' The sad reply was, "This is one of our biggest pains." I know I can't even begin to imagine the sorrow these locked churches must bring to Heaven.

AUGUST 1998

As I was driving, I looked into my rearview mirror at the

woman driving in the car behind me. She was alone, but I could tell by the very evil look on her face that she had a devil's spirit, and probably Sue's devils spirit, in her.

I drove for about another mile, and then I again looked into my rearview mirror. The same car was behind me, and the same woman; however, her body was now a bit slumped and her head was down. Her whole self expressed a total, full, and enormously complete defeat and anguish. God's saint said to me, "They know they are fighting a battle they have lost."

AUGUST 3, 1998

After saying the rosary I heard a gentle voice. I knew this voice was from Our Blessed Mother. She said, "You helped keep the sun out." I did not know what she meant. Then I heard God's saint say, "You prayed the rosary for us, Joyce." Now, I knew my prayers were not for Heaven . . . but my prayers were being *added* to Heaven's prayers . . . for Earth.

✝Please pray the rosary together with God's lights. Add your prayers to theirs (praying for them) . . . as these loving and unselfish lights pray for another day—for us. Love keeps the sun out.✝

AUGUST 11, 1998

I woke up early this morning, about 4:00 a.m. or so. As I lay in bed, still resting, I saw a white spiritual light in my room. I heard God's saint say, "You will get an important phone call today." Well, in the last few days I have been trying to get a loan, I am trying to get a good lawyer, and I have put in a few phone calls for a part-time job. As I lay in bed I excitingly wondered, Who will the call be from? Which one of these will the call be about?

Later that morning a lawyer called me back on the phone, and I now have a good lawyer. I hope. Even though I wasn't totally convinced that this was my important phone call, when I went to work I figured my day of wondering was over, since I work the shift from 3:00 p.m. to 11:00 p.m.

When I got home from work that evening, I had a message on my answering machine from an office supply company. The message said, My special order was in and I could now pick up the ribbon for my printer. After listening to the message I knew this was the important phone call I was to get today. For the last two weeks I have not been able to print anything for my book because I have not had a ribbon for my printer. Now I could get back to writing.

Again Heaven baffled me—as they reminded me what is of true value. That morning I had fumbled about trying to figure out what Earthly objects I might get today, but the important phone call was about writing . . . from the heart.

AUGUST 19, 1998

When I turned on the radio I heard an old song that went something like this, 'Mother Nature is bringing destruction on us.' Then I heard God's saint say, "They will try to blame it on us, Joyce." Now, this is hard for me to explain, but please do not blame destruction on God. I know from previous experiences, that storms and especially thunderstorms, lightning, and other great turbulences in the skies are sometimes brought on as warnings, directed at the devil's spirits. These storms from Heaven do scare, and inevitably help control, the devils when they are doing something evil.

Also, God's saint let me know that sometimes prior to when the devil's spirits are about to cause great destruction on Earth, Heaven has, and will, step in to help us. Sometimes God uses His power and storms to warn the devils before they start. These storms do stop the evil plans before they are carried out, because when the devils are scared they will not cause havoc.

> Remember back to September 18, 1996? (Page 150) That day God's saint explained to me why we had just had some tornados. Saint Robert said these were warnings, saying, "We had to warn them. They wanted to destroy a lot."

Now I know some storms cause destruction. **We must trust in God's Eternal Wisdom. I think that without God's warning storms to protect us, we would certainly have much more evil on Earth, and evil can cause much destruction . . . and destroy our souls.** Also, I am not saying that all storms are for this reason, to protect us, but God's saint has let me know that some storms are for this reason.

You will see that, later on, this message became even clearer to me . . . . There is more.

. . . . .

Later that day, when I was doing my laundry, I was thinking about forgiveness and forgiving someone who had hurt me yesterday. It took a few minutes . . . but I began to feel peaceful and I felt forgiveness for this person. Next, I began to think about what God's saint had said to me before, that God smiled at me a lot. As I opened the door of our apartment complex laundry room, stepping outside, I saw silver and white rays come down on me. The glimmering silver rays were just beautiful. They were thin and straight, while the straight white rays were a bit wider and looked more spiritual than the silver rays. I heard God's saint say, "This is what they look like, Joyce." I thought, This is what God's (Light) rays look like when He smiles on us.

That afternoon as I was driving, I saw the vision of a small white cloud. In this cloud I saw the glimmering silver and white rays, and I heard God's saint say, "Remember this. This is important." The vision was gone.

I realized this was a good, "Remember this . . . ."

Later I again thought, Forgiveness is so very important for our souls, and when we forgive this pleases our wonderful Heavenly Father so much. For now, and for eternity, wouldn't you like to have your Father smile at you . . . sending His rays upon you? Please forgive.

✝Remember Jesus' words, ". . . forgive us our sins as we forgive those who trespass against us. . . ." Do you think that you can enter Heaven with a bitter and unforgiving Heart?✝

AUGUST 31, 1998

The cooler weather is beginning to set in at night, so this morning when I got out of bed my ankles ached a bit as I walked. I thought, Well, the dampness is going to kill me. Then I heard a devil's spirit correct me. Very evilly he said, 'We are.'

✝Dears, try to not be afraid of death, for this is the time when we will meet our Guardian Angel and see God's Great Light. Please lead a good life and pray . . . prepare yourself for your meeting with your Heavenly Father.✝

Later, I knew that I would know when my work here is almost done. Although I hope that this time does not come for a long time.

SEPTEMBER 1998

I was thinking, The devils seem to be getting worse. Things seem to certainly be harder than when I was a child, and things seem to be worse than even ten years ago. God's saint said, "The closer it comes, the more desperate they will get." I knew that as the devil's time on Earth comes closer to an end, they will get more desperate.

SEPTEMBER 1, 1998

The devil's spirits were around last night and they did scare me while I was writing, but I kept writing. Later that night I felt that there was a *very pure* spirit in my room. I became worried for the small pure spirit, because I did not want him to become angry at the devil's spirits. I did not want his pureness to be tainted or spoiled by anger in him; not even by a slightest bit of anger in him.

I said to the pure spirit, 'Please do not have anger toward the devils.' The pure spirit came into me and I felt a great love—a Love for everything that is alive. He was letting me know that he would not have anger. He quietly said, "We have this."

✝God's heavenly creatures are filled with a tremendous love for everything that is alive. What a wonderful, Loving Creator we have!✝

SEPTEMBER 8, 1998

I was sitting in my parked car in front of the church at the quiet monastery, just relaxing and correcting some of the punctuation and grammar on the already written pages of my book. I have to admit, I would never have been a good English teacher, or even a so-so English teacher.

I noticed a group of birds that suddenly and quickly flocked to the ground. The birds were in a tight group and they were all chirping happily. The group was close to a tree that was about fifty feet away from me. Before fifteen seconds had passed there was a lot more birds in the area, and the area was larger, but still, all of the bird chirped happily, walking about in this close-knit group that was now maybe, a twelve foot area.

> I remembered long ago when Saint Robert had said to me, "Watch for the birds." He was telling me where to look for his spirit; birds just love to flock and they chirp so happily in his heavenly, peaceful spirit.

Calmly I kept writing and glancing over to the group of birds. I noticed the tightly knit group move slowly away from the tree and toward the front doors of the church. When the large group of birds stopped for a few seconds in front of the church doors, I thought, Good, the saint will probably go into church to visit Jesus. I kept writing.

I looked up. The group of birds was coming toward my car and they were pretty close. When I realized that the saint was coming to me, I got scared. I'm not exactly sure why.

Then from behind my left shoulder I saw Sue's devil spirit pop up, and very animal-like, she angrily snarled at the saint who was moving closer to me. The birds disbursed and I knew the saint's spirit quickly flew away, high up into the sky. I was so disappointed that I had gotten scared and that the saint had gone away.

Later Donna said, "We are getting you ready." I am not sure why this happened, but I am sure this will all intertwine.

SEPTEMBER 9, 1998

Back to storms.

Last night I was working another 11:00 p.m. to 7:00 a.m. shift in the nursing home. I was sitting in front of a large picture window when I suddenly felt God's saint rush from me. He said, "They did something very bad." Although all of us who were working were sitting around the nurses' station, I heard two people talking in one of the resident's room down the hall. I could not tell what was being said, however, I did think that this was odd, as I had just made rounds and all of the residents had seemed to be asleep.

Now, when God's saint rushed from me, I knew that his spirit had gone outside, through the window I was sitting in front of. Instantly, as he left me, a heavy rainstorm started, and within minutes there was thunder with the heavy rain. I just sat in my chair.

A bit later that night, as I was walking down the hallway, one of the girls I was working with was walking toward me. She looked very scared. She said to me, 'The lightning is going sideways.' At first I thought this was an odd thing to say, then I knew that Sue's devil spirit must have been in the girl. Also, I knew that God's saint was using the storm and the lightning to warn the devils to stop the bad thing they had done. (Although we could not see it, I think the spirit world must have been able to see God's spiritual lightning going sideways.)

Then, as the girl turned and walked away from me, I knew that the devils had stopped their evil plot. All was better now . . . a storm, a warning, had helped again.

I am not sure, but I think the devils tried to take a soul, and take this soul before their time. No one passed away that night.

SEPTEMBER 11, 1998

As I was driving in my car I thought about the president of the United States and the troubles he is having now—the impeachment question. God's saint said to me, "This is for the power." Then I felt a very strong, almost overwhelming, power. Not so strong, but with this power, I also felt a threat. The threat seemed to come at me.

As I am sitting here writing this, a few days after God let me feel this power and threat, God's saint said to me, "Remember the threat."

SEPTEMBER 13, 1998

I was eating breakfast at a restaurant and I saw Donna, her small white spirit fluttered toward my chest, at my heart. I felt her there, seemingly hanging onto my heart. She said, "Follow your heart."

SEPTEMBER 14. 1998

> Remember the Christmas gift I had gotten on December 23, 1997? (Page 197) Right after I had bought a religious gift for the girl I worked with I noticed my gift, a beautiful picture of Our Blessed Mother; and after I had gotten this picture for myself I heard a beautiful heavenly voice say to me, "She will talk to you through this."

I hung the picture of Our Blessed Mother on the wall behind my computer; so I can look at this picture while I type. At times, I have seen images of tears coming from the far corners of this humble lady's eyes in this picture. I have even seen tears overflowing from her eyes. As the image briefly appeared of Our Blessed Mother's tears, I was never really sure why she was looking at me and crying.

Today, when I called my son at 7:30 p.m. he was eating supper. His voice was so depressed, and this made me sad. I waited for an hour, so that he, his father and stepfamily could finish eating. Then I called my son's father. I was so worried for my son, and angry. I asked, 'Why is he so sad?' As usual I was rude to my son's father. I couldn't help it.

After I had gotten nowhere and hung up the phone, I was still worried for my son. Then I remembered what God's saint had told me to do to help my son—I prayed the rosary for him. As I was praying the rosary and walking through my home, God's saint said to me, "You can turn back time." Naive me sat in a chair and concentrated my thoughts on turning back time. Well, it didn't take me too long to realize that I couldn't turn back time by just sitting in a chair and thinking about it.

Still . . . having Faith in God's saint, I continued to pray the rosary. Then I knew what he had meant. I have continually been rude and insulting to my son's father for the last year or so. I know that it is a sin for me to be insulting and unforgiving. Whatever the reason, I should remain calm and be forgiving. God will Judge. (This is something God's lights have been trying to teach me, and I must admit they have been very patient.) I knew this loving saint was now, and again, reminding me to forgive. . . . It was extremely hard for me, but I picked up the phone and called my son's father. I apologized to him for my rudeness. I explained I was so worried for my son.

After I hung up the phone, I again continued to pray my rosary. When I was almost at the end of my prayers, I started to cry. First the tears came from the far corners of my eyes, and then my eyes just overflowed with tears. (Never have my eyes overflown with tears, and believe me I have cried, as we all have.) As I cried, two small heavenly white lights and one small light blue spirit, lit up in my room. I also heard Donna, as she softly said, "This is good." I knew this cry was good for me, but I had no idea why.

Then, as I looked at the picture of Our Blessed Mother, I knew why my crying was good. I especially noticed that Her eyes were

clear, there were no tears in Our Blessed Mother's eyes. In forgiving my son's father, I knew I had been allowed to take back the tears that my sin of unforgiveness toward him, had caused Our Heavenly Mother to cry for me.

I knew this was a gift . . . a gift that was granted to me a while back.

> Remember, on August 13, 1996 (Page 144), I had cried after I had asked Our Blessed Mother if I could take some of the pain and sorrow she bore for sinners?

Because of this, and I did not know it at the time, in Her Grace, she was to allow me to take back some of the pain, sorrows, and tears she bore for my sins. Our Blessed Mother is more loving and wise than I could have imagined.

I *had* turned back time, as my sin from yelling at and not for-giving my son's father was gone . . . and indeed, this cry was good for me; very good. Our Blessed Mother's tears for this sin of mine, was gone from her.

SEPTEMBER 23, 1998

As I was typing, I thought about my brother and wondered how his spirit is now. I was really hoping he had made it; I was hoping he was now a bright spirit of God's. Then I looked at a picture of Jesus, and God's saint said, "When he looks at his children, he is." I knew that although my brother's spirit may have lost his peace for a time, he had, and must surely still have, a real love for his children. The caring from his heart could probably allow in and renew God's great Love and peace.

Later that morning, as I was still typing, I heard my brother's spirit say to me, 'Publish it.' I know that my brother is a good and bright spirit now, and I know that his caring and loving heart has made him bright. I am aware that love makes God's spirits so bright. Please love.

I continued to type away for a while. When I looked at a picture of Our Blessed Mother, God's saint said to me, "There are many more mysteries about her." I knew I would be told some of these mysteries.

On my drive to work God's saint helped me along again. He said, **"It's all in the heart."** These few words mean so much.

SEPTEMBER 24, 1998

The woman who sits beside me at work has been anxious and worried for at least a week now. It seems her very young daughter-in-law is expecting a baby soon, and the girl is having much difficulty adjusting to her huge size. The family really wishes the baby would be born soon.

Again today, as yesterday and the day before, the woman anxiously said, 'When will she have the baby? I wish she would have the baby today.' I knew she was just nervously talking, but I asked God's saint, When will she have the baby? He did not reply, but I could feel this was because he was scared. Then I knew why he was afraid to tell me. He was afraid for the baby. I said to the lady, although I knew she may not have realized what I was talking about, 'They are dangerous. He can't tell you.'

Shortly afterward God's saint said to me, "She will be *surprised*." And I knew the baby would be beautiful. I smiled and told the lady, 'You will be surprised.'

Now, I realized that the devil's spirits were happy because of the anxiety and worry this family felt over the awaited birth of this child. These worries, and God's saint not telling them when the baby would be born, satisfied the devils. The devil's spirits would not bother this child as an infant . . . he would be a beautiful baby. This grandmother would be *surprised*.

✝Can you see how it seemed that God wasn't listening? But actually His Love—and so His quiet—was for a good, final outcome, if you will.

I am glad I was able to tell you this and I hope I have explained it clearly enough . . . . **God is listening. Trust Him. ✝**

SEPTEMBER 30, 1998

I was at work; I wondered what had happened to my mother's spirit, Where is she now? God's saint said, "She's OK." With this I also knew that she was in a lot of pain. I did something I hadn't done before, I prayed for her. "Hail Mary, full of grace, the Lord is with thee . . . ." As I was saying this prayer, I heard some girls walking through the hallway that was outside of the room I was in. They said, 'It smells like incense out here.'

I thought, Our Blessed Mother is here . . . and then I vaguely smelled roses. Shortly afterward I heard Our Blessed Mother's soft voice say, "Why did you pray for her?" I answered honestly, and at the time I knew that this was the only way I could have answered her pure spirit, 'Because I remember she used to make my bed.' (Our house was always clean) . . . I put my head down and humbly added, 'I know this is childish.' I paused, 'For my father.' I knew his spirit would be very worried about her.

I started to cry, first the tears came from the corners of my eyes, then my eyes overflowed with tears. I knew these were not my tears, but again, I was being allowed to take back some of the tears that Our Blessed Mother had cried for my sins. Because of my pride, I was at work and I thought someone might see me crying, I tried to stop my tears. The rose smell left, and the tears stopped coming down my cheeks.

Within minutes, I again became fully aware that my pride is one of the faults I have to overcome. After I had stopped feeling so foolish, because of my pride, I thought, I *knew*, Donna, and our loving Guardian Angels, are so eagerly waiting to *rush up to Heaven* with reports of us doing good.

Now . . . I knew my answer to Our Blessed Mother was not right. I knew I was not praying for my mother for the right reason, but I did not realize why I should have been praying for my mother . . . . I thought for at least fifteen minutes. Finally, I realized why I should pray for her. To help her soul.

✝When Our Blessed Mother asked me this question . . . when I was in her presence, I felt a feeling of complete honesty overcome me. I *could not* have lied if I had wanted to. Within Our Heavenly Mother's pure radiant presence, we are humbled, and most completely honest.✝

OCTOBER 1998

For the last few weeks I have been able to take walks just before work; there are paths that go through some woods about the building I work in. Last night it had rained, so early this morning as I followed the path through the woods, I noticed that the few small ditches the path went over held water. To the left of the path, in a ditch with water, a small, no larger than one foot, white saintly image vaguely and briefly appeared. This very saintly being had his head down humbly, and he said, "There is water here now." I know that the saints pray to God Our Father for water for us. Our substance of life on Earth.

My love has grown so enormously for these very humble, saintly beings. We must also try to be humble, and pray with much humility and love. Please, pray the rosary with and for them. (See August 3, 1998, Page 205.)

Another morning walk; as I was walking this path I saw a tiny chipmunk, his cheeks were just bulging. I thought, He's carrying food back to his home for the winter. God's saint said, "Even the smallest of creatures, we give them this ability so they will know; for you. So we will judge and know. There will be much more light, Joyce."

✝God has made and given us this wonderful and complex Earth . . . . The Earth (balance of nature, etc.) is for us. By our actions here, God will know how to judge us. (Heaven will hold its Peace. For us.) **We are here so God will know.**✝

This did not occur to me at the time, but I would like to add this here: One night, months later, I was watching a special on TV about Noah's Arc. The question arose, how did two of each type of animal find its way to the arc, male and female? I know this is not exactly like the above, but I have no doubt that God's wonderful lights led the animals, one male and one female, peacefully to, and kept the animals peacefully in, Noah's Arc.

One day, as I walked through the woods, I thought, God, I really want to finish this book. (I am ashamed to put this here, but.) I heard God's angel say, "We are sad that this is all that you think about it." I thought about this book. I asked, 'What is it?' The reply was, "A gift." In my eagerness I had forgotten.

I was listening to the radio on my way to work and I heard someone say the word *real* when he was trying to describe something as being genuine or authentic. As I took my walk in the woods I thought about this word again. I thought, We use the word *real* the same as the spirits use the word *true*. *True* is the word the spirits use to describe something as being authentic or unquestionable.

This is hard for me to explain, but God's helpers can and do—through their love—take the burden of our heart's pain and our tears.

> I remembered far back, to the time when I started to cry as I was walking down Main Street (page 5). Later, as I sat on the steps crying, my tears and pain suddenly stopped. It was puzzling to me how this stopped so quickly.
>
> Also, I thought about something that had happened just recently. I had seen a girl crying, then she painfully said,

'God.' I could tell that she was looking for some relief from her pain. Her tears quickly stopped and her pain certainly seemed to be lessened.

Now I know God heard her, and the girl's Guardian Angel had been allowed to take the girl's pain and tears. I would think that all of God's angels, because of, and with their great love . . . can take our pain, and can cry our tears for us. (I was to learn about what happens to some of the tears and pain, God's lights take for us. Later, I will explain it.) Much of this is still not precisely clear to me, but I know our emotions, love, hate, joy, pain, etc. are spiritual. They are of God's spiritual world. . . . There is so much more.

OCTOBER 4, 1998

I was worried about getting my home for boys. I really want it, and of course I want it yesterday. Today is Sunday, and I thought, Before Mass I'll stop in church and pray for a bit.

In church, as I walked toward one of the front pews, I noticed a statue of Our Blessed Mother. She was holding baby Jesus and she stood on top of the world. As I turned and walked toward the statue, I thought, May I come close to you? I heard a woman's soft voice say, "Stop there." I stopped. I knew she was telling me this for my own good. I thought, I want to go closer to her, but I felt some tremendously strong and very protective angels flying swiftly between Our Blessed Mother and me. I knew I was not allowed, nor could I myself take another step to get any closer. I knelt down in the aisle, knowing the woman's voice was Our Blessed Mother's.

Thinking of the boys' home I said, 'When will I have it?' She softly replied, "When you hold the children." I realized there had been times when I was uncaring toward people; times I have not been as compassionate and as full of love toward people . . . children . . . her children. She continued, "When you have the world." I knelt there and thought for a bit, and then I knew these great spirits were gone. I still continued to think about this after I sat down in the nearby pew. I realized, **If you love, you will have the world.**

Later that day Donna corrected me, this is not to be my home for boys, but "God's home for boys." I knew I was wrong.

Also, I would like to say that previously Our Blessed Mother had said to me, "You are not ready." To this God's saint said, "She is wise." I truly agree with her wisdom. I try to be good and especially to love, but I know I have a way to go yet. I am not ready.

OCTOBER 16, 1998

It was Sunday and I was on my way to the 10:30 a.m. Mass. I didn't have much time to get there, so I decided that I would not make any stops along the way. As I drove by a small closed church, which is now for sale, I said, "God." I knew when I said this, that there was someone else's strength in my voice and in the word that I had just said. The strength of this voice came from a man. I thought, God's saint's spirit must be in me . . . I knew he was compassionately pleading to God. Very quickly, at least thirty chirping birds flocked to the front side of the church's small lawn. I thought about the time I was at the monastery and the same thing had happened. I knew, again, God had sent one of His wonderful saints down from Heaven.

I kept driving because I was so worried about being late for Mass; I thought, God would like me to go to church. Then I realized God would probably like me to take some time and talk to His saint. I turned my car around.

I drove by the church, to a parking lot. I saw an even larger group of chirping birds than I had noticed before. The birds were now perched in a large bush to the front side of the church, and I knew where the saint was. He said, "This is important to this area." I realized he wanted this closed church to be open, and he wanted this for the people who lived about this area. (My own thoughts were for a school to be built and attached to the church.) He continued, "I will be big here." I knew this holy saint would be very strong and give much light to this area . . . then I felt he was done talking to me.

As I drove off, I thought, I have just enough time to get to the 10:30 Mass. I asked the saint if he would like to go to my church. I was thinking, This church is closed. I said, 'Today we would have a Sunday service at my church.' I told him I would meet him there. When I walked into my church, I could feel that this heavenly saint was already there . . . .

After the Mass I told our priest that I was almost done with my book. I asked him if he would look at it. (I know I need a little help here and there.) The priest said he was going away to a retreat and he would be back on Friday. (When Friday came I became so busy that I was unable to talk to the priest for some time. I'm not really almost done, but I do want to get things going a bit, and I know I could certainly use some help from a priest.)

As I finished typing this page I was told, "Just think of your heart."

OCTOBER 20, 1998

It was a beautiful fall day. I was in a park, just sitting in my car, resting and writing. There was a very small, almost unnoticeable breeze. I looked out at the paved road ahead; it wound a bit and then went down a hill. To the side of this road was a small grassy area, which then sloped down the hill.

As I relaxed, I thought, Why are the devil spirits so afraid of tornados? Shortly after, I noticed the leaves on the paved road ahead pick up and go into a whirlwind. As I looked at the three-foot or so whirlwind, I thought back . . .

> I remembered the other time that I had seen this similar whirlwind, in November of 1997. The whirlwind I saw as I looked out the window of the nursing home I was working at . . . the whirlwind that spun as I heard the pure voice . . .

As the leaves still swirled, the whirlwind moved them from the side of the paved road to the side of the hill the road was on. Then, most of the leaves in the bottom of the whirlwind, and some of the leaves from the top of the whirlwind, were blown loose from the still swirling whirlwind. The loose leaves were thrown quickly down the hill.

As I watched this I heard the same pure voice I had heard in November of 1997, when I had first seen this whirlwind. Today, the pure voice said, "With the wind they fall down."

✝My question was answered: **Tornados scare the devil's spirits so very much, because with God's wind, they fall—the devil's spirits fall into Hell.**✝

OCTOBER 26, 1998

I had some spare time today so I decided to go shopping. Well, when I came out of the department store I noticed a van for the Shriners Hospital for Crippled Children. I knew where my spare time would lead me next, to this hospital, where I could pray for these poor children.

When I got to the hospital I walked into the children's playroom, where an older man who was playing air hockey with a beautiful red-headed young girl, started talking to me. Although the girl was lying on her stomach on a stretcher and her legs were covered with a sheet, I could still see that her legs were not straight.

I walked next to the girl's stretcher, and to myself, I started to pray to God. Shortly afterwards I felt full of Faith and light. I touched the girl's left leg. When I touched the girl's leg the feeling left me, so I prayed until I had the same feeling again, and I touched her leg again.

I looked up (the ceiling of this room had a huge sunroof) and I prayed to God more. 'Please help this girl.' I felt light and I touched her leg. Then I felt I had no more strength, or light in me to give. I looked up again. I sadly said, 'I have no more left.' I heard a man's voice correct me. He said, "Yes, you do. It's in your heart." I thought, In my heart? I prayed again. I felt love and compassion for the poor girl, and then I felt a light grow from within me. I touched the girl's crippled leg again . . . then again.

Now, I know the girl did not get up off of the stretcher and walk about, but I also know that God hears us pray.

As I was leaving, and walking into an elevator, I heard a saintly voice say to me, "We're staying here." I knew the two saintly spirits that had walked with me to the elevator, went back to the children . . . where they knew they were needed . . . .

NOVEMBER 1998

I was driving on the bridge that leads into the downtown area of my hometown. Before I came to the end of the bridge I saw the vision of a rainbow over the bridge. God's saint said, "You will see a rainbow here." I wondered why the rainbow would be there . . . and when it would be there.

Because my schedule is busy and my father's church is far away, some Sundays I go to closer churches for Mass. However, this Sunday I drove to my father's church. As I was driving, God's saint let me know that the angel Donna was happy because, "This is her church." I had noticed that this angel certainly seems the happiest and most comfortable in this particular church.

> Remember, this church, my father's church, was the first place I had seen the angel Donna? She was talking to my father. (Page 35)

✝Now, this is just my opinion, but just as we have our own church that we tend to worship in, could it be that God assigns, or each angel has, his or her special place to worship in . . . their church here on Earth? Maybe this is related to our Baptism?✝

NOVEMBER 9, 1998

A man at work started discussing religion with me. He said, 'I have no problem with the Catholic religion, except, why should I tell my sins to a priest? He is just another human.' I told him, 'I don't mind going to a priest for confession. I figure I could certainly use the guidance. Just as we have teachers and certain people to guide us in schools and many other things in our life, it also seems that we might be better off having teachers and guidance in our religion.' (Most priests usually try to guide me when I tell them my sins.) Then I said to the man, 'A Priest is human, but he represents Our Lord.'

Although this is not directly related to the above, I would like to write a quotation from my prayer book, *The Pietà*. On page 68: Our Lord revealed to Mutter Vogel, "When a Priest falls we should extend him a helping hand THROUGH PRAYER AND NOT THROUGH ATTACKS! . . . . Every Priest is My Vicar and My heart will be sickened and insulted because of it! If you hear a judgment (against a Priest) pray a Hail Mary."

Now, our priest can say Mass, Consecrate the Eucharist, bless water to it make holy water, and the list just keeps going on and on.

> Remember the time I sprayed holy water on Sue's devil spirit? It was on my second trip and she was in the backseat of my car. Remember at the touch of the holy water she screamed in pain, as if she was burning? (Page 57)

A priest blessed the water, and after his blessing, the water certainly was, without a doubt, holy water. Of course, all we can see is water; we cannot see God's spirit world—yet.

I know Sue's devil spirit enjoys the rain. I have seen her running about in it, seemingly happily, a couple of times. But, holy water burns the devil. Again, I hope I am not too repetitive, but water *does* become holy water *after* a priest blesses it.

NOVEMBER 15, 1998

Today is Sunday, and I went to Mass at my father's church. When it was time to receive the Eucharist, I walked around the back of the church seats and then I turned to walk down the center aisle. As soon as I stepped into the center aisle and faced the front of the church, I felt Our Lord's Heavenly Presence radiating from the front of the church. It was very strong . . . I blessed myself.

I must say, in these last years, every time I have walked by or down the center aisle of all of the churches I have been in, I have felt His Heavenly Presence.

Today, His Presence was the strongest that I have ever felt Him. As I walked down the center aisle I saw Donna's white angel spirit, her large wings were fluttering to close as her spirit went into my body.

✝Later, I thought, Donna might have wanted to receive Jesus also . . .? and I welcomed her spirit to come into me at any Mass she desires. You may also wish to welcome your Guardian Angel.✝

DECEMBER 5, 1998

This evening God's saint told me, "Type," "Just type." I sat at my computer and I typed this:

My son had an operation about five days ago; he had an emergency appendectomy. The specialist took the child's appendix out only hours after seeing him. I was not with my son the evening he had this operation, I was at work, and I did not know about the operation until after it was over. His father and stepmother were with him.

The night before the operation, I had called my son and his stepmother answered the phone. My son and I talked for a short time. After I hung up I became very worried, and about twenty minutes later I called him back. This time he sounded terrible. He said, 'Now I'm sick.' And he quickly hung up the phone. I was worried, so I called back but no one answered the phone. Nervously, I paced throughout the apartment. I saw a white oval spirit appear and I heard God's saint say, "They will have to pay for this." I didn't know what he meant.

I called the police and asked them to check on my son. I knew if I went to his father's house it would only lead to trouble. The police called me back and said the child looked as if he was sick with flu-like symptoms. There was nothing else I could do. Since a month before my son's thirteenth birthday he has lived with his father and stepmother.

Tonight and last night I have my son with me at home. This will be my second and last night of visitation for the week. I am so sad. I know I can take good care of my child, the child I took care of for thirteen years. I realize I was so wrong in signing Physical Custody of my son over to his father, but now there is nothing I can do. I had, at the time, truly thought this would be best for the child.

DECEMBER 9, 1998

A man at work turned to look at me. With sadness, and a little defeat in his voice, he desperately said, 'God gives us the strength to handle everything.' My first reply to him was a simple, 'He does.' Then, as I walked away from him I realized that this man needed a more reassuring answer. I walked back to the man and said, 'God does give us what we can handle, and in very difficult times, in times when we have problems that we don't think we can handle, if we look to and pray to Him for strength . . . we can become even stronger, and closer to Him.'

✝This is our choice, in times of trial. (And we all have these times.) Do you choose to become bitter and hateful, or compassionate and loving? Do you choose to move closer to God? Please don't be tricked. Again . . . do you choose Heaven or Hell?✝

DECEMBER 18, 1998

For the last several weeks I have been working 50 to 55 hours a week at a mail center. Wow, Christmas mail. You can imagine the demand on us. I have just had time to eat, sleep, and work my 5:00 p.m. to 2:00 a.m., or longer shift.

Last night on break I noticed a newspaper on the table by me. I thought, Well, for a change I'll look to see what's going on outside of this building. Not the whole paper was on the table, but I thought, I'll read the part that's here. I looked at the obituaries.

When I read that my favorite cousin had passed away, I said aloud, 'Oh, my God.' I remembered when I had seen her the last time, after Mass. She did not look strong and I had wanted to go and visit her at her home soon, however, because of my work schedule I knew I would not have the time to visit her until after Christmas. I had planned on visiting her first thing after this Christmas job ended. I read that her Mass and burial were to be the next morning, and I definitely wanted to go. Figuring I would go home and rest a bit before attending her Mass.

During the Mass, I saw her white spirit zoom about the church. She said, "I feel good." "I feel so good." She was so happy, she said, "I would not miss my own funeral." I knew she was with her husband's spirit.

Only once during her Mass was she saddened, and this was at the Consecration of the Mass. I felt she was sad, not because her family had no Faith . . . but at their lack of Faith. She was sad because she wanted them to have more Faith in Jesus, in God. She loves them and worries about them so much.

Before I went up to receive Jesus, God's saint told me, "Touch her casket." I had no idea why he told me this. As I walked up the center aisle to receive Jesus, I touched her casket, which was in the middle aisle. I was surprised. As I touched her casket, I felt an energetic, almost electrical, spiritual feeling in the palm of my hand. I knew why God's saint had told me to touch her casket. I knew my cousin was now a light of God's; she was a saint.

✝From this, I have learned to pray much more deeply that we all may have more Faith. **Please . . . do not bring sadness or tears to the departed ones who love you.**✝

Chapter 5

More Guidance, More Answers

1999

JANUARY 1999

As I was praying, I looked to my picture of Our Blessed Mother. From behind the picture I saw a spiritual light, of a light blue color, that seemed to be trying to burst out. This light was so energetic and anxious, that it lifted the picture of Our Blessed Mother off of the wall, just a bit. The light shown from the bottom and right of the picture, and with it I heard a wonderful voice say, We re waiting.

I knew a large group of Our Blessed Mother s (of course, God s) angels are just waiting to come down from Heaven. These angels are eagerly waiting to help me, so I may help you.

JANUARY 9, 1999

I was watching TV today. On E.W.T.N. a priest was explaining the Book of Revelations, Chapter 6, The First Six Seals. When the priest read about the sixth seal being broken opened, he explained, Verse 13, ". . . the stars in the sky fell to Earth—like unripe figs shaken loose from the tree in a strong wind . . ."

> I remembered, there have been three or four times that I have looked into the sky and noticed a star high in the sky, and then it fell. This star would only be visible to me for a second or two after I had noticed it, and it had started to fall. I would notice this in the day or night sky.

> When I had seen this, God's saint would very sadly say, "Joyce, another one just fell." For many a month, I never knew what all this meant—stars falling?

> Today, as I was listening to the priest read from the Bible, I think I know what God's saint meant. The stars are not literally falling to Earth, but (Just my opinion, and I may very well be wrong here, but I feel this because I can feel God's saint's sadness.) some of, a very few of, God's lights from the sky are falling. (This is a spiritual vision.) So some of His angels, saints, etc., even to this day, may still be falling to Earth.

Remember in the Bible it states that God knows the stars, each by their name. God's lights do each have their names. (Again, this is just my opinion of what God's saint meant. He was always so sad when he showed me one of the stars falling, as he would say, "Joyce, another one just fell.")

JANUARY 19, 1999

I'm to work at our church bingo tonight, but before I begin I usually go into the church to pray the rosary. As I prayed the rosary I felt my energy being pulled from me. I looked. Behind the stained glass windows in the back of the church, I saw the shadow of a man who was standing in the outside hallway. Then he turned and walked away. I turned around and continued to pray. Suddenly my lip started to quiver, and I cried. The tears just overflowed from my eyes. I heard Our Blessed Mother sorrowfully say, "It's one of my children." Her sadness was so immense as she cried for this soul . . . her child.

I knew I was allowed to feel some of Our Heavenly Mother's sorrow, the sorrow she has for her children when they do things that are bad. Feeling this Mother's sorrow and her tears, just broke my heart. As I think this would have broken anyone's heart. **Please try to be good. Your Mother in Heaven does cry when you do wrong.**

(This honor was to bring me much closer to Our Heavenly Mother.)

JANUARY 21, 1999

I have been praying the rosary, not one, but usually two times a day lately. Many times I have prayed for my son. Today, as I began praying the rosary I saw a tall, very white spirit, briefly appear in my room. He said to me, "Many children don't have anyone to pray for them." Quickly the white image was gone. I thought for a second. I remembered Our Blessed Mother's tears for her children's sins. Then, as I looked at the picture of Our Blessed Mother, I said, 'I pray this rosary for your children.'

Later that day I called my son on the phone. As I was talking to him I noticed that the 3:00 p.m. prayers were about to begin on E.W.T.N. I told him I had to go, but before I hung up I told him I would say a prayer for him. After I hung up the phone I became so worried about missing some of the three o'clock prayers, that I quickly got my rosary beads and prayed the Chaplet of Divine Mercy for Our Blessed Mother's children.

Then at 3:30 p.m. the rosary began, and I remembered that I had told my son I would pray for him. Quietly, I said to Our Blessed Mother, 'I told my son I would pray for him. Could I pray this rosary for him?' Softly I heard her say, "This is for him." As I prayed the rosary, I felt that some very holy souls were also praying with me.

✝I can see how between January 19th and today, Our Blessed Mother has allowed me to become closer to her. Now I realize **how much our Heavenly Mother loves all of her children, and how she cries for each wrong we do**. I hope you don't mind me saying this again, but if you could feel Our Heavenly Mother's sorrow and tears for us, her children, your heart would just break.

Thank God. She has helped me to become a little more compassionate to all. When I remember her tears, I could not, as I hope you will not, be able to dislike anyone who has a mother like this.✝

Now when I pray the rosary, many times I choose to pray for all of Our Heavenly Mother's children. She is truly, a wise Mother.

JANUARY 27, 1999

We sat in the only subway shop in the town we live in. I heard a man talking about the terrible car accidents that have happened daily in town. Within the last four days there have been four accidents that have been very bad. In two of these accidents, helicopters had to be called in to rush the injured to the hospital. In the last accident, the car slid into a river and a little girl and her parent were trapped in the car until rescued. The man told us that the little girl is now in the hospital in critical condition.

That evening I went to my class at night school. As I drove home, into town, and not too far from home, I felt my car swerve toward the side of the road. It very much felt as if my car had swerved from the wind, and I wondered why this had happened. There definitely hadn't been any strong winds that night, so there was no apparent reason for my car to swerve. It was about 10:30 p.m.

Then, as I looked at the man driving toward me in a truck, God's saint said, "He is the one causing the accidents." I felt the very empty, and angry devil's spirit that was in this poor man. I knew this devil's spirit had caused the very bad car accidents in town within the last few days.

I saw a faint, large, and very angry black spirit rise to the left of the truck. I knew this devil's spirit came from the man to viciously go after God's saint, who was to the right of my car. I heard God's saint say to this devil, "You don't belong here." Then I knew God's saint raised his right hand a little, and after a very brief battle, this bad spirit was thrown into Hell. I knew the rash of vicious car accidents in town was over.

FEBRUARY 1999

As I drove tonight, God's saint said, "There's an army waiting." Shortly afterward, he said, "Look in the sky." I looked into the sky and thought—and felt—it's so huge. He said, "That's how many angels there are." I know when it's time; God's army of angels will come down from Heaven. This army, this Heavenly army, which is huge, is waiting for God to tell them that the time is right.

. . . . .

Just a bit later, in the distance, I saw a white spiritual light that went from Heaven to Earth. However, I knew this light was not like any of the lights from Heaven to Earth I had seen before. I knew this white light was of many flying angels . . . angels flying in a group to Earth.

In front of this vision was a black crow that was perched on one of the several barren branches of a tree. Very animal-like, the bird turned its head to look at the massive amount of angels flying to Earth. God's saint said, "They will all know." I knew, all the devils will know when their time on Earth is almost over. They will see God's huge, white army coming to Earth.

Late in the fall there was an invasion of ladybugs in my town. They were everywhere, and even homes were covered with these bugs. I live in an old apartment, so some of the bugs found their way into my home.

Now it's February and cold outside. I have plants in my home, so some of the ladybugs have decided to stay with me this winter. Well, for days I have been picking up the bugs then letting them go outside. I was really annoyed that my plants were deteriorating. (At the time I thought that the ladybugs were eating my plants, not the bugs about my plants.)

Yesterday, God's saint let me know that I should not be throwing the tiny bugs outside in the cold for the sake of my plants. He said, "There's an order of things." I know he's right, but I have had my plants for so long and I really enjoy them.

So, today, as I threw the bugs outside, I prayed that they might find happiness in Florida, or in a warmer climate. But, the point is—**God has made an order of things**.

†It seems to me that God has organized this order together with awareness. Awareness of a species seems to place it in its order. Or, the more awareness God has given to a species, the higher it is in the order of things. (My opinion only.)†

FEBRUARY 8, 1999

As I prayed to Jesus, a great feeling of humility overtook me. Still praying, I prostrated myself, and then I heard God's saint say, "Thank you. That will last me another hundred years."

> I remembered back to when I was in church praying and I had heard a poor, lonely, and stubborn spirit say, 'That will last me another one hundred years.' (Page 100)
>
> (Of course he was being sarcastic, but this shows you how slowly Purgatory must pass.)

Today as I heard God's saint say this, I knew that our stubborn friend was finally out of Purgatory, and I knew he was now a light of God's. I also realized that someday I will know who our friend is. I thanked God for letting me know this, and I was glad for our friend.

FEBRUARY 10, 1999

I was driving on the highway, Rte. 91, passing by several towns and miles and miles of woods. I thought to Sue, Look at this beautiful Earth. How can't you be happy here? From my heart, I said, 'Thank you, God.'

I felt the presence of God's saint, and then I looked to my right, into the vast, far away woods. On a large hill, I saw a huge white spirit and I heard this spirit say to me, "I take care of these woods." His spirit was vague, but I knew his image was vague because his spirit was so spread out over the woods, as he was trying to cover a large amount of the woods. I knew he takes care of all of the woods in the large area under and about him. Also, that he takes care of all of the creatures, from the smallest to the largest, in these woods. I knew his white spirit did this for God.

FEBRUARY 11, 1999

I sat in church and looked around, wishing that there were more people in church. Then I prayed to God that the churches would be crowded again, as they were when I was a child. I prayed, God, maybe we could do something to bring more people back into the churches. God's saint said, "Even if you did a miracle right here, now, many would not believe." When he said this—I knew that we are in for a great catastrophe.

FEBRUARY 16, 1999

I was praying the rosary in church. As I looked at a statue of Our Blessed Mother I heard her say, "Joyce, put your hands together." The statue of Our Heavenly Mother had her hands together in prayer. She continued, "Now, pray the whole rosary like that." I finished the rosary with my hands together.

At the end of the rosary, I realized that by keeping my hands together, in prayer, I had a certain feeling of light in my hands . . . . I knew this knowledge was another gift.

FEBRUARY 17, 1999

I lost my temper last night and said some angry things to a lady I was working with. Now, when I was at home, I became so ashamed at what I had done. As I sat at my computer typing, I felt Jesus was standing behind me. Then I felt an even stronger shame, because I had lost my temper and from this anger I had said something cruel. Totally ashamed—I stopped typing and put my head down.

I heard **Our Blessed Mother's soft and gentle voice say, "You must have more Love and Compassion."** When she said this it really hit home. If I had more love and compassion I would not have gotten angry.

I also remembered when God's saint had said to me, "Have more Faith and Love." Both this saint and our most Loving Blessed Mother have reminded me to try and have more love.

FEBRUARY 18, 1999

Today I felt much pain in my heart because of something that has been happening in my life, and has been going on for a long time. Then quickly this pain was gone—I knew God's angel had taken this pain from me. (See October 1998, Page 217.)

I had known why some of our tears and pain are sometimes gone so quickly, but now I knew where these tears and pain go. I knew my pain, which was taken by God's angel, in God's justice, will inevitably be given back to the bad people who had caused me this pain. I knew God will see this is done. God knows our pain and suffering.

The people who cause us pain will inevitably know the pain they have caused, and they will feel this pain . . . they will receive this (their) sorrow and pain. God, the Final Judge, will see this is done.

✝Please do not hurt others. God watches us, and He can *feel* our hearts. **I realize we should actually feel sorrow for the poor people who choose to hurt others.** I try to feel this . . . I know our Guardian Angels feel sorrow for these poor souls. They tell me to "feel sorry for them," letting me know that, **We will all face God someday**. However, I must admit, I have a way to go yet before I am as good with this feeling as God's angels and saints are. Let's all pray that our strength, compassion, and Faith will continue to grow.✝

MARCH 15, 1999

I was sitting at home, alone, eating lunch. I felt a strong love, the love that comes from someone loving a child. Then I heard a man's voice quietly say, "We love you as a child." I looked up and saw a small white spirit figure, but only as it vanished.

✝God's love for us is within all of His lights and Guardians. In God's family we are the youngest children, just learning and still growing.✝

(As a mother, I know the love for a child is forgiving, enormous and pure.)

APRIL 1999

As I drove, I turned a sharp corner and went down a narrow street before driving on a small bridge that went over a stream. On my right, I saw, sitting by a large tree before the bridge, the spirit of a boy who was about eight to ten years old. His spirit looked so sad and desolate. He sat with his knees up and his head down. God's saint said, "Joyce, he died there." I prayed for his soul and asked that he now turn to God and light.

Days later I drove on this same narrow road and looked for this same tree, but it wasn't there. I knew what I had previously seen was a vision of the past.

APRIL 8, 1999

After Mass I stayed in the church to pray. When the church was empty I walked to the tabernacle, and as I stood close to one of the walls, God's saint said to me, "Joyce, touch the walls." I put my hands on the church's wall, and in my palms I felt I was touching a very live, heavenly spiritual being. God's saint said, "This is a part of me."

Later the thought occurred to me, that this is why some churches are viciously burned. Evil knows that the church is a part of Jesus.

MAY 6, 1999—FIFTH SUNDAY OF EASTER

I was sitting in church, waiting for Mass to begin. As I looked toward the altar, I noticed that the large Pascal Candle was a bit shorter than it had been the last time I was in this church, two weeks ago. I heard God's saint say, "The candle burns and their time goes, Joyce. They don't know." I looked at the people sitting in the pews in front of me and I felt they were so unaware of this, then I felt such a sad compassion for them . . . God's saint's compassion.

✝Again I would like to remind you, **Please use your time here wisely. WHAT YOU DO WITH THIS TIME GOD GIVES YOU HERE ON EARTH IS SO IMPORTANT. OUR TIME HERE IS ONLY SO LONG . . . THEN IT IS GONE.**✝

I was watching E.W.T.N., and a woman on TV was thanking God for the gift He had given her of motherhood. I am a mother also, and as I had done many times before, I thanked God for the gift of a child . . . He has given me one of His children to take care of.

✝God's saint said, **"Your greatest gift, Joyce, was the love you were able to give."**✝

Later on TV they mentioned The Woman clothed with the Sun, Our Lady of Lourdes. I thought to myself, I know what the sparkling Bright Sunlight is.

I remembered the time that I was looking at my picture of Our Blessed Mother and I thought, Where does the angel Donna come from? I heard a soft reply, "From here." I looked at Our Blessed Mother's heart.

I know Our Blessed Mother is adorned with many angels. These angels are very pure and bright, and their stars sparkle everywhere about, and within their Heavenly Mother . . . as so many sparkling suns.

How wonderful God is to His Mother and her angel . . .

How wonderful this must be for her and her angels . . .

MAY 18, 1999

I was walking through our beautiful park, following a path that goes around several baseball diamonds. At one of the diamonds a children's baseball team, in which the small children must have only been around six years old, were practicing hitting the ball. I stopped to watch as one boy went up to the mound with his bat; he was thin and didn't look very strong. I felt sad for him and I asked God's saint to help him.

Then it was the next boy's turn to bat and I continued to walk. Thinking of the first boy I had watched, I thought, He's my favorite. Please help him. I heard God say, "You must not take favorites." I knew He was also letting me know that not taking favorites is something I should work on to improve my soul. I must admit I do take favorites. God knows us very well.

As I walked, I looked at a man in front of me that was jogging toward me. I could not help but notice the man, and that he had a very evil look on his face. God's saint said, "They will know." He was letting me know that the evil spirits will know if I take favorites. I know that if I learn this lesson, I will grow greatly inside, in both love and compassion.

JULY 4, 1999

It was a beautiful morning, so for the 8:30 a.m. Mass, the small chapel I was in had their windows open. Near the end of the service a strong wind came in through a window and blew by one of the altar candles. I thought for sure the small wax candle would be blown out by the wind. Surprisingly, the candle's light leaned, not away from the wind . . . but toward it. I heard God's saint say, "Against all odds." I knew he meant, I will succeed against all odds. I thought, We will succeed against all odds—here on Earth.

JULY 17, 1999

I was at a wedding service. Two brothers, one that was getting married, knelt before the church's altar. It was so beautiful. I prayed for their souls. Then God's saint said, "They will hardly come to my altar." With this he also let me know that these brothers' souls would only have a bit of God's Light.

✝Jesus has told us to lead a good life, and many of us do without going to church, but . . . . Where is your respect for Our Creator and Heavenly Father, His Son, and the Holy Spirit? Cannot we all just give Him one complete hour of worship every seven days?

In church we receive Jesus in the Holy Eucharist. I am sure that each time we receive Jesus' spirit in the Eucharist, God's Light within us becomes brighter and stronger. (Here and for Eternity.)✝

JULY 24, 1999

As I was writing down a passage from the Bible, I felt a wonderful tingling feeling all over my body. God's marvelous angel Donna said, "When you write from the Bible, you gain a special blessing."

NOVEMBER 24, 1999

It was a beautiful day; the weather was very mild for this time of the year, so I was eating lunch by my open kitchen window. I looked outside. This back window overlooks our apartment parking lot, a bit of woods, and then the backs of some of the homes on the next street. One of these neighbors has a horse, which was outside in his fenced-in area on the other side of a small wooded area.

As I was eating, I briefly saw a black spirit in the woods close to the horse. For that second I think that the horse also saw this evil spirit, because as I saw this spirit angrily looking at the horse, the horse seemed to look back at him as he put his head up, whinnied several times, then paced about before going into his barn. God's saint said, "The horse was very brave." I know the devils want to destroy all that is God's.

Now, I was amazed that the black spirit was at least five feet up on the trunk of a tree; however, he was horizontal. His feet, the bottom of him, was somehow hanging onto the tree, and his head and body were horizontal to his bottom.

About a minute later, after I had gotten over thinking about what I had just seen . . . a pure spirit quietly said to me, "They can do a lot more than you. We have to stay very close." I know all of our guardians are very close to us.

(Today, July 13, 2000, I was typing this page. A black car stopped briefly on the road that goes by my apartment, and then the computer went out, as did all of the electricity in my home, for a few seconds. God's saint said, "They are very strong." I got a bit scared and was going to stop typing for the day, but then I realized I have to continue.)

2000

JANUARY 16, 2000

I was in church at a Sunday service. I felt compassion in myself, then a tear filled my eye. I heard God's saint say, "Because of what will happen." I knew something wonderful was about to happen in this church, and I wondered what it would be.

About five minutes later, most, if not all, and certainly all of the people who were in front of me, stood up and walked toward the front of the church to receive Jesus in the Eucharist. As I looked at the people standing, I heard God's heavenly saint say, "This."

FEBRUARY 2000

After I had finished my grocery shopping I drove through the parking lot, toward the main road and home. I saw a dog with its head out of the open window of a passing car on the main road, but he really noticed me. The dog's eyes began to turn to a very angry stare, and I knew a devil's spirit was in this dog. Then I saw a small white spirit fly by . . . in between the passing car and me, and quickly the dog's attention was turned to the white spirit. I knew I was again allowed to see God's guardians at work.

Again I thought about God allowing me to communicate with His angels and saints. I thought, They won't believe me. God's saint replied, "We are telling you things that are easier to believe now." I know I will be told more, and some of the things I will be told later about God's spirit world will be hard for us to comprehend. They are still going slowly with me, and you. (Written about in the Second Trip, Page 91.)

FEBRUARY 7, 2000

It was the middle of the week, and the middle of the day. I knew the church I was about to drive by would be locked up, but I drove my car onto the small access road that loops from the main road. On this small road, I parked my car in front of the walkway that goes directly to the front doors of the church and the altar.

I heard God's saint say, "Some will be closer than others." I realized, some of us, as spirits, would be allowed closer to God than others. I also realized, that the closer our spirits are to God, the more

Light we will have, the more Graces, the more Peace; and in our human words, the more power we will have.

MARCH 2000

I was watching TV. A father had heard that, years before, an old friend had raped his young daughter. In anger, the father killed the man who had raped his daughter. I felt so sorry for the father's soul. I thought, Someday he will have to face God, and he will have to face Him with this terrible sin. I prayed for God to forgive this father. God's saint said in reply, "It has been written thru the ages." I thought of the times we have been told not to kill another human, and I thought of the fifth Commandment: **You shall not kill**.

MARCH 19, 2000

At Sunday Mass God's saint again reminded me, "You will shake, Joyce." I know that when I see more of the devil's spirits, I will be very scared and I will shake. Devil's spirits are about, but God protects us from seeing these very angry beasts that are not human. When I see more of them, I know it will be for a reason and I hope God will give me the courage to continue to write. **Only God could give me this courage and strength.**

> I remember, months ago, when I felt very energetic and strong, I said to God's saint, 'I am strong. I don't need God.' Well . . . within a minute . . . I felt as if I was no more than a weak mass of nothing. Then, I knew God's strength had left me, and as I realized **God gives us our strength**—I became strong again.

Our Loving, and *very* patient Father did not punish me, but, He *did* let me know . . . .

MARCH 22, 2000

I was at work. The work was so overwhelming that I couldn't help but get a little discouraged because I had to work so hard. God's saint said to me, "You will be rewarded for your work." I knew that in Heaven, we will all be rewarded for our labors. He will justly weigh our efforts and work, as only God could. Your work is most certainly of value.

MARCH 28, 2000

I was hoping I would not run into a man who pulls a lot from me because he leaves me very tired. Then, with God's saint's help, I thought, What about his soul? What about helping his soul, and souls? I knew I must have more patience and not worry about being tired.

✝I realize powers are not important to God's lights. What is important to them is helping souls. **God's lights give up so much to be here on Earth to help us.**

God's saints are what we all should strive to be, very loving and caring toward our brothers and sisters, and not selfish. (As I just retyped this, I thought, This is so much like what our Catholic religion, and many other religions teach us to be. We should all take such pride in our religions.)✝

APRIL 2000

At Mass . . . as I looked at the altar, God's saint said to me, **"It will be the center of the universe."**

APRIL 5, 2000

I looked about. It was such a beautiful day. Saint Robert said, "There will be another spring."

APRIL 16, 2000

At the Consecration of Sunday Mass today I cried; I knew these were God's saint's tears, and he was in me crying. I looked in front of me, into the emptiness, and I knew this saint was thinking of, and looking at, some of the horrors in Earth's future. Now, I felt his emotions—I'm sure not his full emotions—however, he did not let

me see his vision. I am sure this was to shield me from the horrors that he saw.

APRIL 18, 2000

Not until today, as I looked at the trees in bloom and the flowers blossoming everywhere, did I fully realize what Saint Robert had meant on April 5, 2000. I knew that God had again granted us another spring. The spirit world realized that this wonderful gift was just given to us. I knew prayers, ours and many of God's loving lights' prayers, were heard.

. . . . .

Later in the day, I was retyping the beginning of this book. Sadly, I remembered that my mother's spirit so desperately wanted to tell them . . . but her spirit cannot communicate with us. She won't be able to tell them. God's angel said, "You will."

APRIL 19, 2000

Retyping again today. As I typed the word *mall* from the beginning of the book, I mistakenly typed the word *Mass*. At the same time, I saw one of God's tiny white stars light up on my keyboard and say to me, "Type this." I thought for a minute, and then I realized how much I, and my life, have changed. I used to go to the mall, now I go to Mass.

APRIL 29, 2000

Passover has just gone by, and I thought, Many of the first followers of Christ were Jewish. Saint Robert said, "They choose to break bread with Him."

MAY 3, 2000

I was reading in the newspaper that there are now many adults entering the Catholic religion. Saint Robert said, "They are getting ready." Although this was all he said, I knew by the bit of strength in this saint's voice, that God, His spirits, and the world, are getting ready for The Battle.

MAY 9, 2000

Dears, it is not by mere chance that the balance of the Earth has continued for so long. Today Saint Robert said, "We must keep the cycle going."

MAY 25, 2000

I was sitting at work and became very tired and tense. Although I couldn't see the girl in the work cubicle beside me, I knew a devil's spirit was in her and she was pulling my energy very hard from me. I thought, This is terrible. Down here on Earth—this is terrible. God's saint said, "Heaven was terrible." My first thought was, This is such a strange thing to hear about Heaven. We always think of Heaven as being the most peaceful and beautiful place.

Then I knew that before and during the war in Heaven, Heaven must have been terrible. Angels turning bad and pulling from other angels; and the good angels, as Saint Robert had very sadly said before, "You should have seen the angels just lying there."

. . . . .

Later in the day, I was thinking about a girl I had known. She seemed uncaring and she pulled a lot of energy from people. I think she was aware she was doing this. I wondered, Where is she now, and is she still doing this? God's saint said, "She is choosing."

✝Now, would you choose Heaven or Hell? When you choose to be caring or uncaring, giving or selfish, loving or hateful . . . you choose Heaven or Hell.✝

MAY 26, 2000

Saint Robert said, "She will show you how." I knew he meant my Guardian Angel, Donna, will show me how to be good, and I knew he was referring to my past as well as my future.

> But, I thought back . . . it took years. I had a lot of anger, greed, selfishness, and so little forgiveness for so long. God's saint and angel Donna so patiently watched me fail again and again . . . and I know they cried for my errors for so long.

Yet, even now, as far as I think I have come, I know I still have further to go . . . however, these wonderful lights have not given up on me. **Thank God for His patience and His patient Helpers.**

MAY 30, 2000

I woke up about 10:30 p.m. and turned on the TV. There was a special on about a past president of ours. As the program started to show the prisoners of Beirut I got up to turn off the TV, however, just before I got to the TV a tiny star lit up and I heard, "Watch this." I sat back down. The show went on and told of the president's arms deal with Iran and our country's arms deal with Russia. Then I felt it was OK to turn off the TV so I did; and I went back to rest.

I thought hmm . . . our country has made a lot of money selling war machines to other countries, vaguely I thought of Israel. Then I thought, There must be other countries we also make money on by selling them our war machines. Saint Robert said, "Remember this . . ."

(Again, he said, "Remember this.")

MAY 31, 2000

I was going to make myself a roast beef sandwich, and I went to take a few slices of meat out of the deli wrapping I noticed blood on the wrapping. Saint Robert said to me, "There is blood in this."

Then I knew the evil spirits stopped him very quickly before he could say anything else to me. I still wonder what he wanted to tell me.

JUNE 2000

I was reading the *Maronite Voice*, Volume 6, Issue No. 10, June 2000, Page 11. "Pope Reveals, Third Fàtima Secret." The third secret seemed to be that the Pope would be attacked and shot, as he had been. Saint Robert said, "There will be more." I knew there would be more attempts on this Pope's life, and the Popes who follow him.

A thunderstorm was starting and as I listened to the thunder I thought, God, thank you. Now some will be saved. I was thinking God is using His power (storms) to control the devils, and I was hoping some people could, and would now freely choose to be good. Donna flew through my room and said, "It doesn't stop them. It just delays them." I knew what she meant. We will have a bit more peace for a while, but the devil's spirits and *our choice* . . . is only delayed.

Please try to be good, no matter what.

There was a great fire burning in the western part of the United States. As I prayed for the end of the fire, Saint Robert said, "This has been going on long enough." I knew God and His lights are now a bit angry with us, and this fire will not stop soon. **I fear we are at a turning point, and we may see the deterioration of the Earth's cycle.**

JUNE 4, 2000

Months ago, as I was walking through a parking lot, I was kicking up dust. Saint Robert said, "It will be this dry." I knew we were in for a drought.

Today, and for well over a month, we have had a lot of rain; however, my thoughts went back to Saint Robert telling me about the dry weather. As I looked at a tree, and even felt a bit of life coming from it, this saint said, "This is for them." I knew the rain we are now having is to raise the underground water level, so the trees will not die in the dry weather to come.

When I was at work I told a girl about this and she laughed, saying, 'Why do the trees get it and not us?' Well, later when I was at home, I thought, We have not been the best of children. Hard times may be what it takes to bring some of us closer to, and even back to God. The trees and Earth will give us more time to be saved.

So every day when I look at the rain I sadly think, The underground water level is still rising. The drought will be that much longer. God Loves us . . . and He wants to save all of us.

JUNE 8, 2000

I was at work and I started to really worry for my hometown. I was hoping the people who had lived there did not, and the people who live there do not, have many sins on their souls. Saint Robert said, "The lightning will hit the ground lightly there." I knew that on the Judgment Day, the day when we will have the big storm, God's great lightning will not hit the ground in my hometown hard . . . there will be no need, as not that many will fall. (The lightning hitting the ground will open it up, and the devils will fall.)

JUNE 15, 2000

I haven't slept well for three nights now; I am so worried for my son, who is living with his father and stepfamily. This morning as I drove to work, I was still worried. I was thinking about evil spirits and all of the children of God who choose to be so cruel to their brothers and sisters.

Then I felt just a little of Our Blessed Mother's almost coldness toward these bad children. I knew this Mother's coldness was because she had watched for so long, as these bad children were so cruel to their siblings. I understood how this Heavenly Mother can look at some of her children and no longer have the same love in her heart for them . . . I thanked my Guardian Angel for allowing me to understand Our Blessed Mother and Heaven more.

A bit down the road a saint said to me, "You'll understand more as we go along."

JUNE 25, 2000

During Mass we prayed The Creed. As we said, " . . . He will come again in glory to judge the living and the dead, and His kingdom will have no end . . . ." The words seemed to be louder than the rest of the prayer. Then Saint Robert said to me, "This is what they believe." I knew, as I looked at the people in church saying this prayer together, that this is what they hope and wait for, our time in Heaven. (This was a wonderful gift, as are all of God's gifts.)

JULY 6, 2000

I slowly walked toward a window in my living room, the window that faces the main road in front of my apartment building. I heard an ambulance drive by and saw its lights flashing. As I looked down at the lights, my left eye just filled with tears. I knew these were the tears of the saint that was in me. He said, "They took him, Joyce."

✝Please lead a good life . . . so that God's angels may protect you; not only in your lifetime on Earth, but also protect your eternal soul after your body's death—so that God's lights may guard and protect you from the evil that does wait.✝

JULY 8, 2000

After church I came home to write. As I put my floppy disk into the computer, God's saint said to me, "This is how you will fight."

JULY 11, 2000

A priest was saying Mass, and had his hands together in prayer. God's saint said to me, "Joyce, there's so much power in those hands and he doesn't know it."

JULY 12, 2000

I was in church early this morning to pray, at least two hours before Mass was to begin. I said my rosary in the empty church. At one time I walked up to the tabernacle and touched the stand it was on. As I touched it I felt a spiritual circle, of a little more than an inch, in the palm of my hand, and I heard, "This is where we touch."

When I completed my rosary, I again touched the stand. I heard, "Remember this."

(This was a very good, Remember this.)

JULY 18, 2000

I was the only person sitting in church, and it was at least one hour before the 8:00 a.m. Mass. As I sat in the corner saying my rosary, I could hear, but not see, a man who came in the front doors of the church. (He was around the corner.) He moaned a bit, it was an unusual moan, and then I couldn't hear him anymore. I continued to pray the rosary.

Before I finished my rosary I saw him, as he very nonchalantly, walked up the center aisle toward the altar. He turned his head and saw me sitting in the corner, under the statue of Our Blessed Mother. Then he turned and left the church.

✝I realized one of the reasons why Jesus comes down to Earth (is present) and into his churches, so he can see how we freely choose. I was awed that Our Lord, Our King, quietly comes down here to face our disrespect, as well as our love.✝

JULY 19, 2000

I was watching a Mass on TV. As I looked at the parishioners I thought, God, they are all so old. Then the TV showed the priest and Saint Robert said, "Even the priests are getting old." I thought, What is going to happen? What is going on? God's saint calmly replied, "You'll see." Once before I was worried about the churches and he had given me the same reply, "You'll see." I wonder what will happen?

JULY 25, 2000

I was watching the news. The Middle East Peace Talks have broken down, there is no peace agreement. As I walked through the house, Saint Robert said, "**It is time to separate.**" I know God will be watching, as the people affected by this *choose* to react.

JULY 31, 2000

I would like to show you how perfect and knowing God's angels are.

> Months ago, after I had parked my car and was walking toward the back door of my apartment, I vaguely saw the white spirit image of Donna in front of my apartment door. I heard her say, "Come on, Joyce." I was tired, so as I walked I put my head down and quietly replied, 'I'm coming.'

Today, as I walked from my car to the same back door, I felt Donna's angel spirit in front of my apartment door again. She said, "Come on, Joyce." But today, along with her loving care, I also heard in her voice, "We will have to fight a bit of a battle here

tonight." I knew that this battle would be small in comparison to the large battle God's angels will have to fight to protect me in the future. And I knew that before this other battle is to happen, Donna will let me know.

AUGUST 2, 2000

I was thinking of how much I love my son, how much I want to cook for him, keep his clothes clean, and to just watch him sleep, safely in our home . . . . Then as I thought, To serve him. I remembered when God's saint had said, "We are here to serve."

✝I now know—to Serve . . . is to Love.✝

AUGUST 3, 2000

Today I mailed out letters to the editorial department of some local newspapers. I wrote about the drought to come after this abundance of rain stops. (June 4, 2000) As I put the letters in the envelopes, I heard God's saint say, "You are fighting." I thought, This is my first effort to publicly write about one of my visions.

AUGUST 5, 2000

Today I understood the following about God's saint telling me to "Remember this . . ."

- When he showed me the vision of the future on November 17, 1996 (Page 160). I knew that although the two women were seemingly fighting on this busy Main Street . . . no one cared, everyone was <u>indifferent</u>.
- On May 30, 2000 (Page 245) this saint wanted me to remember that our country makes money by selling war machines.
- A few days ago I heard a single mother brag to several men that she had two other children. One of her children stood by her; she had very tight and skimpy clothes on and was trying to look very pleasing to the men. When the men left,

the mother told the little girl, who must have only been eleven or twelve years old, 'Keep trying.' As I walked away Saint Robert said, "Remember this . . ."

In these cases this saint wanted me to, Remember this, because when the time comes for His children's chastisement, he wants me to remember our sins.

AUGUST 6, 2000

My heart is very saddened when I see a person who knows that a bad spirit is in or about him, trying to get rid of this spirit by telling it to go into or about another person. Also, many times this person tries to get rid of this bad spirit by telling it to go into a person who knows nothing at all about bad spirits. Therefore, the poor innocent person, is a victim indeed.

Of course, you may tell an evil spirit to go, but please, not to go into someone else. If you are badgered by evil, pray to God for help—trust Him. Turn to God, His angels and saints, and Heaven. It is a terrible thing to have a devil about you, but it is worse for you to deliberately try to send this evil after one of your <u>brothers or sisters</u>. So please, in this trial, choose to become closer to God and Heaven. This may not be a short or easy trial for you. (Again, these underlined words are words that God's helpers gave to me as I wrote.)

AUGUST 15, 2000

Months ago, as I watched three people walking down the street, Saint Robert said to me, "One out of three will fall." Dears, out of every three people, two will be saved and one will fall.

AUGUST 19, 2000

I was allowed to feel some of God's wonderful saint's Love again. As I was driving I noticed a boy, about ten years old, crossing the road with his bike. He was caught somewhat in the middle of the road and he stood there, quickly looking both ways, before peddling his bike across the street. As I looked at the alert child, I thought, "Magnificent." I was totally awed by this creation of Gods . . . this child, this human.

Also, I knew that in those seconds, that I had felt this Heavenly awareness, any, and all, of God's human creations, would have awed me. Our bodies, our spirits, our minds, are just magnificent. This creation of Gods is just Magnificent! I knew God's saint had allowed me to feel some of God's awe and Love for us.

After I passed the child and this feeling left me, I looked into the sky. I saw a large group of birds flying overhead . . . I knew where God's saint was now. He said, "This will be one of your best pages." I wondered, How?

Later in the day I drove through a wooded area. It had rained the night before, and when I saw the rays of sun coming through the very light fog and the trees, I stopped my car. It was beautiful. God's saint said, "It's still coming down." I knew what he meant—God is still sending us His Light.

I parked my car. God's saint said, "Stay in your car for a while." I sat in awe at the beautiful sights before me—The Light and Life of God. Water fell from a few of the leaves in the trees, and I thought, God is also still sending us His water. I began praying the rosary, "Glory be to the Father, the Son, and the Holy Spirit . . ." I again thought of the child on the bike and the magnificence of creation, and human creation. Continuing the prayer I truly meant, from my heart, **"Glory be to the Father, the Son, and the Holy Spirit . . ."**

I realized this is one of my best pages, but not because of anything I have done—because of God's Creations and His continual Light to us . . . His Love.

AUGUST 24, 2000

I was at Mass. Saint Robert said, "When they mix equal parts of wine and water." I knew he was referring to the day when the priest mixes equal parts of wine and water at the Consecration of the Mass; however, I do not know what will happen on that day.

AUGUST 28, 2000

I had worked the 11:00 p.m. to 7:00 a.m. shift, and gotten out of work early. So I wanted to see if there was a seven o'clock Mass in the nearby church, but there wasn't, and the church doors were locked. I sat in my car in the empty parking lot, deciding to wait and pray the rosary.

As I prayed, I looked behind the church at their park and baseball diamonds. I noticed a large group of birds sitting peacefully on a tall light pole. Then I saw a crow that was flying about and cawing very loudly, seemingly at the peaceful birds. Finally the crow flew toward the birds, and finding a shorter pole that was just big enough for himself, he perched there, quietly. I thought, This crow is so much like the devil's. Unsettled as they watch 'humans,' who are peaceful and settled. They watch, very unsettled and angry, knowing that a large group of us will go to Heaven—Heaven our Home. Can you imagine the pain and emptiness the poor devil souls must feel, knowing that they will never be able to go home?

After the crow sat peacefully on the pole, close to the other birds, I felt, Well, at least here on Earth the devils get some relief. They are not in Hell—I knew Our Blessed Mother, who loves all of her children, is happy for this bit of (peaceful) time these bad children have on Earth.

As I continued to pray the rosary I said the prayer from Fatima, "Oh, my Jesus, forgive us our sins. Save us from the fires of Hell. Lead all souls to Heaven, especially those in most need of thy Mercy." I realized that this prayer was given to us from Our Blessed Mother's love. She wants us to pray to Jesus to save us from the fires of Hell; because after a spirit goes through the fires of Hell . . . it is

too late for them. Their souls lose much humanity. (July 22, 1996, Page 141)

Please pray this *very* good prayer to Jesus, with His Mother—Our Blessed Heavenly Mother.

AUGUST 30, 2000

I was thinking, soon I will be able to print my book and make it known. Saint Robert said, "Then you will begin to fight." I know that when I am writing I am fighting, but printing my book will begin my fight.

SEPTEMBER 2000

As I drove home I saw dust on the side of the road blow about in one place and I heard the gentle, pure, voice from the past. The voice that came with the whirlwinds. He said, "It will come." I knew he was telling me that the long dry time God's saint had told me about, will come.

SEPTEMBER 1, 2000

As I read the newspaper I saw a name that certainly seemed to be a Jewish person's name. Then Saint Robert said, "Joyce, you have to be patient with them. You are going to do a lot of damage to them."

Later in the day I was wondering if I should write what God's saint had told me today. He said, "This must be written." I asked God to help me to have patience when I need it.

SEPTEMBER 4, 2000

I was watching the Jerry Lewis MDA (Muscular Dystrophy Association) Telethon, and I heard two speakers that are affected by neuromuscular diseases, speak. It seems that researchers are close to a cure. God's saint also said, "They are." Then I saw a spiritual light in the room and I heard Donna say, "It was God's Light."

Now, I know this angel said *was* instead of *is* or *is to be*. She said this as if there is a cure now. To God's lights, whom I am sure can travel through time very easily . . . *was* and *is* can be very easily transposed in their speech. So, when they talk to me, sometimes they use past tense for future events. (I'm sure this was not an error on God's angel's part, but something else God has allowed me to write about.)

SEPTEMBER 5, 2000

Today I sat in church, saying my rosary before the morning Mass was to begin. I looked up at the Jubilee 2000 emblem. I noticed there were five birds in this circle, not four, as I had seen last week. Then I realized that last week when I had seen only four birds and God's saint had talked to me, this was a vision. At that time I didn't write down what God's saint had said to me, but let me tell you:

About one week ago I was looking at the Jubilee 2000 emblem. I saw one large white bird and three other birds in this circle. I thought it was a little odd, as the white bird was twice as large as the other three, equal in size, birds. As I looked at the three birds, with their wings open and all touching the one large bird, I felt the three were not only touching . . . but were connected to the one. Saint Robert said, "It will support the other three." My thought was the Catholic religion will support the other three, very related religions. I wondered what three religions our Catholic religion would be so connected to.

Later I knew that the three, connected to the one, was a vision of the future.

SEPTEMBER 14, 2000

Today I went to our city's cathedral. As I walked into the rectory, out walked a group of people. They told me they were leaving to go stand across the street from the abortion clinic, where they

were going to pray the rosary for the babies. Well, the timing seemed just right and they invited me to go with them and also pray the rosary. So I walked along with them and prayed. However, the rosary turned out to be the complete three mysteries and three to four songs.

As we prayed I noticed a white butterfly by the clinic building. God's angel, Donna, said, "It is very pure." I know these babies' souls are so pure. Also, she said, "Other angels are here, to take the soul (babies' souls) and record this on the mothers' soul."

✝This is very sad. Please pray that the mothers' hearts are changed *before* this is recorded . . .✝

SEPTEMBER 21, 2000

I was lying down and trying to sleep for the night. I felt an unusually hot, almost burning, feeling on the back of my neck. I knew I was feeling the end of a devil's spirit's finger as he touched my neck. I knew that he knew I realized his finger was touching me. He said, 'I don't care.' God's saint said to me, "He won't be here long." My thought was, He must be a soul that has just turned into a devil. He is misbehaving and God's saints, through God, will not allow him to be on the Earth too much longer. God's saint continued, "Now you see one of the sins."

✝Please do not choose to live your life with the outlook of: I don't care. I don't care about my brothers or sisters. I don't care about anyone or anything. This choice, this lack of love, this emptiness, will inevitably stay with our souls for eternity.✝

OCTOBER 3, 2000

I was driving home and I looked over to the river. The water in the river was down, and as I looked toward the banks of the river I could also see at least a foot and a half of the riverbed. God's saint said, "It's getting lower." I knew, of course, that he realized I could see that the river was getting lower, but he was also telling me that the underground water level was getting lower, too.

Remember this saint telling me several months ago (June 4, 2000. Page 246) about the underground water level rising in preparation for the long, dry spell to come? (I know this drought has not come yet and I know the underground water level is going down. I do not know what God has planned, but this is what God's saint had told me.)

Then I saw a vision of God's large, beautiful rainbow in the sky; however, this vision was vague. God's saint said, "It's coming." And I knew he was happy.

Now, the vision was vague, but I knew this was because our saint was telling me, The time for God's great rainbow in the sky is coming; this event that will signify the end of the bad times and evil on Earth (also see August 19, 1997, Page 188). However, our time, our terrible times, the end of times, which we much get through *before* the rainbow comes—are only beginning. **Therefore, God's large rainbow is not here, but just beginning to show.**

OCTOBER 6, 2000

Years ago, I had thought about the people in the Middle East fighting over the land there. So I had asked God's saint, 'Who does this land belong to?' He replied, "To the people who were living there."

Today, after I decided to write this, God's saint said to me, "Wash your hands." I did. When I was washing my hands with the soap I had taken from the pump of my soap dispenser, a bit of the soap dripped from the dispenser. As I noticed the soap begin to fall, God's saint continued, "This is how their blood flows."

OCTOBER 18, 2000

As I drove home on the freeway, I admired and was in awe at the beautiful colors of the trees and brush along the side of the road. There were several vibrant shades of green, red, and yellow; and these colors were even mixed together alongside the road. I said to God, 'Thank you.'

I felt God's saint in me as he sadly held back his tears. He said, "You are the only one that said, 'Thank You.'" I knew he meant, I was the only one who said this, today.

OCTOBER 26, 2000

As I was waking up this morning, I heard a child crying. This child said, 'It hurts.' God's saint said to me, "Don't forget." (God's Children's home.)

I have been waiting for some work to be done for me, again I have been waiting too long. I thought, I will put more time into my work for this book.

OCTOBER 29, 2000

Today in church, before the Mass started, I saw someone being very cruel to someone else. I thought, Even in church . . . this is very bad. God's saint again said, "He is getting mad." At least three times in the last few months this saint has told me that God is getting mad.

After receiving Jesus in the Eucharist, I went back to my seat and knelt down, putting my head on the back of the pew in front of me. I prayed, Please, help them.

Jesus said, "Joyce, touch me." I thought . . . ? Then I put my hand on the pew my head was on. — I know Jesus *is here* helping us.

Previously Our Blessed Mother had said to me, "It is the good children that protect the bad children." The saints' and angels' prayers have protected us for so long, but . . . .

NOVEMBER 2000

In the past years I had noticed that when the season of fall comes, the birds and ducks flying south for the winter would fly in very organized and formed groups, usually in the form of the letter V. The leaders, and these groups, most certainly seemed to know where they wanted to go, and flew straight in one direction.

This fall, and just beginning this year, the groups of birds and ducks seemed very confused and didn't fly too far before almost one-half, one-fourth, or one or two from the group, would turn and fly in another direction. No longer did they form the letter V. In fact, I remember looking into the sky and seeing as many as two very confused groups of birds flying in different directions. These groups would make sudden turns at any time, and even lose part of their group to other groups flying in yet other directions. They seemed very confused and were not organized at all. I watched this for well over a month. The migrating birds were a mess.

Today, and for the first time this fall, I saw a group of migrating birds flying in an organized group, forming the letter V, and they certainly seemed to know where they were going. God's saint said, "There's still time." Now, from this group, a smaller group formed and flew in another direction. Then the groups of blackbirds were no longer organized and they seemed to fly in disarray. As I watched this, I saw that these groups of flying black forms had jagged wings, and I realized that this was now a vision, which was no longer of birds but of devil's spirits.

We still have time.

I was waking up and I was still pretty drowsy. I heard God's saint say, "You will rush them along, Joyce." I saw a vision of just the back of my head, and my back and hands, as I was rushing a group of very young and innocent children along. The unaware children were walking through what seemed to be an open doorway. I felt that I was rushing the innocent and unaware children along to protect them from the very evil spirits that were in back of me. In the vision I vaguely saw an evil spirit, and felt there were more with him, looking at the innocent children and eagerly wanting to get to them; however they couldn't.

Yesterday, I had a very hard day and God's saint must have had one also. I think this may have been part of the reason why God, through His saint, allowed me to have this vision of the future. These visions, or powers, do not come from me, but from God and the Holy Spirit.

NOVEMBER 1, 2000

Years ago, Jesus said to me, "My blood shall make you white." I felt I was a spirit and standing in front of his white spirit; and as He pushed on His heart, His spiritual red blood squirted out of his heart into my spirit. (I did not want to write this when it happened because it made no sense at all to me.)

Today, at the All Saint's Day Mass, the first reading was from the Book of Revelations. "He said, 'These are the ones who have survived the time of great distress; they have washed their robes and made them white in the blood of the Lamb.'"

NOVEMBER 5, 2000

During this morning's Mass the priest was leading the people in prayer. He said, "Pray for the unity of the churches of the East and West." God's saint said to me, "It will happen."

NOVEMBER 8, 2000

I was in church, I felt such a feeling of love and peace toward the people around me. I knew that this wonderful love for each other, and this peace, awaits us in Heaven. God's saint said, "If they only knew."

NOVEMBER 27, 2000

This morning I was watching the thick, black clouds break up in the sky; this left a large opening in which there was no black clouds. I finally realized what God's saint had meant long ago (July 3, 1996 at 8:50 p.m. Page 136) when he said, "We're going to really open up the skies, Joyce." There will come a time when God and His lights will push away the dark clouds, opening up the skies; for the great amount of souls to be raised to Heaven. God will call those to His Right.

NOVEMBER 30, 2000

I was so tired today. I said, 'God, I'm tired.' His saint replied, "It was worse in Heaven." Pause "Much worse." (I was not going to write this, but . . .) Our Blessed Mother said, "What he is telling you is important."

✝Later this saint said, "God must separate." I saw an image of a black spirit. **This is why we are here on Earth, to separate the good from the bad. Heaven will not have another war. Heaven will hold its peace. God is watching . . . .✝**

FROM HERE ON IS WHERE THE COPYRIGHT OF 2000 ENDS, AND APRIL 2001 BEGINS. I HAD TO MAKE NECESSARY CHANGES TO THE COVER, SO AT THE SAME TIME I DECIDED TO ADD THESE FOLLOWING PAGES. ALSO, I CHANGED THE PAGES BEFORE PART ONE BEGINS, HOWEVER THE REST OF THE BOOK IS THE SAME AS BEFORE.

DECEMBER 15, 2000

I was driving to work on the freeway. I turned to look at the car and driver that were in the lane to my left. Although the car was behind my car, I could still see the driver and I heard God's saint say, "She still wears her habit." Yes . . . there was a nun driving the car. She was wearing a full nun's habit, all in black, except for a little white above her forehead. (And, white, I think, on both sides of her face. I wrote this after I had stopped my car) She looked so very young and very pretty.

Curious, I looked again . . . a woman who was not in a nun's habit was driving the car. I slowed my car down to let this car pass me so that I could get a better look at the driver of the car. This businesswoman, not a nun, drove her car past me. I knew I had seen the vision of another spirit, a spirit of one of God's holy nuns. I thought, Well . . . another one of God's army is here on Earth, another fighter (a nun) to help save our souls.

Then I noticed a truck driver that was *traveling* on the other side of the freeway. As the truck and driver bounced around a bit on the road, I heard God's saint say, "We must keep moving along." I realized that time keeps going on; and I must keep writing. (You are really going to enjoy God's helpers "fighters.")

. . . . .

Later in the day, as I walked up the stairway to get to my apartment, I briefly saw a black spirit crouched on the railing to my left. Then I felt a spirit on me and I knew this dark spirit must have jumped on my head and attacked me. Of course this attack only lasted for less than a second and I barely felt it. I was not hurt. Our Guardians are here with us.

DECEMBER 16, 2000

This morning I woke up early. As I lay in bed thinking about the bad spirit attacking me yesterday, I again had a wonderful awareness that His guardians keep us safe. I said, 'Thank you, Father. Thank You.' God's saint said, "He just likes to hear that from time to time."

Please, thank Him.

. . . . .

Later that morning I started to get angry at someone. As I looked at the door in front of me I saw the vision of a large tear as it slowly slid down the door. I heard, "We cried for them." This was not the first time, but one of many times, that I have heard God's lights say that they have cried for one of us (because we choose to sin). I was no longer angry because of the hurt this person had caused me, but I felt sad for him. I know God is well aware of His children's choices, and His good children's tears.

I had previously heard on the TV that a Palestinian refugee had driven his car into some Israeli people, and then he himself was killed. Several people were killed by his car. I know that God does not take a human killing another human lightly. I became really worried for the soul of the man who had killed. God's saint said, "This is the first man you know of that will be a devil."

Days later I again asked God to please forgive this man. A bit later I felt some of the feelings from the man before he had driven his car into the people, killing them. I knew God had let me feel this, and I knew it was just a bit of this man's feelings. The feeling was very bad, and I knew this man was bad. Again I knew this man *was*, or would be, a devil.

Later, on February 16, 2001, as I wrote about the above event, and as I wrote the word *was,* Donna's tiny star lit up and she sadly said, "Was." I knew this man who had killed is now a devil.

PLEASE, DO NOT KILL !!!!!

DECEMBER 17, 2000

After I had gotten out of bed, I thought a bit about the devil's spirits and how they spend so much of their time pulling energy from us and from God's lights. I thought, It's terrible to spend all of this time just pulling. God's saint said, "Their motto was, 'Power.'" I thought, This is very sad. They completely turned their backs on their Father.

. . . . .

Later this morning I was thinking about the time I was in church on December 8, the holy day of the Immaculate Conception of the Virgin Mary. After I had received Jesus in the Eucharist, I went back to my seat and prayed for all souls. I heard God's saint say, "Pray for all of those that are here." I knew that all of the people in this church . . . sitting scattered about; would be saved.

After Mass, as I walked to my car, I told a friend about what

God's saint had told me the day before. On that day, when I was looking out of a window, I saw the vision of rain coming down, even though there was no actual rain. God's saint said, "It will rain, even though it was not supposed to."

Today, I finally realized what God's saint meant when he said to me, "It will rain, even though it was not supposed to." I realize that the dry time God's saint had told me about months ago (June 4, 2000, Page 236)—the dry time to come—which will come, has been delayed. I am getting more time—we are getting more time—from God.

.....

I was reading the Sunday paper today and I noticed the heading: "Tornados Kill 10 in Alabama." I remembered last week when I had seen the vision of a tornado in the sky, and again on Friday I saw another vision of a tornado. I know that through my vision of last week God was letting me know about a tornado to come, and today I knew that this vision was of the tornado that came to Alabama. Also, I knew that the vision of the tornado I had seen on Friday was of another tornado to come. For years I had seen visions of tornados just before they happen. God has allowed me into His spirit world.

At other times, I have felt myself shake as if I were standing in an earthquake; however, everything around me would be still. Or I have seen something shake as if it were in an earthquake, but everything else would be still. With this, God's saint had said to me, "It will make the ground shake" or "It's coming." I knew that shortly, usually within days—somewhere, an earthquake was going to happen.

Now, God has never told me where these quakes or tornados would be (and I know this has to be explained). There is a very good reason for this. Remember, before tornados or earthquakes happen I had seen visions of them or felt them—*this was a spiritual awareness*—God allowed me to see and feel things that the spirit world knows. So, when He lets me become aware of these events to come, I am also sure that the spirit world of angels, saints and devils know this. However, I am sure that when God lets His spirit world know about these events, *before they happen*, that these are also *warnings* to the devils—warnings to help control them.

Also, importantly, as the devils do not know where the tornados or earthquakes are to happen, the evil spirits are more controlled . . . *everywhere*. God is wise.

> Remember on October 20, 1998 (Page 220), a pure voice said, "With the wind they fall down." With a tornado some devil's spirits are swirled about and may even fall down into Hell. I am also sure that with an earthquake, some of the devils may fall.

DECEMBER 22, 2000

I have rarely seen my brother's widow or children. I did not live in my family's home state for a very long time, and now I have so little free time and hardly anything that I could offer them. I feel so bad. As time goes by, our relationship has not gotten any closer.

Today I purchased a gift certificate, which I brought over to my sister-in-law's house with some clothes for them. Just as God's saint had told me, I was not invited into their home. However, as I was driving down the street I started to cry. I know this widow is having a very hard time of it. I thought, Why doesn't anyone try to help her? Jesus, told us to help the widows. God's saint said, "They do." But I know there is still so much want in this family.

After I stopped crying, God's saint reminded me of what he had told me before I had gone to their house, that I would not be invited into their home. I thought, It was OK. I was very glad to have been able to give her and her children something, and I wish I could have given them more. A few minutes later he said, "Thank you, Joyce." And I knew I had received a blessing for helping this widow and not expecting anything in return.

Even though it was early in the evening, it was dark outside. As

I was driving home I saw a young teenager standing alone at a bus stop; he looked so scared. I asked God's saint to please give my blessing to this teenager. He replied, "We have nothing either. We give it all away."

Dears, how many thank-yous we must owe God's lights . . . who receive and give so freely.

DECEMBER 28, 2000

I was thinking about our prayers for Peace. I asked, 'God will they listen to me?' The reply was, "It will take a lot of these." With this, I saw the vision of a tornado.

2001

JANUARY 9, 2001

I was watching E.W.T.N., The Way Home. A priest was talking about the Holy Spirit and how important He is.

> I remembered long ago, when I was just beginning to thank God and Jesus. Then one day God's saint quietly told me, "Don't forget the Holy Spirit."

JANUARY 10, 2001

I was delivering the printed pages of my book to the bookbinders. As I walked through the building and went to open a door, I looked to my right. I noticed Saint Robert's vague, white image. He was standing above some steps, five or six steps up, on a landing, and then the steps continued up and around a corner. I am sorry, but I did not write down what he said right away, so I can't give you the exact words of this light of God's. But, what he did say was in reference to, "You have come this far" or "You are here." At the time

my thought was, Great, I have climbed some steps. I am that much further along the way.

JANUARY 12, 2001

Not until today did I realize the full meaning from the vision of January 10, 2001. Remember God's light was standing on a landing . . . which of course was wider then the five to six steps below him. And he also had more steps before him. Now I realize that I have completed my climb above the first steps; however, I am now on the landing. This landing is somewhat of a turning point for the steps, and this landing is, of course, larger than the steps, my steps. I am at a bit of a turning point and at a larger step forward, on my journey for God.

I have become closer to God and to completing my first book; however, I must get this book into stores and market and sell the book. I must write articles about the book, advertise, and make speeches to help God. I hope to continue writing, maybe to even finish another book. I also plan to someday start a non-profit organization, so that I can get started on God's boys' home, His home for abused and neglected children. This landing I am now on is large, larger than the steps I had previously climbed.

JANUARY 21, 2001

As I was typing I thought about something that was very sad and I started to cry. I looked up to the picture of Our Blessed Mother that is on the wall in back of my computer. I heard her soft, tender voice say, "You must cry." I thought, Yes. I know that after I cry, after I let go of my sorrow, I do feel better. We must cry.

JANUARY 24, 2001

I am a Roman Catholic from an Eastern Catholic Rite. Although we are under Pope John Paul II, in Rome, just as other Roman Catholics are, our Catholic Rite, the Maronite Rite, has a few differences in the way that we worship God.

Today, as I watched E.W.T.N., the introduction to the Chaplet of Divine Mercy, I realized that God's choice of me is another part of His Divine plan. We are moving closer to the time when the church will become One. I know it will be a while in the future before His church becomes One.

JANUARY 25, 2001

I was watching E.W.T.N. and some prayers came on the TV to stop abortion. I began to pray the first of the three "Hail Mary's . . . ." God's saint said, "It won't." I knew abortion will not end. He sadly continued, and I could feel a bit of his compassion as he said, "If you could see them all." I vaguely saw the image of many babies, many babies lying beside many other babies, and a few Heavenly spirits flying above the peaceful babies. The babies were lying on a cloud and seemed to all be wrapped in soft, white blankets, or the white cloud.

. . . . .

I noticed a large amount of smoke coming from a smokestack. I saw the vague image of a rainbow in the smoke and I heard God's saint say, "It's coming." (October 3, 2000, Page 257) I looked across the freeway and I noticed a small truck driving fairly fast, with three cars about and behind it. The three cars seemed to be following the truck. I knew one of God's saint's spirits, the one who had let me see this vision, was in the man driving the truck; and I knew that devil's spirits were in the men driving the three cars about him.

JANUARY 26, 2001

I remembered when I was watching a TV show about an event that had happened hundreds of years ago. Now, I'm sorry that I did not write down right away what God's saint had said, but he said something like, "Do not spend your time on the past." I knew I

should learn about and work for now. This should be our concern, today.

. . . . .

A woman I know is married for the second time. She said her first marriage was annulled, but she had to fill out much paperwork to get this done. She is now married a second time and this is also the second marriage for her new husband. She told me she hasn't yet tried to get her present husband's first marriage annulled. I could tell that although she was sad that she doesn't fully participate in her church at this time, she was still a bit irritated because of all the paperwork she had to fill out to get her first marriage annulled. I felt so sad for her. God's saint said, "God will remind her that it was, 'Because of the inconvenience.'"

JANUARY 27, 2001

I was standing beside my car and about to open the car door when I saw a snowflake fall in front of me. I knew that it would be snowing soon. I realized that the closer my visions get to the actual event happening that I see in my visions . . . the closer it will be to the time when God will take back His world.

. . . . .

I was praying the rosary as I drove my car on the long road to work. As I prayed, "Our Father who art in Heaven . . . ." I felt such compassion and sorrow for Our Heavenly Father. I know He must cry immensely for His children's sins. I asked to take some of Our Father's tears for His children.

I saw a large spiritual tear fall to the road in front of my car. This tear had several specks of silver in it. God's saint said, "This is one of them." I thought, God's tears . . . !! I'm ashamed to say that I was so amazed at what I had seen, that in my amazement I had lost my compassion. God's saint continued, "You will take a river."

(We can take God s tears.) God s angel Donna said, You will do what we can t. I know that there are times that I can use my physical body to work with and to help do some things for the spiritual angels and saints. Our team will work together.

.....

As I did the dishes I looked out of the window. I saw a very vague white image and I heard God s saint say, You did a lot of writing today. I know there was a March for Life in Washington a few days before, and there must have been many prayers said on that day. Now, even though God s saint s image was vague today, I know he is strong. This is the first time I have seen his image in some time, and also he has been talking much to me recently. I thought, Prayers help strengthen God s lights. I then realized that through the prayers of priest, nuns, and holy people, that God s lights would have been made even stronger. The stronger the Faith and Love, the stronger the results, or light.

JANUARY 30, 2001

Mother Angelica Live was on TV tonight. Although I was very busy typing, I stopped and heard one thing she said. She lovingly said, What good is it to know when a hurricane is coming? It would be good to know where it is coming to save lives.

This is where one of God s gifts to me helps. I know approximately when a tornado or earthquake will happen (within days) but I do not know where or the exact time. (See December 17, 2000) These visions of the future that I see, or feel, are spiritual knowledge, and also warnings to the devils. The devils know that some of them will fall when God uses His power to create a hurricane or a tornado. So, these warnings, and because it is now known where these hurricanes or tornados will happen, control the bad devils—

everywhere. They do not want to fall. God is wise and His spiritual warnings are Powerful. Trust God.

JANUARY 31, 2001

I felt a wonderful warmth. God's saint said, "You will always be warm." When your spirit becomes one of God's spirits of Light . . . you will receive Heaven's warmth. Please be Good.

FEBRUARY 7, 2001

Two days ago I went to a meeting to look into starting a non-profit organization. I was trying to start on God's home for boys. Wow, at this time it's overwhelming, a lot of work. I realized that I can't write, distribute my books, sell them, and also start the home. I had to put the papers for the home away for now.

FEBRUARY 12, 2001

I was watching James Robinson and his wife on TV. God's saint said to me, "They will be afraid of you, Joyce."

FEBRUARY 15, 2001

I was thinking of the vision I had a while back, on September 5, 2000 (Page 256), when I had been saying my rosary in church and looking at the emblem of, The Jubilee 2000. Today, as I thought about this past vision, God's saint said, "You must draw it." So, this is what I had seen when I was looking at the emblem. (The vision is explained in more detail on September 5, 2000. Please realize I am not an artist.)

> Remember, God's saint said, "It will support the other three."

MARCH 17, 2001

This is my second year of teaching religious education at the church. I must say, This year I have more confidence than I had last year. I am teaching seventh graders instead of first graders. Boy, was it hard to keep those first graders in their seats. Because I know so little about my religion I was really reluctant to 'take on' the seventh graders, especially since this is just my second year of teaching (and learning), but there was a real need for teachers, so here I am.

As I was preparing for my class and reading the class book, I felt that I should open my attendance book. (The book that I have my students' names on.) After opening the book I looked at the students' names, however, I was unable to read any name clearly. God's saint said, "We will open this book for you." I knew that as we help Jesus on Earth, this is recorded in Heaven's Book. Please help Jesus. Open your heart, and again, **Use your time here wisely**.

Give and gifts will be given to you; a good measure,
packed together, shaken down, and overflowing will be
poured into your lap. For the measure with which you measure
will in return be measured out to you.

Luke 6:38

May this not be the end . . .
but for you,
the beginning of Forever.

Index

From the Heart, *Conversations, Visions, and Answers from God's Angels and Saints*
may be purchased or ordered through your local bookstore.
Please refer to ISBN 0-9708645-2-3
Or, telephone me at 1-413-747-5602.